GEOLOGY OF ANZA-BORREGO: EDGE OF CREATION

Author Paul Remeika in North Fork Fish Creek. LL

Geology of Anza-Borrego: Edge of Creation

Paul Remeika
and
Lowell Lindsay

Produced by Sunbelt Publications
as one in a series of
California Desert Natural History Guides

KENDALL/HUNT PUBLISHING COMPANY
2460 Kerper Boulevard P.O. Box 539 Dubuque, Iowa 52004-0539

Sunbelt Publications, Inc.
POB 191126
San Diego, CA 92159-1126. All inquiries should be accompanied by a self-
addressed, stamped envelope.

Library of Congress Cataloging-in-Publication Data

Remeika, Paul, 1950-
    Geology of Anza-Borrego : edge of creation / general text and
  photographs by Paul Remeika ; climate chapter and book design by
  Bill Hample ; introductory text and editing by Lowell Lindsay.
        p. cm. -- (California desert natural history field guides ;
  1)
    Includes bibliographical references and index.
    ISBN 0-932653-17-0
    1. Geology--California--Anza-Borrego Desert Region.   I. Hample,
  W. G.   II. Lindsay, Lowell.   III. Title.   IV. Series.

QE90.A64R46   1992
557.94'98--dc20   92-33102
                                                            CIP

ISBN 0-932653-17-0

Printed in the United States of America
10   9   8   7   6   5   4   3   2   1

TABLE OF CONTENTS

* Asterisk indicates the title of a self-guiding ABDNHA/ABDSP brochure, available at the Visitor Center

Co-author Lowell Lindsay and Grossmont College Extension geology class in granitic boulders atop Ghost Mountain. HF

LIST OF MAPS AND CHARTS BY TOPIC OR TRIP

Dr. Pat Abbott, SDSU geology professor, and ABDNHA field trip at Superstition Hills Fault, three years after 1987 surface rupture. LL

PREFACE AND ACKNOWLEDGMENTS

Soon after World War Two, Dr. Horace Parker published the *Anza-Borrego Desert Guidebook* to conduct increasing numbers of tourists through this vast, wilderness expanse. Simultaneously, researchers were discovering a magnificent living museum and natural laboratory that supplied yet more pieces in the great puzzle of California desert geology, biology, and archaeology.

As these scientific findings appeared in academic and travel publications, awareness of the unique value of this area soared. Nowhere else in the nation was there such a large and varied desert preserve and outdoor classroom so near to urban centers for recreation and scientific research. The great vision of its founders in 1933 was finally and thoroughly validated.

Meanwhile, Copley Press published Diana Lindsay's *Our Historic Desert* in 1973. This book, part of the widely acclaimed Copley series on the history and culture of the San Diego and Baja California region, was based on the author's master's thesis at San Diego State University. It was the first comprehensive treatment of history in San Diego's desert region and included substantial material on the natural and scientific features that had justified the creation of one of the nation's largest desert preserves.

With Doc Parker's guidebook no longer available, Wilderness Press published *Anza-Borrego Desert Region* by Lowell and Diana Lindsay in 1978. This road and trail guide, including a separately available map of the region, is frequently updated and is now in its 3rd edition (1991).

The Anza-Borrego Desert Natural History Association (ABDNHA) began its publications program in the late seventies. Association books currently in print include: *Anza-Borrego Desert State Park - Photographic Words and Images* by Paul Johnson, Mark Jorgensen, and Harry Daniel; *Cacti, Shrubs, and Trees* and *Weekender's Guide*, both by Johnson. ABDNHA is also credited with Manfred Knaak's *Forgotten Artist - Indians of Anza-Borrego and Their Rock Art,* 1988 winner of the national Ben Franklin Award for publishing excellence.

ABDNHA's latest publication is *Geology and Paleontology of Anza-Borrego Desert State Park* by park ranger Paul Remeika, an earth science interpretive specialist. This thesis presents, for the first time in a single work, a comprehensive view of Anza-Borrego's geologic history and prehistoric biota. It was supported, in part, by the Brainerd Grant Fund for scientific research in desert disciplines. This text is the basis for other earth science studies and publications including the current geology book and a forthcoming paleontology book, both by Remeika. The adoption of such terms as "boulder factory" and western barrier", used by Jorgensen in the book noted above, are examples of the contributions of ABDNHA publications to interpretive science.

Geology of Anza-Borrego: Edge of Creation by Paul Remeika and Lowell Lindsay, is based upon and derived from the ABDNHA geology material. The association's contribution to educational, scientific, and interpretive activities in Anza-Borrego is thus acknowledged as essential. It has become recognized nationally as a model of accomplishment of stated goals in these areas. Credit for these accomplishments is spread through many volunteers and staff since founding in 1971. Representing all these, Sunbelt Publications sincerely thanks founder and Chairman Harry Daniel and Executive Director Betsy Knaak.

The next publication in the Sunbelt series, by archaeologist Ken Hedges, will depict the native Americans of the western Colorado Desert. Topics on history, myths and legends, and wildlife will follow. These publications are part of a California desert natural history series coordinated with related class and field trip programs at Grossmont College of Extended Studies. Participants in these programs test the written material for usability and interest for the typical desert enthusiast. Field trip services and interpretive materials that are contributed by class members are gratefully acknowledged.

Paul Remeika, lead author of the current book, is a career ranger with the California State Park System, curator of geology of Imperial Valley College Museum, and paleontology coordinator at Anza-Borrego. He is in high demand as facilitator and instructor for many professional and volunteer earth science organizations and projects. He has published several research papers, based on extensive field analysis, which cast significant new light on various elements of stratigraphy and paleontology in the badlands of Anza-Borrego. He is a recipient of the Brainerd Grant for paleo-research on petrified wood. He is credited with the first discovery and identification, within the park, of several kinds of vertebrate fossils, rare footprints and trackways, and various petrified wood species.

Paul received his degree in geology and recreation administration from San Diego State University and is planning his Master's degree in paleontology. He is an active member of the Society of Vertebrate Paleontology and the Geological Society of America. His next book will be about the paleontology of Anza-Borrego.

Additional contributors to this work include: Dr. Richard Phillips, late geology professor with the University of San Diego; George Miller, late curator of paleontology of the Imperial Valley College Museum; Bill Hample, aerospace engineer and desert climatology researcher; and Nancy Schmidt, geologist with the Arizona Geological Survey.

Technical and professional expertise has been essential in the work. Critical review of various portions of the text was provided by Dr. Pat Abbott, geology professor at San Diego State University, Will Estavillo, curator of mineralogy at the San Diego Natural History Museum, and Dr. Richard Phillips. The symposium abstracts in the appendix are symbolic of the major contributions of local volunteer and professional scientists to research and interpretation of regional desert natural history. These efforts are organized by Dr. Jim Rickard, as president of the Anza-Borrego Foundation which sponsors the biennial Desert Scientific Symposium series, and Grace Rickard, park volunteer naturalist program coordinator.

Contributions of the book production team are recognized as follows (computer graphics are based on originals drafted by Paul Remeika): Patton Brothers for cover production, Hample Associates for book design and computer charts, Mike Connolly for field testing the roadlogs as a senior intern project for Francis Parker School, and Jon Lindsay, physics student at Stanford University, for technical review of the text.

Park staff assistance was superb as always, thanks to District Superintendent Dave Van Cleve. We particularly appreciate input from Jim Meier, sharing his years of north park area expertise, Mark Jorgensen, long term interpretive guru of Anza-Borrego natural history, and Fred Jee who can make lizards laugh, rocks roll, and volunteers LEARN.

Publications such as this are only a part of a much larger system of interpretive and educational resources in a most exceptional state park. This interpretive system is based on a highly effective three-way partnership of state park staff, ABDNHA members, and the park volunteers who operate the visitor center. In addition to a wide range of projects, including daily naturalist programs in season and frequent field trips, this team also operates one of the finest and largest desert book stores in Southern California with all proceeds "dedicated to Educational, Scientific, and Interpretive Activities."

PHOTO AND DESIGN CREDITS

Photos as noted in captions:

AY	Al Young	DZ	Diane Zuchl	LL	Lowell Lindsay
BH	Bill Hample	FS	Fred Schreier	MC	Mike Connolly
CP	Copley Press	HF	Hal Fisher	PR	Paul Remeika
DL	Diana Lindsay	JL	Joe Lemm	SB	Steve Bauer
				SP	State Park Files

Text by Paul Remeika except:
Introduction, Appendices, and Editing by Lowell Lindsay
Chapter 6 (Climate) by Bill Hample
"A New Look at Old Desert Topography" by Dr. Richard Phillips

Charts and Maps by Paul Remeika except:
Geologic Time Scale by Lowell Lindsay
Tectonic Plate Boundaries and the Gulf by Nancy Schmidt
Sedimentation and Folding by George Miller
Geologic Time Correlation Scale by George Miller
Anza-Borrego Region Map by Lowell Lindsay

Maps used by permission of Kendall/Hunt Publishing Company:
Peninsular Ranges Province
Salton Trough Province
Generalized Fault Map of Southern California

Cover Design by Court Patton using computer graphics integrated with photos and maps by Paul Remeika.

NOTES ON THE TEXT

Technical terms are minimized and are defined when introduced. Terms defined in the glossary are in **bold type** when first used in a chapter. Definitions are based on the *Dictionary of Geological Terms*, edited by Robert Bates and Julia Jackson, of the American Geological Institute. MYA refers to "millions of years ago." Geographical names are based on the park map, USGS maps, or are in quotes with origin explained (e.g. ... as used in *Weekender's Guide* by Paul Johnson). Named geologic formations are based on common usage or are the subject of abstracts in the appendix. Where formation names are new or informal, they are followed by the notation (new term) when first used in a chapter.

Checkpoints on paved road logs utilize the state and county post mile marker system wherever possible. Few are noted on State Highway 78 because they are difficult to spot. On the other hand, credit to San Diego County because its bold green markers are very easy to see. Odometer references are used as a secondary locater system. Readers should be aware that few odometers agree and even the same one will vary from itself over time. (This is obviously and especially true on dirt roads.) Post mile markers are fixed and are the best reference. Mile zero or the origin of each trip is selected to make elapsed odometer miles into whole numbers at their respective post mile markers (e.g. the 1.0 mile checkpoint, Hellhole Canyon View, on Trip No, 1 is Mile Marker 17 on County Highway S-2).

A detailed discussion of a single topic is generally offered only once in the road logs although examples of that topic may be frequently encountered throughout the trips. The topical chapters of Part I, cross-references in the roadlogs, and the index will help the reader to better understand the larger themes that emerge from observation of the land. Photographs and charts, too, serve as carriers of these themes.

Lowell Lindsay
San Diego, California
September 30, 1992

Grossmont College geology class studying the anticline in Split Mountain. TK

INTRODUCTION TO THE STORY

TROUGHS AND TEMBLORS - Rifting and Slipping

Hellhole Canyon was named by an early Borrego cowboy after deciding it was "one hell of a job to get wild cattle out of it." Picture him brooding up there in the boulder factory of Culp Valley, perched on the rim of Hellhole. Perhaps he was sensing a larger truth about the entire Salton Trough, of which the Anza-Borrego region is the western edge. Among other things, much of the contents of Arizona's Grand Canyon have been lost, eroded away, into this vast hole, structurally a part of the great and growing rift that is the Gulf of California.

Twenty thousand feet of these sediments mask the rumbling birth of new earth crust beneath the Salton Sea and Gulf waters. The great western barrier mountains of the Lagunas and San Ysidros are being lifted more than a mile into the sky as part of this rifting and earth birthing. Anza-Borrego is, indeed, on the "edge of creation."

This desert region lies astride one of the most active seismic regions in North America. It bears witness to one-half billion years of continental building, breakup, and burial. As part of both the uplifting Peninsular Ranges and down-dropping Salton Trough, it is literally land in motion. Compounding the tectonic excitement, the area slips northwest with much of Southern and Baja California, grinding against the North American landmass along the massive San Andreas Fault Zone. No less significant is Borrego's five million year vertebrate fossil record, perhaps the best preserved and most continuous recent mammal sequence known in North America.

This non-technical book introduces the desert enthusiast to the fascinating story of the genesis and continuing transformation of this turbulent land. Eight field trips, five on paved and three on primitive roads, journey through deep time both in the desert and along the western barrier mountains. They illustrate major themes and features of earth science uniquely displayed in the Anza-Borrego region. This region, host to nearly 1000 square miles of state park sprawling over three Southern California counties, offers one of America's most significant desert preserves for recreation and scientific study.

The Elsinore and San Jacinto fault zones slash the region from end to end, lifting up mountains and dropping down valleys. This drama is played against the larger backdrop of the awesome San Andreas Fault Zone, that great grandfather of California earthquakes, just across the Salton Trough. Anza-Borrego has a front row seat to the westward march of this sliver of North American continent as it muscles much of coastal California out of its way along the San Andreas.

From the tip of Baja to Los Angeles, peninsular or mobile California is being driven northwest by elemental forces called tectonics. These same forces are also responsible for the opening of the Gulf of California, of which the Salton Trough is the buried and delta-dammed northern extension. The story of Anza-Borrego's landforms is largely that of tectonic mountain building episodes alternating with erosional and depositional cycles. This all occurs on the edge of a very active continental and seafloor encounter zone. A brief survey of current tectonic theory is thus in order.

GEOLOGIC TIME SCALE

ERA	PERIOD	EPOCH	Millions of Years Before Present
CENOZOIC	QUATERNARY	Holocene	0.01
		Pleistocene	1.9
	TERTIARY (Neogene)	Pliocene	5.4
		Miocene	23
	(Paleogene)	Oligocene	37
		Eocene	53
		Paleocene	65
MESOZOIC	CRETACEOUS	Late	
		Early	136
	JURASSIC	Late	
		Middle	
		Early	190
	TRIASSIC	Late	
		Middle	
		Early	225
PALEOZOIC	PERMIAN	Late	
		Early	280
	CARBONIFEROUS (Pennsylvanian)	Late	
	(Mississippian)	Early	345
	DEVONIAN	Late	
		Middle	
		Early	395
	SILURIAN	Late	
		Early	430
	ORDOVICIAN	Late	
		Middle	
		Early	500
	CAMBRIAN	Late	
		Middle	
		Early	570
ORIGIN OF EARTH	PRECAMBRIAN		4,500

THE CRACKED EGGSHELL - Summary of Tectonics

The cracked eggshell description of the earth's surface is a simple but surprisingly accurate depiction of reality. Like the ragged but aligned segments of a cracked eggshell, the seven major and many lesser tectonic plates of the earth's crust confront each other at their edges. These encounters are of three kinds: "divergent" or crust being born, "slidepast" or crustal plates jostling past one another, and "convergent" or crust being subducted and consumed. New crustal formation and divergence occur at spreading centers, usually but not always in mid-ocean (e.g. Gulf of California). Slidepast, resulting in major seismic activity, occurs at major transform faults along plate boundaries (e.g. San Andreas Fault Zone). Convergence, featuring the largest quakes and volcanic eruptions, occurs at plate collision boundaries (e.g. Philippine Islands).

As with their living passengers, the crustal plates themselves may be said to be creatures that are born, journey on, and pass away. Even in the passing away, the consumption of old crustal seafloor diving beneath continental crust, there is birth of new landmass. This takes the form of volcanic material venting onto the surface as well as subterranean cooling of vast blocks of magma rock (granitic batholiths) that will later be uncovered as the bedrock of great mountain ranges.

The Anza-Borrego region, as the western edge of the Salton Trough, is experiencing two of the three possible plate margin encounters. Divergent crustal creation occurs below the Salton Sea whereas slide-past plate contact is revealed in extensive earth shaking and heaving along the major fault zones. This complex tectonic condition is currently unrivaled in any other major landmass except East Africa. Such unique geology demands an exploration of its origin in deep time and observation of its expression on the land. The Anza-Borrego desert invites such exploration.

FIELD TRIP SUMMARY - Geology on the Ground

Bounding the park north and south, both the Santa Rosas and Coyote Mountains display evidence of five hundred million year old Paleozoic sea bottom with shadowy traces of the creatures that dwelt therein. While many pages and chapters of the storybook of time since then are missing, those that remain chronicle a fascinating geologic saga.

The eight field trips in this book explore the major regimes of Paleozoic sedimentation and metamorphism, Mesozoic batholithic intrusion, Cenozoic continental rifting and volcanism, and Plio-Pleistocene sedimentation. Geologic highlights include:

1. MONTEZUMA GRADE - Hwy S-22 west (batholithic intrusion, metamorphism, exfoliation in the "boulder factory," pegmatite veins and dikes)

2. BORREGO-SALTON SEAWAY - Hwy S-22 east (major strike-slip faulting, basin/range topography actively developing, river delta sedimentation)

2A. FONT'S POINT - Borrego Badlands (lakebed sedimentation, alluvial deposits, basin uplift, homeland for mammoth and camel)

3. YAQUI PASS - Hwy S-3 (pediment forming, detachment faulting, pegmatite veins and dikes)

Selected Geologic Features By Trip And Time Sequence

MILLION YRS.AGO	REGIONAL GEOLOGIC ACTIVITY on West Coast of North America	TRIP #1 HWY S-22W MONTEZUMA GRADE	TRIP #2 HWY S-22E SALTON SEAWAY	TRIP #2A - prim. road FONT'S POINT
.00-.01 .01-1.9	CENOZOIC ERA, QUARTERNARY PERIOD, HOLOCENE EPOCH Peninsular Range uplift and Salton Trough subsidence ongoing. Lake Cahuilla forms/dries intermittent. PLEISTOCENE EPOCH Desert forms 10 - 15,000 YA. after last ice age peaks, 18,000 YA.	CULP VALLEY: "Boulder Factory" weathering continues. Desert Varnish "Western Barrier" mtns. continue uplift along Borrego shear zone.	CLARK BASIN: Numerous quakes in San Jacinto Fault Zone. LUTE FAULT: BORREGO BADLANDS OVERLOOK: view west: (correlates to Font's Point notes to right).	Erosional retreat and uplift of Font's Pt. and Ocotillo Rim continuing. FONT'S PT. WASH: Font's Pt. Sandstone. Ocotillo Conglomerate
1.9-5.4 5.4-23	TERTIARY PERIOD (NEOGENE) PLIOCENE EPOCH Peninsular Ranges - commence current uplift and tilting of block to west, Colorado River delta dam complete - seas barred from basin MIOCENE EPOCH Gulf of Calif. opens up. Baja rotates clockwise, continuing NW slip. Rolling plains/swampy west coast of Mexico commences breakup into NW trending longitudinal blocks.	"Western Barrier" mountains commence uplift along Borrego shear zone.	TRUCKHAVEN ROCKS: Canebrake conglomerate. ARROYO SALADA and PALM WASH: Diablo Formation.	RAINBOW WASH (UPPER): Borrego Formation (lake) RAINBOW WASH (LOWER): Diablo formation (Colo. River delta)
23-65	TERTIARY PERIOD (PALEOGENE) Major river flowing westward from Sonora Mtns. Small deposits of riverborne cobbles scattered in AB area. Thick deposits found on San Diego coastal plain, with fan apex near San Vicente reservoir.	LOWER CULP, MONTEZUMA VALLEYS: intermontane erosional surfaces.		
65-136	MESOZOIC ERA, CRETACEOUS PERIOD Late in period - coast ranges erode to rolling plains region. Early in period -batholithic intrusion. Ancestral coast ranges elevated to "Andean heights."	CULP VALLEY: Chemical weathering of granitic mass begins. Pegmatite dikes form late in period.	COYOTE MTN. and SANTA ROSAS: mixed granitics plus metasediments	
136-208	JURASSIC PERIOD Pangea (world continent) breakup. Farallon (East Pacific) plate subducting North American plate.	CULP VALLEY: Metamorphic inclusions in boulders		
208-245	TRIASSIC PERIOD West flowing river delta, shallow marine environment	Julian Schist outcroppings		
403-505	PALEOZOIC ERA, ORDOVICIAN PERIOD Marine environment west of continental land mass. Carbonate and organic deposits on seabed.	MM 15.5 and 15: abrupt shift from darker, ancient metamorphics to lighter, newer granitics.	"Anza's Angel", light streaks on SANTA ROSA MTNS.: marbleized metasediments	

TRIP #3 HWY S-3 YAQUI PASS	TRIP #4 HWY 78 SAN FELIPE CORR.	TRIP #4A prim. road FISH CREEK	TRIP #5 Hwy S-2 CARRIZO CORR.	TRIP #5A Prim. Road. VALLECITO BADLDS
YAQUI MEADOWS: Pediment erosional surface.	TEXAS DIP: San Felipe Wash beheaded from lower Borrego Valley		CARRIZO OVERLOOK: Mesa Conglomerate	ARROYO TAPIADO: mudcaves in pseudokarst. Concretions weather out.
		SANDSTONE CANYON: Olla Member of the Canebrake Conglomerate	AGUA CALIENTE: hot springs along Elsinore Fault Zone	Palm Spring Formation - locally derived basin-margin sediments (similar to Lake Henshaw area). Hueso Member (sandstone)
SHIPROCK: Detachment fault, Miocene sediments on granitic bedrock.	HARPER CANYON FAN: Canebrake Conglomerate BORREGO MTN. WASH: Split Mtn. formation fault contact with West Butte granitics NUDE WASH: Detachment fault features - erosion surface.	DROPOFF WASH: Diablo Formation (Colorado River delta) SPLIT MTN (so. entr.) Imperial Form. (shallow marine) Upper Boulder Bed (marine landslide) Anticline, mile 3.8 Gypsum Beds (marine) Lower Boulder Bed (terr. landslide) Split Mtn. Form. (fanglomerates)	TABLE MTN. (Jacumba) and VOLCANIC HILLS: Alverson Formation volcanic extrusions related to Gulf spreading and crustal thinning.	Tapiado Member (mudstone) ARROYO SECO DIABLO: Diablo Formation "Diablo Redbeds" (delta silt, sand, clay)
		SPLIT MTN. (no. entr.) commence fanglomerates		
MESCAL OVERLOOK: granitics with pegmatites, some mylonization.	SAN FELIPE NARROWS: pegmatite dikes	FISH CREEK WASH: granitic cobbles and clasts	GRANITE MTN: Bands are granitic/pegmatite intrusions late in period.	
			BOX CANYON: metasediments similar to Julian Schist	
	NARROWS EARTH TRAIL: metasediments in fault contact with granitics. Surface faulting visible.		COYOTE MTNS. metasediments similar to Santa Rosa Mtns.	

4. SAN FELIPE CORRIDOR- Hwy 78 (desert geologic processes, antecedent stream, pediment vs. bajada)

4A. FISH CREEK BADLANDS- Split Mountain (catastrophic landslides, "pages of time" sedimentary exposures, anticline, Colorado River delta deposits, marine shell beds, windcaves)

5. CARRIZO CORRIDOR- Hwy S-2 (major slumps, Elsinore fault zone, Julian schist, hot springs, Carrizo Badlands, basin rotation, volcanism)

5A. VALLECITO BADLANDS (lakebed and delta sedimentation, mud caves and pseudokarst, playground of the great mammals)

The relationship between time and place is the organizing concept. The evidence of many different events in time may be seen in a single place. Conversely, evidence in many different places derives from single episodes in time. For example, a single vantage point in Split Mountain reveals a million years of deposition. On the other hand, meandering camel tracks from a single episode in earth time may be encountered in many locations throughout the badlands.

Metaphors of story, stage, and song emerge from the scientific reading of the rocks. "Pages of Stone," for example, is the lyrical description of a major series about the geology of our western national parks. In the same vein, "Gaea's Symphony" evokes the ancient earth goddess whose name lives on in such words as "geology" (earth study) and "geometry" (earth measurement).

GAEA'S SYMPHONY - Geologic Themes in the Region

The several themes that emerge lend a sense of symphony or drama to the geological story of Anza-Borrego. These themes seem to weave, and repeat, throughout the narrative.

1. TECTONICS AND THE BAJA BREAKAWAY - global forces controlling the birth, growth, and consumption of ocean beds and their continental cargo.

2. MAJOR FAULT ZONES - the rumbling architects of Anza-Borrego's northwest trending topography.

3. MOUNTAIN BUILDING, OROGENY -

(and concurrently...)

4. MOUNTAIN DESTRUCTION, EROSION -

"Every valley shall be lifted up, every mountain brought down and rugged places made a plain."
    --Isaiah 40

5. THE THREE BASIC ROCK GROUPS - each in turn revealing the story of the geologic activity in a given area: igneous = volcanic flow or granitic intrusion; sedimentary = deposition from highland or marine sources; metamor-

phic = transformation of pre-existent, generally ancient, rock through intense heat, pressure, or chemical alteration.

The dramatic story in turn may be divided into four movements or acts with surprising correspondence to major divisions in the geological time table:

"A Primeval Sea Bed" (Paleozoic Era, 225-570 MYA)
The original marine sedimentary country rock, metamorphosed and uplifted by later granitic intrusion into today's marine metasediments; some are distinctly visible as light colored stripes high on the Santa Rosa Mountains.

"Ancient Mountain Roots" (Mesozoic Era, 65-225 MYA)
The region-wide Peninsular Batholith intrusion, uplifting California's margin to Andean proportions with subsequent leveling to a rolling plains environment; the "boulder factory" of Culp Valley and granite monoliths of the "western barrier mountains."

"Continental Breakup and Volcanism" (Cenozoic Era, 5-65 MYA)
Opening of the Gulf of California and volcanism in the southern park area, coupled with the initiation of the massive San Andreas and related fault zones that slash Southern California and create Borrego's basin and range topography.

"Borrego's Living Past" (Plio-Pleistocene Epochs, .01-5 MYA)
Shallow marine sea, severed from the Gulf by the Colorado River delta dam, yielding to a fresh water and alluvial environment; final mountain uplift, rain barrier, and post-ice age warming and drying.

World class fossil deposits in nearly unbroken sequence from marine to river delta, savanna, and finally desert; prehistoric creatures whose names reach the heights of fantasy and the deeps of legend including Imperial Mammoth, Giant Tapiado Pig, Long-Limbed Camel, Giant Anza-Borrego Zebra, Ancient Rabbit, Progressive Rabbit, Sabertooth Cat, Spectacled Bear, Bone-crushing Dog, Giant Vulture, Ass (*Equus asinus*) and Half-Ass (*E. hemionus*).

The stage is thus set for the Anza-Borrego story, a name that symbolizes the cultural and natural history of the park. Captain Juan Bautista de Anza was the Spanish explorer who opened the overland trail from mainland Mexican for colo-nists to settle San Francisco in 1776, substantially contributing to the Hispanic heritage of California. Borrego is Spanish for the elegant but elusive bighorn sheep that yet rule the area's mountain ramparts. Fade then to the beginning of time in Paleozoic mists and the genesis of a desert land.

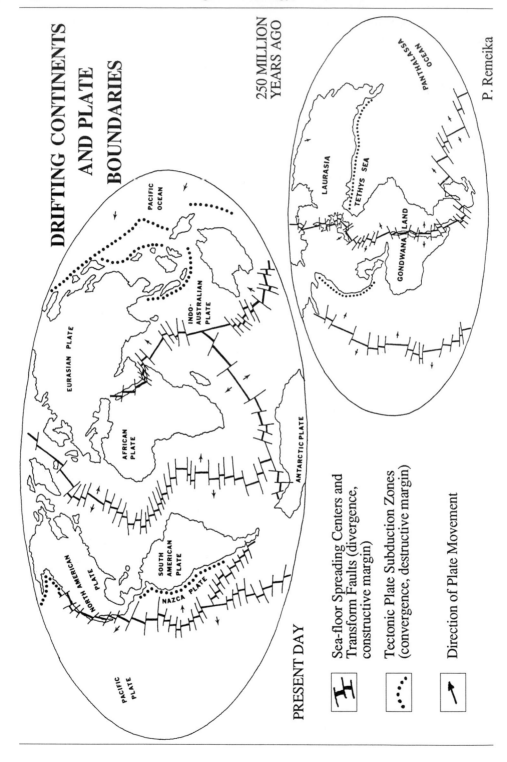

DRIFTING CONTINENTS AND PLATE BOUNDARIES

250 MILLION YEARS AGO

P. Remeika

PANTHALASSA OCEAN

LAURASIA

TETHYS SEA

GONDWANA LAND

PACIFIC OCEAN

EURASIAN PLATE

INDO-AUSTRALIAN PLATE

AFRICAN PLATE

NORTH AMERICAN PLATE

SOUTH AMERICAN PLATE

NAZCA PLATE

ANTARCTIC PLATE

PACIFIC PLATE

PRESENT DAY

Sea-floor Spreading Centers and Transform Faults (divergence, constructive margin)

Tectonic Plate Subduction Zones (convergence, destructive margin)

Direction of Plate Movement

PART I - REGIONAL GEOLOGY, AN OVERVIEW

Chapter 1

DEEP TIME - THE GEOLOGIC CHRONICLE IN ANZA-BORREGO

PREVIEW OF A LAND IN MOTION - 500 MillionYears

To think in deep time, as earth scientists do, we must reset our perceptual clock to units of millions of years ago (MYA). Imagine a satellite-based, time lapse movie camera operating at the rate of one frame per year, starting a half billion years ago, and focused on today's Anza-Borrego region. The drama reveals the face of the land, and sea, changing constantly and violently. Periods of tectonic peace are generally absent.

Five hundred MYA, sea bottom layers and their entombed creatures are deposited, later to be lifted into the sky while the mountains themselves erode to form new continental depositions. Between 70-100 MYA, vast granitic clusters, hundreds of square miles in extent, congeal into mountain building blocks. These rise up and intrude, radically changing or metamorphosing overlying rock layers, and wear away again. Twenty MYA, the western edge of the continent starts breaking up as it overruns the East Pacific seafloor spreading zone.

Soon thereafter, volcanoes burst forth and the great San Andreas transform fault system is activated.The Baja California landmass rifts from mainland Mexico as the Gulf of California unzips north along the spreading zones and connecting faults. Mountain blocks are broken apart. Some are upthrust to become desert-forming rain barriers to the west while others slump into the vast Salton Trough/Gulf of California structural depression.

About 4 MYA, the Colorado River delta finally dams off the upper Salton Basin as the Anza-Borrego lowlands transition from a marine environment to fresh water delta and lake beds and finally floodplain deposits. During and soon after the last ice age, the desert forms a mere 12 to 25 thousand years ago.

Today's symptoms of ongoing massive geological upheaval in the area include its highly varied topography, geothermal activity, hot springs, and several recent large scale earthquakes. Small, frequent earthquake "swarms" near Brawley are clear indicators of ongoing seafloor spreading and production of new earth crust beneath the five mile thick sediments of the Salton Basin.

So the drama continues. Across and around Anza-Borrego's cactus-studded desert floor, spreads a landscape born of tectonic unrest. Massive earth fractures slash sharply drawn mountain ranges from arid valleys and basins. Major fault zones, thinning earth crustal slices, subsiding basins, upthrusting mountains, and on-shore seafloor spreading zones unite in a geologic performance played few places on earth, and no place else in North America.

A PRIMEVAL SEA BED - Paleozoic Era (225-570 million years ago)

Time scarred as they seem, the igneous granitic rocks that predominate in the mountains of Anza-Borrego are not the oldest rocks in the area. These igneous rocks are relative youngsters and date from the late Mesozoic Era, approximately 80 MYA. Along the eastern edge of peninsular California mountains, an intermittent thin spine of primeval Paleozoic metasedimentary strata can be found dating to about 500 MYA.

Dominated by layered rock visible in the Santa Rosa, San Ysidro, and Coyote Mountains, the preexisting Paleozoic roof pendant rocks illustrate several hundred million years of Borregan development. These metasediments are all that remain of a great sedimentary accumulation that was laid down in an ocean environment that existed here during the Ordovician Period of the Paleozoic Era. These old marine sediments, including shales, sandstones, and limestone, built up gradually, about one inch per century, until they had amassed a thickness well above eight thousand feet. Here and there faint traces of invertebrate fossil organisms document this distant beginning.

Laying the groundwork for today's distinctive terrain, the original sediments were metamorphosed by tremendous heat and pressure. This resulted from the molten emplacement of the widespread Peninsular Batholith from beneath, into the metasedimentary, roof pendent country rock, from 70-100 MYA. Limestones were metamorphosed into marble, sandstones into quartzite, and sandy shales into schist and gneiss.

Contorted white streaks of marble from this episode are visible high in the Santa Rosas from throughout Borrego Valley. Good examples of metamorphosed sedimentary rock stripe the face of Indianhead at the mouth of Borrego Palm Canyon (Field Trip No. 1, Visitor Center) as well as Carrizo Peak in the Coyote Mountains (Field Trip No. 5, Carrizo Badlands Overlook).

ANCIENT MOUNTAIN ROOTS - Mesozoic Era (65-225 million years ago)

The precipitous slopes of the Peninsular Ranges, which form some of the most impressive vertical faces of any mountain barriers in North America, hint at the violent genesis of this land. The evolutionary curtain for this act, known as the Nevadan Orogeny or Revolution, rises on the west coast of North America about 150 MYA. The mountain building activity took place as a result of a major collision between two very large tectonic plates - the eastward moving Farallon (or East Pacific) Plate and the westward creeping North American Plate. The North American overrode the Farallon, bending and crumpling crustal rocks at depth in violent episodes. Over millions of years, heat and pressure upwelled molten material into the original Paleozoic sedimentary country rock.This molten magma then hardened and crystallized into a granitic superstructure, or batholith, far beneath the earth's surface.

Borregan granitic rock consists of many individual igneous intrusions, or plutons, collectively referred to as the Peninsular Batholith. By themselves, these intrusive rocks are light-colored and coarse-grained, composed of quartz and feldspar sprinkled with darker minerals such as mica and hornblende. Local rock types range from dark gabbro and diorite to light-colored granodiorite and tonalite (Field Trip No. 5, Tierra Blanca Mountains).   There are also minor intrusions of cream-colored pegmatite material that penetrated cracks and crevices from latter stages of the rising plutonic magmas (Field Trip No. 1, Culp Valley).

As the Mesozoic Era closed, 65-70 MYA, a prolonged period of crustal compression and displacement occurred along the rising eastern margin of the Peninsular Batholith. This included widespread overfolding and thrust faulting. Across Anza-Borrego, stacks of metamorphosed sedimentary rock and fragmented plutonic rock were violently shoved westward several miles, up and over younger batholithic rock materials (Field Trip No. 3, Ship Rock).

Much like the large-scale thrust faulting that occurred in the Rocky Mountains, this period of deformation reflected regional uplift of the entire area, extending from the San Jacinto Mountains southward into Baja California. As the land slowly rose, the countering forces of erosion began at once to bevel down the landscape. Grain by grain, boulder by boulder, the exposed bedrock cover was stripped from the ancestral highlands, with some of the sediment then transported in a westerly direction down flooding rivers and coming to rest along San Diego's low lying continental shelf.

CONTINENTAL BREAKUP, VOLCANISM - Cenozoic Era (5-65 million years ago)

By the beginning of the Eocene Epoch (53 million years ago),the older mountains had been reduced by erosion to a broad rolling plain. Mild erosional surfaces across the Peninsular Mountain highlands formed backdrops and broad intermontane valleys across Anza-Borrego. It was a time of tremendous sedimentary deposition. For nearly 10 million years, great rivers with their huge system of tributaries carried their sediments westward. Eroded debris from inland Mexico (present State of Sonora) was spread over highland plains and along San Diego's low-lying coast, coming to rest as a series of conglomerate, sandstone, and mudstone deposits. Remnants from these times still exist in a few scattered locations within park boundaries, representing the depositional history of Anza-Borrego's early Cenozoic Era.

Indianhead Peak (elev. 3,960 ft.) dominates the San Ysidro crest above the Borrego Springs Shear Zone which delineates the uplifted mountains from valley (basin) sediments (elev. 800 ft). FS

The sediments that underlie most of the Borregan landscape began to be laid down about 20 million years ago during the Miocene Epoch.The Miocene was a remarkable time of mountain building, earthquakes, erosion, deposition of sediments and volcanism, each of which played important roles in the formative development of today's unique park setting.

Anza-Borrego was actually attached to the North American landmass when Baja California first began splitting away from mainland Mexico. This splitting started along the ancestral San Andreas Fault system, about 20 million years ago. As a result, parts of Anza-Borrego - the basins - began sinking, actively filling up with sediments, while other parts - the mountains - began rising. This tectonic mountain-building episode is intimately related to plate tectonic movements. Pressures deep within the earth began to physically break apart the crust along a giant fissure zone of complex faults. This zone is now referred to as the Salton Trough/Gulf of California structural depression.

It was a time of basin and range block faulting and fragmentation of the crust, accompanied by a related generation of detachment faults that evolved across southeastern California. This was all controlled by plate tectonic motions, as the Pacific Plate gradually moved northwestward, relative to the North American Plate. They are separated by the San Andreas Fault Zone and its attendant fault zones that broke the continuity of the land into huge blocks of exposed bedrock along fault lines. This process continues today with Baja and southwest California riding the Pacific Plate northwesterly.

Concurrent with the vast pressures that were creating lateral shifting and crustal extension in the Gulf of California, volcanic activity also manifested itself, reflected in the upwelling of hot molten material onto the earth's surface. Volcanoes erupted from magma chambers below the periphery of the Salton Trough Depression. Voluminous basaltic lava flows reshaped portions of the topography. Named the Alverson Formation, these volcanic events continued unabated, eventually dying out between 18-14 million years ago. Most geologists believe that these eruptions and lava flows mark the onset of continental rifting within the Gulf of California.

The volcanic ejecta gave rise to some of the area's most inhospitable scenery - the laid-bare terrain where the Volcanic Hills, Table Mountain near Jacumba, and remote areas in the Fish Creek Mountains now stand.

Midway through the narrow labyrinth of Split Mountain Gorge, is a sequence of rock strata deposited during this same period of time and derived from the uplifted flanks of the ancestral Vallecito and Fish Creek Mountains. The arrangement of rock here is like no other, representing reddish-colored braided stream deposits and thick boulder fanglomerate deposits. Most of the colorful stripes in the canyon walls belong to the Split Mountain Formation. This unique setting was several million years in the making, recording the rejuvenation of the Borregan landscape during the Miocene Epoch.

BORREGO'S LIVING PAST - Recent Epochs
(0.1 - 5 million years ago)

Today, park visitors to Font's Point, Diablo Dropoff and the Carrizo Badlands Overlook (Canyon Sin Nombre) are rewarded by views of basins, once sediment filled, that have been dramatically altered by weathering and erosion. These desolate and arid badlands of Anza-Borrego are unusually rich in fossil specimens of the Pliocene and Pleistocene Epochs.

The fossil-containing layers of sediment reflect various environments of

A NEW Look
At OLD Desert Topography

In the 1920s a student named Rollin Eckis was denied his graduate degree because his thesis presented a theory that was too "far out." Mr. Eckis, now the retired president of Atlantic Oil Inc., presented his theory in 1988 to the San Diego Association of Geologists. This time he had a responsive audience. His theory - the northern and western ends of the Anza-Borrego Desert are dominated by massive landslides. Those ranges like Pinyon Mountain and Granite Mountain are huge slide blocks from the Peninsular escarpment.

As the Salton Sea depression opened and the Peninsular Ranges rose, great blocks detached from the Peninsular Batholith and slid into the opening on low angle slip plains, or detachment faults. Impressive secondary slides followed.

Take a new look at the desert. The mountains that surround the visitor center could be secondary slides from the main slide blocks. Note that "granitic rock" south of Tamarisk Grove Campground is really large angular boulders, not solid rock. And those "backward facing" slopes high on the mountain sides that lean inwards rather than toward the valley, are a sure sign that you are looking at a landslide rather than solid rock.

This once "outlandish idea" answers many geological questions about the Anza-Borrego region - and provides an entire new set of questions to ask.

Dr. Richard Phillips
University of San Diego
November 5, 1989

deposition. They include, in ascending order from early to later, shallow-water marine muds and sands of the Gulf of California, sands and silts of the ancestral Colorado River drainage, and locally derived lakebeds, floodplains, and alluvial fan sands and gravels.

During the early Pliocene Epoch, about 5-4 million years ago, a shallow marine sea occupied the eastern edge of Anza-Borrego, inundating the Vallecito-Fish Creek basin and half of the Borrego basin. The earliest invasions of the sea were tentative. The extensive gypsum beds, now being mined near Fish Creek, were formed as the first advances of the sea evaporated and left their minerals behind. As the earth's crust continued to sag, layers of marine sediments (named the Imperial Formation) were laid down within this void. Consisting of gypsum, turbidite sandstone, mudstone and calcareous sandstones, the marine environment supported a multitude of intertidal shellfish. Over 200 invertebrate fossil species have been identified - snails, periwinkles, starfish, sea urchins, barnacles, corals, oysters, and clams. Near the top of the Imperial Formation, delta mudstones and channel sandstones became predominant, indicating changing environmental conditions as the sea withdrew and water became shallow. Within the Carrizo Badlands the transition from the marine to non-marine is characterized by alternating brackish, tidal flat layers of the Diablo Formation (new). (See Appendix abstract regarding elevating Diablo to formation status.) This Diablo Formation is the delta-plain of the ancestral Colorado River. It contains a wealth of petrified wood, mostly early forms of California laurel and cottonwood.

About four million years ago, Anza-Borrego was located closer to the mouth of the Colorado River than it is now. It was another time of tremendous sedimentation. As early as 3.8 million years ago, ancestors of modern horse *Dinohippus*, and camel, *Megatylopus*, lived and died in the region of the Fish Creek badlands. Their remains have been found along with camel type footprints along Fish Creek Wash.

Above the Diablo delta sediments, the Palm Spring Formation in the Vallecito Badlands contains the remains of some of the most spectacular land mammals that ever lived. Over 100 varieties of large grazing herbivores, carnivores, aquatic mammals, microtine rodents, amphibians, and reptiles have been found. Together this unique assemblage represents one of the richest concentrations of Pliocene and Pleistocene vertebrate fossils in North America, five to one and a half million years ago. A major value of this assemblage is its unbroken sequence of several million years with the Borrego Badlands to the north nearly completing the sequence into recent time.

The Vallecito-Fish Creek Basin, shown on most maps as the general Carrizo Badlands, is easily differentiated into three classic badland areas: Vallecito, Fish Creek, and Carrizo (specifically defined). The Vallecito Badlands is named for mudhill exposures in the Vallecito and Arroyo Tapiado drainages including West Mesa. These sediments include locally-derived lakebed, riverine, and floodplain deposits of the Palm Spring Formation.

The Carrizo Badlands, as specifically defined, are named for Carrizo Creek and include mudhills exposed throughout the Coyote Mountains and Carrizo Impact Area. Sediments are shallow marine deposits from the Imperial Formation and Colorado River delta deposits from the Diablo Formation (new).

The Fish Creek Badlands are exposed along Fish Creek Wash, and include all of the mudhills from Split Mountain (marine Imperial Formation) through Diablo Dropoff Wash (delta Diablo Formation) to Sandstone Canyon (terrestrial Canebrake Conglomerate).

During the late Pliocene and early Pleistocene Epochs, these badlands looked vastly different from today. Ground sloth and mountain deer roamed here. Herds of grazing equids (horses, zebras, and asses) and camelids (large species of camel and stilt-legged llamas) were also plentiful, according to the rich fossil deposits found in the area. Each was spied upon by predatory cats, such as the saber-tooth *Smilodon gracilis* and *Smilodon fatalis* (our state fossil), as well as the American lion, *Panthera atrox*. There were abundant canids (dire wolves and coyotes), too. Airborne, above open grasslands and sagebrush, daily flybys of hawk, eagle and giant vultures such as *Terratornis incredibilis*, worked over carrion and microtine rodents.

To the north, the Borrego Badlands chronicle the latest chapter of evolutionary trends and climatic changes. Dating from the middle to late Pleistocene Epoch, between 1.5 million to about 300,000 years ago, the area was home to resident Columbian and Imperial mammoths, *Mammuthus columbi*, and *M. imperator*, camels and horses (including *Equus bautistensis*, the western plains horse), sloth, deer and bears that were larger in size than today's grizzly.

The Pleistocene Epoch was also a time of dramatic and dynamic mountain building. Dating back 1 - 2 million years ago, and continuing today, the Borregan landscape, included within the Borrego Badlands, began to rise; All this was driven by the same tectonic forces that widened the Gulf of California, rifting Baja California away from mainland Mexico.

Pressure on the layered sedimentary strata was so great that they broke into several fault-blocks. The uplift of the Santa Rosa, Coyote and San Ysidro mountain ranges steepened gradients, causing streams draining from these highland sources to run fast and strong into the low-lying basins. The badlands scene today at Font's Point, is the result of water cutting into soft sandstones, mudstones and claystones of the Borrego Formation and Ocotillo Formation. Exposed to view, this barren geological layer cake encompasses earth history and the evolutionary procession of life. Many are the stories of cast-off shells, petrified wood and shards of bone - each comprising an important window into Anza-Borrego's past.

The final and current uplift of the mountains of "the western barrier" commenced during the latter part of this period. The mountainous backcountry surrounding the community of Borrego Springs is a part of the Peninsular Ranges Province, a segment of the backbone of Southern California. The "rainshadow" effect of these rising ranges contributes to the desert climate as we know it today.

These mountains are the most prominent feature of the Borrego landscape. To the northeast are the mighty Santa Rosas with several peaks that top eight thousand feet. The San Ysidro Mountains to the west form a natural western wall and drainage divide to the Pacific Ocean. To the south stretch Pinyon Ridge and the Vallecito Mountains, and southeastward, the Fish Creek Mountains. Farther south, the Laguna, Jacumba, and In-Ko-Pah Mountains are concordant across the border with the Sierra Juarez and San Pedro Martir ranges of Baja California.

The powerful forces beneath these dynamic and rising ranges are closely related to those causing the rifting of Baja and the sinking of the adjacent Salton Trough and Gulf of California. The next chapter descends below sea and earth crust in search of these forces.

Los Angeles County Natural History Museum diorama of fossil camel skeletons, similar to the Pliocene discoveries in the badlands of Anza-Borrego. PR

TECTONIC PLATE BOUNDARIES AND THE GULF OF CALIFORNIA

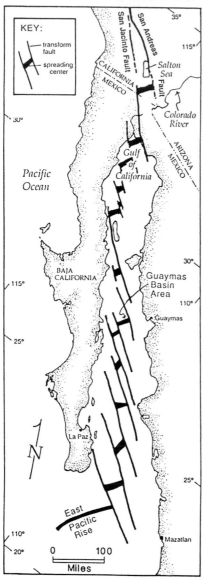

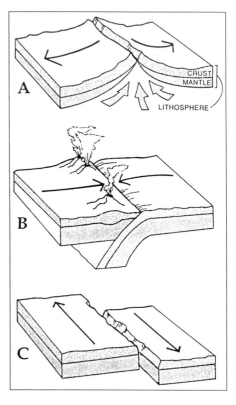

Three types of plate boundaries and relative plate motions:

(A) Divergent (plates move away from each other); the process of sea-floor spreading creates new oceanic lithosphere,

(B) convergent (plates approach each other); the process of subduction destroys lithosphere,

(C) transform (plates slide past each other without approaching or diverging); transform faulting is the corresponding process.

Transform faults and spreading centers in the Gulf of California.
Modified from Moore, 1973, p. 1886.

Modified from Sawkins and others, 1978, p. 165

Chapter 2

A HELL OF A HOLE: SALTON TROUGH AND THE SEA OF CORTEZ

THE SALTON TROUGH - The Big Rift

The Salton Trough didn't just happen. Its origin is closely linked to the complex extension of the Gulf of California (Sea of Cortez) into the Californias, Alta and Baja. It is a child of a wild geologic process that began here less than five million years ago, when waters of the Sea of Cortez lapped the shore north of Palm Springs.

This structural depression, including the Coachella Valley, Imperial Valley, and the Anza-Borrego region, extends 120 miles from the Mexican border to San Gorgonio Pass. Within its depth, two immense tectonic (crustal deforming) systems clash, causing a sediment-filled crack in the earth's surface four times deeper than the Grand Canyon.

It is here that the sea-floor spreading centers of the East Pacific Rise march up the Gulf of California. Here these centers meet the notorious San Andreas transform fault zone which runs northwest five hundred miles through San Francisco. Sea-floor spreading centers emit fiery new ocean floor material from the earth's cauldron while the San Andreas is the wrenching slip zone between the Pacific Plate and the North American Plate. The result of this rift and fault meeting produces one of the most active seismic systems in North America.

The Salton Trough, as a classic, fault-bounded, basin continues to stretch, thin, and sink about one inch per year. This conforms to its larger identity as the northernmost extension of the subsiding Gulf. This regional structure is dominated by the San Andreas Fault Zone on the northeast side and the San Jacinto Fault Zone on the southwest, or Anza-Borrego, side.

The 350 square mile Salton Sea divides the long and narrow trough. The northern half, Coachella Valley, is the apex of the total Salton Trough-Gulf of California structural depression. Coachella is Spanish for shell, referring to the delicate, bone-white, fresh-water shells that occur along the flanks of the San Jacinto Mountains. The southern half, Imperial Valley, includes the Salton Sink and is largely below sea level. Before the accidental creation of the Salton Sea in 1905, the area claimed the lowest elevation in the Western Hemisphere at 274 feet below sea level. With the surface of the Salton Sea at minus 235 feet, Death Valley now rates top (or bottom) score at minus 279 feet. (For comparison, the Dead Sea in Palestine is the world's deepest land trench at minus 1286 feet.)

This is a classic region for studying how the crust of the earth has deformed. There are localities in Nevada that approach it. The eastern side of the Sierra Nevada has parallel scenery; parts of Death Valley compare, but none of these equals it in complexity and current activity. The entire area is alive. The earth is riddled with faults of great magnitude that rupture often and regularly. The scars of faults are everywhere, reshaping the topography and marking an area that is sinking faster than it can be filled with sediments. It is veined with fresh volcanic vents and mineral-laden hot springs where Vulcan continues to stoke his fires.

The larger earthquakes in the trough region (including the powerful M7.5 Landers earthquake) are primarily caused by crustal rock structures adjusting to the rifting stresses and strains of continuing continental breakup. Northwest-trending fault systems have propagated in a stair-step fashion up the Gulf and explain the pattern of pull-apart features beneath the alluvium of the Colorado River delta.

Commencing about five million years ago, the Gulf of California unzipped like a horseshoe opening to the south, with the tip at Cabo San Lucas rotating 148 miles away from the Mexican mainland. Driven by plate interactions, the Pacific side rifts apart from the North American side, along the Gulf/Salton Trough axis.

The Anza-Borrego region spreads along the western edge of the Salton Trough, with the Salton Sea (elev. minus 235 ft.) in its basin, as seen in this view east from Travertine Palms. Only the 42 foot high Colorado River delta dike separates the minus 274 foot floor of the basin from the Gulf of California. LL

In addition to rifting, the relative motion has obliquely stretched and thinned the crust, which continues to collapse. A result of continental rifting is that Anza-Borrego moves closer to San Francisco by about two inches each year. A result of crustal collapsing is that the Colorado River delta dam, now about 40 feet above sea level, will eventually be breached by Gulf waters. Thus will a marine seaway, floored by oceanic crust in the Salton Trough, be redeveloped. This evokes a fanciful image of Yuma, Palm Springs, and Borrego as northern Gulf seaports rather like Guaymas, Puerto Penasco, and San Felipe today.

Spreading centers are the source of another type of seismic activity known as earthquake swarms. These are rhythmic expansions and contractions, announcing the movement of molten rock underground. They occur frequently in the Imperial Valley and Gulf margins. The only difference between spreading centers in the Gulf and in the Salton Trough is that the latter are buried under a thick accumulation of sediments from the Colorado River.

Young volcanic intrusions of rift-related magma into the sedimentary succession have resulted in the development of numerous geothermal features - dynamic, near-surface links to the underworld of plate tectonics. Here and there, hot springs, fumaroles, mudpots which resemble miniature volcanoes, and occasional puffs of ash and vapor, are surface expressions of internal heat from active spreading centers beneath the desert floor. This provides an ideal arena for geothermal power.

The energy of the system has also given rise to the major uplift of the Peninsular Range mountains to the west. Beginning about two million years ago, the uplift continues. This has resulted in an arid change of climate as the rising mountains cast a rain shadow over much of the Colorado Desert. Related deformation has tilted, warped, folded and faulted much of the sedimentary basin fill around the margins of the Salton Trough.

THE COACHELLA VALLEY - Apex of the Trough

The range-bounded Coachella Valley extends northward a distance of 50 miles from the Salton Sea to San Gorgonio Pass. It is a deep and narrow basin which is the northern apex of the Salton Trough. This is, in turn, the northern extension of the Gulf of California. The Coachella Valley is bordered on the northeastern side by the Little San Bernardino and Cottonwood Mountains, and on the western side by the high San Jacinto and Santa Rosa Mountains. Since Pliocene times (3 MYA), the ever-widening Coachella Valley has received a vast amount of material from these adjacent highlands. As determined from exploratory wells, it may contain up to 14,000 feet of nonmarine sediments.

At the northwest end of Coachella Valley, San Gorgonio Pass marks the constraining bend in the San Andreas Fault, part of the structural knot of Southern California's Transverse Ranges, which include the San Bernardinos and San Gabriels. This fault borders the northeast side of the Coachella Valley and displaces in a right-lateral sense. (Right lateral refers to the relative motion of an object across the fault line from the observer moving to the right.) The result is that the San Bernardino Mountains slip relatively to the right (southeast), in relation to the San Jacinto Mountains block. This relative slip is evidenced in rocks exposed in the nearby Orocopia Mountains (northeast block) which have their counterparts exposed in the San Gabriel Mountains (southwest block). Total displacement of the San Gabriels to the northwest may exceed 190 miles since the Pliocene Epoch (3 MYA).

San Gorgonio Pass is guarded on the south by the abrupt, magnificent mountain profile of Mount San Jacinto. The precipitous drop, 9000 feet to the desert floor in less than six miles, is the steepest escarpment in North America after Telescope Peak in Death Valley. At 10,831 feet, this two mile high skyscraper outranks all other aeries of the Peninsular Ranges. Only nearby San Gorgonio, on the north or opposite side of the pass in the San Bernardino Mountains, reaches closer to the Southern California clouds at 11,502 feet.

IMPERIAL VALLEY - Delta Dammed

Just east of Anza-Borrego and south of the Salton Sea (-235 feet below sea level), the sediment-filled Imperial Valley extends beyond the international border to the head of the Gulf of California at El Golfo de Santa Clara. Measuring up to 36 miles wide, this depressed structural basin is the southern portion of the Salton Trough. Most of its alluviated floor lies below sea level, protected from the Sea of Cortez only by the broad, 40-foot-high Colorado River delta. It is one of the nation's most productive agricultural areas.

Before its damming, the Colorado River had one of the greatest silt loads of any river in the world. Over a period of several million years, the river built a natural delta just below what is now the Mexican border. Since the Pliocene (2 MYA), this barrier has pushed the ocean back, isolating the Salton Trough from the Sea of Cortez. Filled mainly with river and lake deposits, the valley has undergone many cycles of flood and desiccation. Raging river waters wandered freely, flowing northward into the basin or southward into the Gulf.

At present, this natural dike is actively eroding along a shallow shoreline where the never-ending conflict between sea and land recurs with every rise and

The rich fauna of the Sea of Cortez is pictured here in Bahia Refugio in the Gulf of California. PR

fall of the tide. This drainage divide is only 40 feet above sea level, a subsiding toehold that will eventually yield to marine processes. The invading sea will once again inundate the Salton Trough in a watery grave.

Mountain boundaries flank the valley east and west. The eastern edge is lined by a chain of relatively low desert ranges - Cargo Muchacho, Chocolate, and Orocopia Mountains. Summits along this crest are around 1000 feet with some exceeding 1400 feet. The much higher western edge is the Anza-Borrego region, which includes the Vallecito, Fish Creek, and Coyote Mountains with the Laguna crest beyond. Some summits and ridges are over 5000 feet.

Rocks of the Imperial Valley tell complicated stories of continental drift, sea-floor spreading, and abundant seismic disturbances. These are all vital signs in a crustal anatomy undergoing dynamic change. It is here, in a desert pulling itself apart, that the East Pacific Rise manifests itself via geothermal power plants, high heat flow, earthquake swarms, natural hot springs, mudpots, and recent volcanism along the Salton Sea's southeastern shore. These are reliable indicators that new crust is forming out of hot mantle material from active spreading centers. These centers are hidden beneath a veneer of five million year old Pliocene to recent delta sediments under the southern end of the Salton Sea.

GULF OF CALIFORNIA - Submarine Supercrack

Geologically speaking, the key to understanding Borrego is to understand Baja and the Gulf of California. Anza-Borrego's mountains are near the northern end of the long Peninsular Ranges. Her basins and badlands echo their parentage as part of the rift basin which is now occupied by the Gulf and Salton Sea. This great rift, almost 1000 miles long and 60 to 150 miles wide, is a supercrack bounded on either side by fault block mountains.

At the close of the Eocene Epoch (about 36 MYA), the entire Baja Peninsula was fixed to Mexico's west coast. Mature, through-going river systems flowed across a gentle countryside, bringing river sediments westward to the coastal plain. Its rock and structures evolved as a continuation of an ancient geologic system massed along the Sonora and Sinaloa coasts of the westward-moving North American continental plate.

What caused this stretch of coastline to break apart? The mechanism was apparently the same as that which produced the features of western North America's Basin and Range Province. This began during the Miocene epoch about 23 MYA and continues today. This mechanism is the override of the East Pacific Rise by the westward moving North American continent. This rise is a dynamic sea-floor spreading center, similar to the Mid-Atlantic Ridge, which marks the diverging boundary and upwelling of magma between two tectonic plates. It marks the centerline of the Gulf of California from which Baja and the Mexican mainland continue to spread.

This complex process of spreading center override and tectonic plate collision broke apart crustal blocks into a new orientation of fracture zones and systems. Plate collision included subduction, the underflow of oceanic material beneath the continent. This resulted in violent seismic, volcanic, and orogenic (mountain building) activity throughout the western continent. The 1980 eruption of Mt. St.Helens in Washington State is evidence of remnant subduction activity which began with the breakup of western Mexico in Miocene times.

The expanding series of down dropping basins, bordered by uplifting mountain ranges, is characteristic of the Mojave Desert and Great Basin regions. Earthquakes and volcanic activity here bear witness to buried and consumed tectonic plates and yield footprints of a possible northern extension of the East Pacific Rise coming ashore. The East Pacific Rise may be hard at work, embedded between such heights and depths as the snow-covered Sierra Nevada, Death Valley, and Utah's Wasatch Mountains. Locally, much of the topography of Anza-Borrego owes its tectonic origin to related activity during this time of oblique subduction beneath the continental margin.

The gross effect of plate reorganization resulted in the eastward-moving Pacific block rotating away clockwise, relative to the continental edge. Pres-sures were great enough that this change in direction initiated the rifting that literally sheared off land from the North American Plate. This included 55,000 square miles that became Baja California and a slice of southwestern California. Incorporated onto the Pacific side, the newly liberated San Andreas Fault Block, today one of the longest peninsulas in the world, rafted away from mainland Mexico. This severance left in its wake the mouth of the Gulf of California.

Seismic data reveals a narrow, well-defined belt of submarine spreading centers inside the mouth of the gulf, a young rift basin. Beginning about 7.5 MYA, spreading widened the mouth of the gulf by one-quarter inch/year. Cumulative into the early Pliocene Epoch, it was enough to admit a northward marine transgression of ocean water and sediments that reached Anza-Borrego in the form of the Imperial Formation, about 5-6 MYA.

The East Pacific Rise is a key actor in the continuing drama of the gulf. This rise cleaves the sea-floor with a series of obliquely parallel ridges, each terminated by a transform (major strike-slip) fault.

Advancing northward, in an unzipped succession of pull-apart features, this remarkably huge wound widened the gulf as it went. It reached the south end of the Salton Trough by 4.5 MYA. By 4 MYA, the apex of the gulf embayment had dilated crustal rocks beyond Palm Springs.

The gulf today is world known for massive aggregations of resident and migratory waterfowl, marine mammals, and great fish schools featuring over 650 species. During the Pliocene Epoch, this waterway was even more fruitful, with the existence of the Panamanian seaway and a link to the Caribbean. It was probably the northernmost range for members of Caribbean and tropical eastern Pacific faunas, strikingly represented by the fossil shellfish of the Imperial Formation in Anza-Borrego. Prominent are *Turritella* (turritellid shells), *Ostrea* (Oysters), and *Conus* (cone shells). Biological affinities of these extend throughout both Caribbean and Pacific.

Chapter 3

LAND THAT DANCES: THE MAJOR FAULT ZONES

INTRODUCTION

Since the beginning of the Pliocene Epoch 5 MYA, crustal stretching, thinning, and rupturing caused the Salton Trough to subside below sea level. It does not subside gently. The frequency of felt and recorded earthquakes attests to the region as seismically active.

Three prominent northwest-southeast trending fault zones (the San Andreas, San Jacinto, and Elsinore) have played important roles in the crustal deforming evolution of the Salton Trough and adjacent mountains. Earthquakes and faulting provide visible, bone-shaking evidence of North America's most pronounced example of a seismically active divergent tectonic plate boundary. This chapter is the story of these fault zones.

"Earthquakes Shake Valley"; "Quakes Jar Wide Area Around Borrego Springs"; "Quake Biggest Known in Desert"; "Twin Quakes Jolt Area, "Aftershocks Keep Desert on Edge." Newspaper headlines only scratch the surface. Some scientists say, in the geological maelstrom of the Salton Trough, that the twin Richter magnitude 6.2 and 6.6 earthquakes that struck here in 1987 or the one-two punch magnitude 7.5 and 6.6 temblors of June, 1992, were no more than a passing yawn compared to the real whoppers of yesteryear, or "The Big One" expected to uncoil along the southern San Andreas Fault Zone within the next 30 years.

One of the first recorded accounts of an earthquake in the Salton Trough comes from the personal diary of Friar Thomas Eixarch in 1767. Camping along the river bank of the Colorado near the future site of Fort Yuma, his entry on April 25th tells us: "At night there was an earthquake, but it was of short duration. Since I have never experienced such a thing, I was frightened to see how the ground shook. On the following day, Yuman Indians confided to Eixarch that the ground always shakes like that and " . . . usually trembles three or four times."

Little did Eixarch realize that this event stemmed from complex interaction between Pacific and North American tectonic plates, accounting for basin subsidence and boundary mountain-building. Here, where faults have cracked landward from Gulf spreading centers of the East Pacific Rise, the earth's rocky crust has thinned considerably. It ranges from 12 miles thick under neighboring ranges like the San Ysidros to less than three miles thick beneath the sedimentary fill under the Salton Sea.

These transform faults, transforming or offsetting spreading center forces at an angle to the northwest, tear at the land horizontally and deepen the Salton Trough rift as a classic "pull-apart" land feature. The pliant crust of this rift has been and continues to be deformed across a broad and splintered belt, as the Pacific Plate pulls obliquely away from the North American continent along a series of major strike-slip or transform faults.

In the Imperial Valley, these transform faults - the San Andreas, Imperial, Brawley, and Cerro Prieto - are the principal discontinuities which facilitate east-west crustal extension. They are not simple cracks but connect by hot, seismically active, spreading centers offset in an en echelon pattern, a geological term suggested by progressively offset rows of troops. Such a pattern is similar to the ridged segments that mark the East Pacific Rise on the floor of the Gulf of California. The only difference between Gulf and Imperial Valley spreading centers is the lack of topographic expression of the latter, buried under the sedimentary sheet of clay, silt, and fine sands from the Colorado River.

The sedimentary rocks of the Salton Trough-Gulf of California exhibit almost every kind of deformation known on the earth's crust. Fracturing, faulting, and folding affect almost everything. Most of the rock formations have been altered beyond recognition, metamorphosed, intruded and extruded, tipped on end, turned upside down, thrust over, rotated, and offset many miles.

Faults within the Salton Trough have caused about 20 large earthquakes (greater than magnitude 6.0) since 1899. Most of these events have occurred in the western part of the Trough, on the subparallel Imperial, Superstition Hills, Coyote Creek, Clark, and Brawley faults. These are all part of the diffuse San Jacinto Fault Zone, one of the most seismically active areas in all of North America. The patterns of its earthquakes are typical of motions occurring along

Clark Dry Lake occupies the low point of the Clark Basin, a crustal thinning, pull-apart feature between the rising Santa Rosa Mountains (right) and Coyote Mountain (left), all of which is controlled by the Clark and Coyote Creek strands of the San Jacinto Fault Zone. FS

strike-slip features, by which brief main shocks are followed by hundreds of aftershocks and swarms of smaller events, vibrating the entire Salton Trough.

At present, the Trough has a clear claim on earthquake frequency with over 11,000 measurable tremors per year. That's an average of 30 per day or one every 48 minutes. Each quake, no matter how large or small, is charted as sequences of nervous peaks and valleys on rolling seismographs. A battery of instruments -accelerometers, creepmeters, strainmeters, tiltmeters, leveling lines, geochemical sensors, magnetometers, and a dense network of seismometers - measure fault movements. Part of the Global Positioning System ground stations receive radio signals beamed from Dept. of Defense satellites 13,000 miles high. Distances measured between ground stations and satellites can be used to calculate distances along a fault to within one-half inch accuracy.

Seismologists have been consistently in agreement that Southern California is overdue for a catastrophic shaking. They had predicted a 60 percent chance of a magnitude 8.0 or more occurring within 30 years in the Southland. This includes a 30 percent chance of this quake occurring on the Coachella Valley section of the San Andreas fault. Now there is much higher concern. The strong M7.5 Landers earthquake was the strongest in the coterminous United States in four decades and the worst quake inland Southern California has ever seen in historic times. It triggered a robust twin jolt of M6.6 at Big Bear and an unusual aftershock sequence that has baffled scientists and made seismologists nervous. For the first time, the Governor's Office of Emergency Services and the San Diego County Office of Disaster Preparedness issued a formal "earthquake alert" for more damaging earthquakes to come. Is this a sign that the notorious San Andreas is primed to unleash an even larger quake? Are we getting closer and closer to the "Big One" above magnitude 8?

THE SAN ANDREAS - Salton Sea to San Francisco

An ominous line of reddish crushed rock is exposed in a narrow zone at the mouth of Painted Canyon, east of Mecca in the Coachella Valley. From the graded roadway, it is a short hike to see where movements along the main line of the San Andreas Fault have upended these sediments, similar to Borrego's Ocotillo Formation, on one side. They are pinned against highly deformed, crushed granitic and volcanic exposures on the other side in an awesome display of nature's muscle.

The mystique that surrounds the infamous San Andreas Fault continues to attract scholarly and popular attention. This great shear zone slices 650 miles of California from Cape Mendocino to the Salton Sea. It visibly proclaims the boundary where Pacific Plate grinds against North American Plate, separating Southwestern and Baja California from the rest of the continent. Relative north-west motion of this area, also known as peninsular California, averages about two inches per year with a horizontal displacement of several hundred miles.

This fault is a complex system of roughly parallel fractures that branch and interlace within a zone. Like other major fault zones, pressure ridges, beheaded or truncated alluvial fans, sags, and fault scarps clearly mark its trace. The zone varies in width from less than one mile at Point Reyes to nearly 40 miles in Southern California. Tectonic plate motion is translated into surface evidence across coastal plains and hills, inland valleys, mountain ranges, and the Mojave and Colorado Deserts.

The largest and most destructive temblors in California have occurred on the San Andreas. The northern segment experienced horizontal displacements of

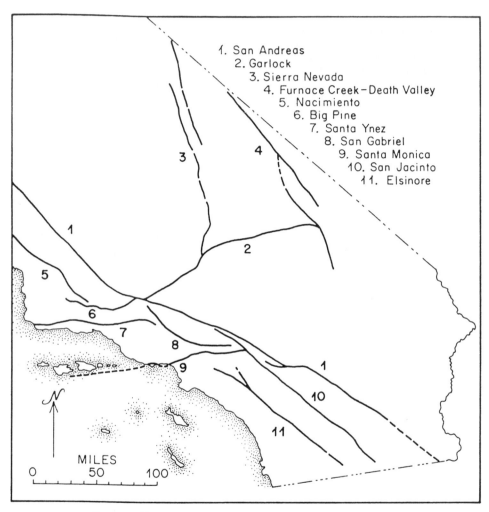

1. San Andreas
2. Garlock
3. Sierra Nevada
4. Furnace Creek–Death Valley
5. Nacimiento
6. Big Pine
7. Santa Ynez
8. San Gabriel
9. Santa Monica
10. San Jacinto
11. Elsinore

Generalized Fault Map of Southern California
*(From **Geology Field Guide to Southern California** by Robert P. Sharp,
copyright 1975, reprinted by permission Kendall/Hunt Publishing Co.)*

15 feet during the San Francisco quake of 1906, Richter magnitude 8.3. The nearby 1989 Loma Prieta quake, magnitude 7.1, was on a scale not recorded in the United States since the massive M9.2 knock-out punch that paralyzed Alaska in 1964. The 1857 Ft.Tejon quake, magnitude 7.9, ruptured the surface between Cholame and Cajon Pass with 30 feet of horizontal displacement.

The southern segment stretches 110 miles from Cajon Pass to the Salton Sea and is, statistically, the most dangerous portion of the entire San Andreas. This is based on the lack of "major" quakes (Richter magnitude 7) in the historical record, producing a seismic gap in space and time. However, there have been half-a-dozen good-sized events of magnitude 6.0 or greater near to, but not directly on, this segment of the San Andreas since 1986. Are these advanced warnings, foreshocks of an even bigger one?

This scenario is not unlike stress build-up and seismic events prior to the damaging M7.1 Loma Prieta shocker (1989) and devastating M8.3 San Francisco quake of 1906. Surprisingly, the Landers event likely did little to relieve pressure on the San Andreas. In all probability it increased the stress level and activity in the region. Allan Lindh, chief of the USGS Seismology Branch, says that the San Andreas is "loaded and ready to go." It may happen tomorrow, next month, or next year. No one can say with certainty, only that it might come sooner than previously predicted.

On July 7, 1986, a wrenching earthquake rumbled through the Coachella Valley, abruptly jolting millions of Southern Californians from their beds. The epicenter of the temblor, which stopped the clocks at 2:21 a.m. and registered M5.9 on the Richter Scale, struck northwest of Palm Springs on the Banning strand of the San Andreas Fault. Lasting only 30 seconds, the initial jolt caused widespread power outages. It buckled and cracked highways, damaged bridges, knocked mobile homes off their foundations, triggered rockslides and swayed high-rise buildings from the Nevada state line to the Mexican border.

At the same time, the Colorado River aqueduct was damaged in several places, causing more than 975 million gallons of water to be diverted out into the desert. The earthquake was followed by hundreds of aftershocks that kept desert residents jittery, with 20 rated at M3.0 or higher.

The San Andreas Fault Zone remained calm until April 22, 1992. At 9.52 p.m., the area east of Desert Hot Springs moved again. Following on the heels of a moderate jolt registering 4.6, the M6.1 Joshua Tree earthquake shattered the peace of the Coachella Valley and Morongo Basin. The powerful temblor knocked out electric power and telephone service to many communities, and rocked buildings from San Diego to Santa Barbara. It was the biggest temblor in the lower 48 states since the M7.1 Loma Prieta quake of 1989, and was quickly upstaged by the M6.9 Ferndale quake in Northern California on April 25th. Frightening aftershocks in the M4.8 range rocked the Salton Trough, causing seismologists at Cal Tech in Pasadena to issue a warning that this shaker, related to the San Andreas Fault, could be a foreshock to something much bigger.

All the recent temblors in the Salton Trough pale in comparison to the monster juggernaut 7.5-magnitude Landers earthquake which ripped through the region at 4:58 a.m. on June 28, 1992. It was California's strongest earthquake in 40 years, the third most powerful this century, and was 4 times stronger than the Loma Prieta event.

Within seconds, surface rupture scarred a swath of destruction 43 miles long, with a record-setting 21 feet or more of right-lateral, strike-slip displacement. The epicenter of this megaquake was above the northeastern edge of the

Coachella Valley, in the Morongo Basin, beneath the sparsely populated high desert community of Landers. In the maelstrom that followed, shock motion, travelling at speeds of two miles per second, shook and shook and shook the Salton Trough for almost one minute, jarring the Anza-Borrego region.

Incredibly, its enormous fury was felt all over the West, as far east as Denver, Colorado, as far north as Boise, Idaho and Seattle, Washington, and as far south as Cabo San Lucas, Baja California, Mexico. The initial jolt spawned instantaneous rumblings hundreds of miles away in Utah, Nevada and the Owens Valley along the eastern base of the Sierra Nevada. It also caused low-level seismic swarms in volcanically restless hot-spots beneath Mount Lassen, Mount Shasta, and the Long Valley Caldera near Mammoth.

Three hours later, a powerful M6.5 aftershock ripped through Big Bear in the San Bernardino Mountains, 20 miles west of Landers and less than 10 miles from the San Andreas Fault. In the aftermath of these two major quakes, hardest-hit Landers suffered buckled roadways, broken water mains, electric outages, and numerous homes and business destroyed or damaged. Two weeks later, the earth continued to quiver from over 5,000 aftershocks. Damage in the quake-riddled areas is estimated at $92 million. Due to the sparse population, only two deaths were reported.

Much of the problem in Southern California is centered in the Transverse Ranges. The steadily increasing compression at the northern end of the Salton Trough-Gulf of California has created, through time, a structural knot. This knot is the Transverse Ranges, which trend east-west, extending inland from Santa

Horizontal slip-strike faulting along a "plunging anticline" accounts for this fracture, which incorrectly appears as a result of vertical motion, at the north entrance to Split Mountain. SB

Barbara to the San Bernardino Mountains. The southern half of the San Andreas Block is attempting to get around the corners of this immense obstacle by splaying out into half-a-dozen seemingly unrelated smaller faults. In doing so, interaction on the west has produced a region of overthrusting and crustal shortening, as evidenced by the 1971 San Fernando quake (M6.6), 1987 Whittier-Narrows quake (M6.1), 1990 Upland quake (M5.5), and 1991 Sierra Madre quake (M5.8).

From the southeast end of the San Bernardino Mountains to Cajon Pass, the fault bends abruptly, running east and west. This "big bend" in the fault has been seismically quiet since 1680, and is commonly regarded by earth scientists as being locked. As a result, pent-up strain has become acute.

To help alleviate strain, much of the motion in this region is believed to have been taken up by strike-slip interaction along younger faults sub-parallel to the San Andreas. There is also the remote probability that the "Big One" may not occur directly on the San Andreas but perhaps along a fault running sub-parallel to it. In the Yucca Valley and Morongo Basin, geologists regard the Landers event as evidence of a new fault zone in the making. Northward-trending underground stresses widening the Salton Trough may be attempting to take a shortcut around the steadfast bulwark of the transverse ranges along a previously unknown avenue of least resistance. Maturing through the Plio-Pleistocene (1-5 MYA), many second-order magnitude splays and branches of epic portent evolved in Southern California, most notably the San Jacinto Fault Zone and the Elsinore-Chino fault zone.

Unlike the San Andreas, slippage on these faults has generated most of Southern California's earthquakes. In combination, these subparallel belts have effectively sliced up the continental margin of the Pacific Plate. As a consequence, Anza-Borrego annually experiences hundreds of minor and several major temblors. Some say that this rivals the claim of Parkfield, in central California, to be the "Earthquake Capitol of the World."

SAN JACINTO FAULT ZONE - A Contender for the Title

The region is of considerable interest to earth scientists. Many suspect that an entirely new regional tectonic era has arisen, and it involves Anza-Borrego. Instead of opening headward towards the constraining bend in San Gorgonio Pass, they believe the energy expended in the Salton Trough is being offset up several corridors of weakened rock. One of them, to the west, cuts diagonally across Anza-Borrego as the San Jacinto Fault Zone.

Today, more than ever before, the San Jacinto is where the action is. It is the driving mechanism behind the mood of the land, responsible for the features that loom over Anza-Borrego. Signs of faulting and change are everywhere. Note the faceted spurs along Coyote Mountain and east of Clark Valley on the face of the Santa Rosa Mountains. Numerous well-preserved fault-scarps, deflected drainage courses, sags, shutter and pressure ridges, aligned valleys, offset alluvial fans and other large-scale features apparent at the surface, all show geologic recency of movement.

This style of deformation - high seismicity, compression, stretching, and general upset - corresponds to the periodic outboard transfer of tectonic energy from the San Andreas Fault to the San Jacinto Fault system. While there is still debate on the subject, many geologists regard Anza-Borrego as part of the emerging tectonic boundary between the Pacific and North American Plates.

This then, should be a more important celebrity than the southern segment

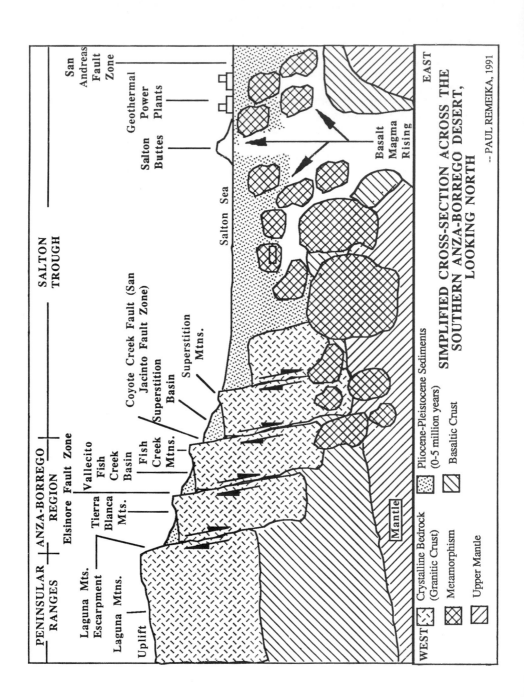

SIMPLIFIED CROSS-SECTION ACROSS THE SOUTHERN ANZA-BORREGO DESERT, LOOKING NORTH

-- PAUL REMEIKA, 1991

of the San Andreas Fault. The San Jacinto main fault has a 40 percent chance of shifting again before the end of the century. Its related smaller faults demonstrate similar probabilities. The Imperial Fault has a 50 percent chance of repeating the M6.7 El Centro quake of 1940. The Coyote Creek Fault has a 10 percent chance of rupturing with a fury at least that of the M6.5 Borrego Mountain quake of 1968. The Clark strand has a 30 percent chance of producing a magnitude 7.0 event between the Truckhaven Rocks and the town of Anza.

On April 9, 1968, the M6.5 Borrego Mountain earthquake sent seismograph needles jumping nervously up and down on rolling graphs, as the earth's surface broke along 31 miles of the Coyote Creek Fault. Rocks tumbled down in Split Mountain Gorge. Visitors atop Font's Point sucked a quick breath when six feet of rock, holding up the tip of the point, collapsed underfoot. Four days after the quake, the earth was still moving. Hundreds of aftershocks triggered appreciable displacements on the nearby Imperial and Superstition Hills faults.

The San Jacinto may also be responsible for the alarming northward progression of activity within the Brawley Seismic Zone, beginning with the M6.6 Imperial Valley Quake of 1979, the M6.4 Westmoreland quake of 1981, and the 1987 M6.6 Superstition Hills quake. All of this suggests a change in strain across the region.

On the evening of November 23, 1987, an earthquake more powerful than the October 1st M6.1 Whittier-Narrows Quake rocked the Imperial Valley and jostled Anza-Borrego. The temblor, registering M6.2 on the Richter Scale, was located 16 miles east of the Fish Creek Mountains on the Elmore Ranch crossfault near the agricultural town of Westmoreland. It was preceded by two strong foreshocks of M4.0 and was followed by several after-shocks stronger than M5.0.

At 5:16 a.m. the next morning, Westmoreland and Borrego residents got a chilling wake-up call. This time a magnitude 6.6 earthquake occurred in the same general area as on the previous evening, sending frightened residents rushing into the streets. The main shock, rupturing over 14 miles of the Superstition Hills Fault, was Southern California's strongest earthquake in six years and the second major quake in 12 hours. As it rumbled through the Colorado Desert and Baja California, it injured 94 people and contributed to two deaths. The epicenter was located on the northwest end of the Superstition Hills Fault, three miles closer to the Fish Creek Mountains than the shaker of the previous evening. This is the same trace that also ruptured in response to the 1968 Borrego Mountain Earthquake.

The 1987 pair spawned a series of 45 aftershocks, measuring up to M4.9, that whipsawed the desert for 10 days. This one-two punch shattered windows and cracked walls but did not cause serious damage in Borrego Valley. In the park, cave-ins and rockfalls occurred in the usual areas - Split Mountain, Arroyo Seco del Diablo, and along Arroyo Salado. Boulders and landslides also covered sections of pavement along Montezuma Grade and at Yaqui Pass.

Professor Phil Kern, of San Diego State University, notes that the San Jacinto is very active, having produced 13 major seismic events near or greater than M6.0 or larger since 1899. It has been several years since the Superstition Hills Earthquake of 1987. The Anza gap, between Anza Valley and Coyote Mountain, has a pronounced lack of seismicity. This locked portion, 13.5 miles long, is bounded on either side by areas of high earthquake activity. It may well be the probable location for the next big shaker.

It may therefore be that the San Jacinto Fault Zone deserves the title of

"Granddaddy" of Southern California faults, but why? How can the one to two million year-old San Jacinto be the credible heir to the title of the 25 million year-old San Andreas?

First, the San Jacinto, geologically speaking, is a child of the San Andreas. The motion of the latter has been inhibited by the tectonic knot of the Transverse Ranges at the constraining bend of San Gorgonio Pass.The San Jacinto is a continuous zone of seismic strain release and right-lateral, strike-slip motion that has demonstrated and dominated active tectonic instability of Southern California in historic times since 1800.

Second, the San Jacinto has a remarkably straight course, a more direct natural extension of the San Andreas that tends to be the principal crustal discontinuity south of Cajon Pass. This alignment conveniently straightens the transform boundary, assisting the Pacific Plate to bypass the constraining bend of San Gorgonio Pass. Finally, geologic measurements across the Salton Trough indicate that some strain release has been taking place along the San Jacinto Fault Zone, not the San Andreas.

SAN JACINTO FAULT ZONE - A Tour Through the Area

The San Jacinto diverges from the San Andreas Fault near Wrightwood, striking southeast from the San Gabriel Mountains through San Bernardino along the west side of the San Jacinto and Santa Rosa Mountains to Anza-Borrego. Upon entering the desert, the fault splays into a number of subparallel and branching faults of the same strike and character - Coyote Creek, Buck Ridge, Clark, San Felipe, Superstition Hills and Superstition Mountain. Cumulative right separation is about 15 miles. There is no deceptive absence of earthquake activity along these faults. All are very active and capable of producing large, destructive earthquakes, as evidenced by the recent Arroyo Salado, Borrego Mountain, Coyote Mountain, and Superstition Hills events. In addition there is a great deal of microseismic activity.

Structural details along the San Jacinto are especially well displayed along two separate, major strands of this system, the Clark and Coyote Creek Faults. The most obvious fault in the area is the Clark Fault. It is the more direct extension of the San Jacinto into Anza-Borrego.

This master break can be followed from San Jacinto and Anza Valleys, down along the east side of Table Mountain to Horse Canyon, trending sharply along the west side of Buck Ridge, Rockhouse Canyon and extending across Clark Valley. Beyond Palo Verde Wash, the fault is concealed under intensely deformed sediments of the Borrego Formation in Basin Wash and the San Felipe Hills. To the south, the fault steps to the left, into the Brawley Seismic Zone with its attendant spreading ridge, probably becoming the Imperial Fault. Unknown prior to the 1940 M6.7 earthquake, the Imperial Fault trends into the Cerro Prieto Fault and its related geothermal field on Baja California.

The position of Coyote Mountain and the Santa Rosa and San Ysidro Mountains is the result of relatively recent movements along major strands of the San Jacinto Fault Zone. Some blocks have been squeezed up a mile or more above sea level, just a bit faster than erosion can tear them down. Others have been fragmented into elongated slices of rock. All move either laterally, vertically, horizontally, or a combination of these.

Counterbalancing this uplift, intervening blocks have sunk where fault lines diverge. Borrego Valley, more correctly called "Borrego Basin," is one of these. Another is Clark Valley. The eastern side of Clark Valley is an impressive

5,700-foot escarpment of rock (Santa Rosa Mountains). But the valley's most interesting aspect of relief is its interior drainage, the result of tensional stresses that are pulling the crust apart.

This closed basin didn't exist until relatively recently. Its exterior drainage formerly flowed south into the Borrego Basin. But subsidence of the Clark basin, coupled with uplift in the Font's Point area northeast of the Borrego Sink, has resulted in Font's Point being nearly 700 feet above the floor of Clark Valley which blocks Clark Valley's former southerly drainage.

The triangular graben of Clark Valley is bounded by the magnificent escarpments of the Santa Rosa Mountains and the Coyote Ridge block. This enclosed basin is undergoing rapid subsidence, elongation, and tilting, part of a widening oblique transform motion along the fault.

Remarkably recent surface expressions, including zones of crushed crystalline basement rocks and fault gouge, aligned canyons and arroyos, seeps and springs, sag ponds, deflected drainage and fault scarps, indicate recurrent movement along nearly the entire length of the fault.

The best known of these youthful fault features is Lute Ridge, across from Rattlesnake Canyon. Recent geologic mapping shows that this distinct scar across the landscape is a classic fault scarp. It is the largest known of its kind on the North American continent, developed in recent, unconsolidated sediments. Although it extends two miles in length, fresh scarps and scarplets indicate about 2,100 feet of recent displacement, with progressively smaller offsets in sequentially younger alluvial fans nearby.

Desert View, on Hwy 79 southeast of Julian, overlooks the Earthquake Valley Fault striking southeast along the San Felipe Mountains, past Scissors Crossing and Sentenac Cienega, into the Pinyon Mountains. LL

The largest strike-slip faults record horizontal movements of the earth's crust that are many times greater in magnitude than the impressive vertical movements which result in the relief of mountains and basins. For example, the upthrown Coyote Mountain, pushed up over one mile to make the Coyote Ridge block, contains cataclastic rocks that correspond to similar beds along the southern end of the Santa Rosa Mountains. The total offset of the Santa Rosa Cataclastic Zone within Anza-Borrego is 15 miles. Also, geologists have found that some of the deep-gullied Truckhaven Rocks on the east side of the fault have been displaced sideways 16 miles. Today their western counterparts are located in and around Butler Canyon, northwest of Clark Valley.

The Coyote Creek branch serves as a through-going, northwest-trending series of en echelon splays that document many episodes of recent movements, which are characterized by high seismicity, linearity, continuity, and fault-produced topographic features. It can be easily followed from Turkey Track down through Coyote Canyon, where it uses Box Canyon to separate the Pleistocene Ocotillo Formation of the Coyote Badlands (westernmost equivalent of the Borrego Badlands) from the elongated Coyote Ridge block on the east. This block behaves geologically as a single unit, enclosing the northern end of Borrego Valley.

From the Pegleg Smith Monument, the fault trends southeast, folding sediments of "Mammoth Cove" while truncating the entire western edge of the Borrego Badlands. Beyond, the projection of the fault follows the Anza Trail, obscured beneath alluvium along San Felipe Creek. South of Borrego Mountain, the fault steps left, deforming the Ocotillo Badlands, to become the Superstition Hills and Superstition Mountain Faults. It was along this stretch that surface rock ruptured for a distance of 31 miles during the 1968 M6.5 Borrego Mountain Earthquake and 1969 Coyote Mountain aftershock. Field studies following the Superstition Hills Earthquake of 1987 also found surface ruptures across an extended region of the Brawley Seismic Zone

The repeated seismicity of the earth's crust in this area has provided ample information on fault geometry and slip movement. Although individual events have been quite small, the cumulative effect over the past several million years is considerable. The amount of crustal shift experienced along the Coyote Creek Fault during the Borrego Mountain Earthquake was three feet. Substantial horizontal displacement, such as that between the Coyote and Borrego Badlands, occurs when such movements are repeated. The same holds true for sites of significant uplift like Coyote Mountain and Borrego Mountain. Late Quaternary slip rates have been estimated at almost one inch per year along the Coyote Creek Fault near Borrego Valley.

This is a good area to observe the "coal car" interpretive concept of stacking rock sediments from highlands onto lowlands. The image is that of canyons and water courses from mountain ranges serving as "conveyor belts". These conveyer belts bring sediment downslope to the "loading bays" of tectonically mobile basin floors as if the basin floor at the foot of the canyon were a waiting railroad coal car. As the coal car moves tectonically to the northwest the "car" (basin area) behind begins receiving newer alluvium from the canyon conveyer belt.

An excellent example can be seen along the mouth of Rattlesnake Canyon across from Lute Ridge, along the Clark Fault. Here the relatively stable canyon debouches sediments from the northeast across the fault strand. The southwest block moves laterally, carrying these sediments into Clark Valley. The older sediments from Rattlesnake Canyon are therefore those that are farthest into Clark Valley, northwest of the canyon mouth. This pattern is repeated in many locations where lateral or strike-slip faulting is occurring at the base of a mountain range.

ELSINORE FAULT ZONE - The Carrizo Corridor

This is the third of the major fault zones of the Salton Trough and Peninsular Ranges and is part of the San Andreas complex of right lateral faults. The Elsinore is parallel to its larger cousin, the San Jacinto. Named after the classic pull-apart trough between Temecula and Corona, the Elsinore extends some 125 miles from the Laguna Salada fault near the Mexican border to the northern end of the Santa Ana Mountains.

The Elsinore is a series of major northwest striking fractures that run along the western side of the Coyote Mountains, up through the Tierra Blancas, Mason Valley, Banner, Julian, Warner Springs, Temecula, and eventually becomes the Whittier-Narrows Fault in the Los Angeles Basin. The Whittier segment was responsible for the destructive M6.1 temblor that jolted the Los Angeles Basin on October 1, 1987. Numerous hot springs mark the trace of the Elsinore and related faults including Guadalupe Canyon in Baja, Jacumba, Agua Caliente, Warner Springs, Murrieta, and Glen Ivy.

The Elsinore zone in the Anza-Borrego region includes the Agua Tibia --Earthquake Valley Fault, San Felipe Fault, and Vallecito Creek Fault, any of which are capable of generating major quakes. The impressive landscape along Highway S2 in the Carrizo Corridor substantially results from the combined effect of these faults. Its southern continuation is the Laguna Salada Fault,which was responsible for the major M7 quake that destroyed portions of San Diego in 1892.

On January 25, 1988, a moderate-sized M5.1 earthquake rattled northern Baja California and Anza-Borrego. Centered on the east side of the Sierra Juarez Mountains, the quake was felt for hundreds of miles, even into central California. In the mid 1950s this same region had been struck by an unusual swarm of moderate and strong quakes, including a M6.8 temblor in 1956 that destroyed several villages.

Banner Canyon, which separates Volcan Mountain from the Laguna crestline at Julian, displays numerous examples of high angle fault expressions, including a linear canyon, steep mountain walls, truncated sediments, slump blocks, and vegetation stripes marking the fault trace. As recently as August 11, 1992, a Magnitude 3.4 quake was recorded in this area. A major strand separates at Banner up and over Rodriguez Canyon into Mason Valley.

The Tierra Blanca Frontal Fault, which is prominently displayed between Agua Caliente and Bow Willow, was the site of a 1973 M4.8 temblor. This fault, one of the principal lateral strands of the Elsinore, extends down to a depth of 1.8 miles. It separates the western barrier mountains from the sediment-filled Vallecito-Fish Creek Basin.

Mapping suggests that offset along here, between Aqua Caliente and the Coyote Mountains, is about 4.2 miles. Maximum potential of this fault is rated at 7.1 (equal to the devastating 1989 Loma Prieta quake in San Francisco). Evidence of historically recent displacements can be seen along the foot of the mountains. During these quakes it is possible that as much as 20 feet or more were added to the difference in height between the basin floor and the crest of the Tierra Blanca Mountains.

This strikingly youthful fault scarp is still visible as a prominent bench-like surface rupture, cutting across the base of the mountain front from Canebrake Canyon to Mountain Palm Springs, and beyond. It is probably no more than a hundred years old, formed as a result of the M7.0 Laguna Salada earthquake of 1892. It clearly rivals similar fault scarps along the eastern Panamints in Death Valley and the Hilton Creek Fault scarp of the eastern Sierra Nevada.

Since the Late Pleistocene, deformation has significantly changed the landscape along the Carrizo Corridor. For example, east of the fault the entire Vallecito-Fish Creek Basin has been downdropped along its western margin, and rotated up to 26 degrees in a clockwise sense. Lesser lateral faults - Middle Mesa, Salt Springs, Little Devil and East Mesa - distribute this slippage across the grain of the badlands setting.

"Slickensides," smooth surfaces visible on slip planes of a surface fracture, are an expression of the Elsinore Fault Zone at the southwest edge of the Agua Caliente campground. LL

COLLAPSING MOUNTAINS - A View from the Top

Atop the crystalline rock pasture of McCain Valley, capped by 4,140 foot Sombrero Peak, vistas across the Vallecito-Fish Creek Basin and Carrizo Corridor are wide angle and seemingly endless. Nowhere else does the ground fall away in such a cavalcade of descending mountain blocks - Laguna, Tierra Blanca, Fish Creek, and Superstition Mountain. The visible descent plunges from the Laguna Crest to below sea level in the Salton Trough. The invisible descent continues another 20,000 feet beneath Salton's sediments to bedrock. Geophysical evidence indicates equivalent rock structures at bedrock depth and on Sombrero Peak add up to a distance of over four miles of vertical displacement.

The evidence is strong. These descending mountain blocks may have been detached from the brink of the Peninsular rooftop to form their present stair-step topography, interspersed with low basins. A similar condition is believed to account for Death Valley's Tucki Mountain detaching and sliding down from the eastern Panamints. Stretch marks between the ranges are suggested as the mountain blocks sink deeper into the depths of the Salton Trough, similar to a set of dominoes tipping sideways. This may be a local result of regional crustal spreading, thinning, and Peninsular Ranges uplift in an active zone of tectonic plate margin fragmentation.

Some blocks are finding it hard to keep head and shoulders above the ground (Superstition Mountain). Some sag and collapse throughout their entire length (Tierra Blanca Mountains). Others sag at one end but elevate at the other (Coyote Mountains).

While the Peninsular crest has been bodily uplifted and tilted to the west, the land east of it has been broken by the cluster of range-bounding splays that comprise the Elsinore Fault Zone. No one fault takes precedence. Each has broken and worn down the mountains until its bedrock bones are exposed. Thus, in the southern part of Anza-Borrego, the single steep rift wall of the Lagunas yields to a stepping down of mountain blocks. These ranges stand like flotillas of drowned buttes and battlements, offering an extraordinary diversity of landscapes and range of habitats. To explore them is to discover Anza-Borrego anew.

A Grossmont College geology class explores the depths of Canyon Sin Nombre beneath complex folds of Diablo sandstone along the Elsinore Fault Zone where ancient Paleozoic metamorphic rocks are in contact with Pliocene sediments. DZ

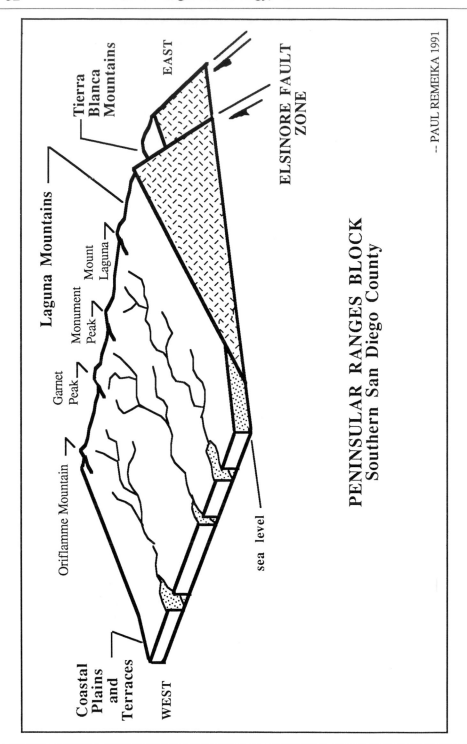

PENINSULAR RANGES BLOCK
Southern San Diego County

-- PAUL REMEIKA 1991

Chapter 4

MOUNTAIN BUILDING AND THE ROCKS OF FIRE

BORREGO'S BACKBONE - The Current Uplift

Elevated mountain walls dominate the western edge of the Colorado Desert and Anza-Borrego with precipitous and denuded eastern slopes ascending quickly to serrated mountain crests five to eight thousand feet high. Many of these walls are fault scarps which feature active faulting. Unbroken, save for inter-montane passes, these mighty escarpments of monolithic rock are part of a major mountain chain, the Peninsular Ranges.

This long, nearly straight chain is almost 1000 miles in length from the San Jacinto Mountains to the tip of Baja California. Its width varies from 50 to 120 miles, structurally even including some coastal islands anchored off-shore. North of the border, it extends 140 miles to San Gorgonio Pass, sharply truncated by the San Andreas Fault Zone (the Banning Fault), from the San Bernardino Mountains of the Transverse Ranges.

These dynamic mountains, named after the Baja Peninsula, are in the full vigor of their youth and continue to build. While the beginning of the current uplift is quite recent, one to two million years ago, the component rocks are old with some up to 500 million years old. From nubbins to hills to peaks the Penin-sular Ranges have climbed skyward five, six, ten thousand feet, cutting off the incoming Pacific rains and drying out the landscape in its eastern shadow. And, with each seismic shudder in its roots, the climb continues.

Beginning in the late Pliocene Epoch (2-3 MYA), renewed tectonic activity along the western Salton Trough began the unique sequence of events that lifted the Peninsular Ranges mountains into rainshadow prominence. As Baja rotated away from the Mexican mainland, compressive energy uplifted the unbroken profile of the Santa Rosas, culminating at Toro Peak (8,716 feet). Beyond, approaching the structural knot of San Gorgonio Pass, these same forces raised the San Jacintos even higher. Mt. San Jacinto (10,831 feet) thus has one of the greatest unbroken vertical rises of any mountain mass in North America.

Structurally, this is a great block of granitic rock of the Mesozoic Era, (70-100 MYA) overlain, in part, with secondary pendants and screens of older and uplifted marine metasediments of the Paleozoic Era (250-500 MYA). Occasional volcanic rock is encountered too, dating from the Miocene Epoch (15-20 MYA). Just as an animal's body is supported by its spinal column, the entire Baja Peninsula and much of Southern California is protected and supported by this crustal backbone.

These mountain blocks have been tilted westward, forming an asymmetric profile. While the eastern slopes are steep, short, treacherously rugged, and lightly clothed with vegetation, the long and gentle western flank rolls and pitches on an average gradient of six percent through pine forests, oak wood-lands, and dense chaparral to the coastal plains. Along the crest, are rich subalpine forests of ponderosa and lodgepole pine (San Jacinto Wilderness), or broad oak meadowlands and Jeffrey pine (Laguna - Cuyamaca Mountains). Lower elevations feature impenetrable thickets of deerbrush, manzanita and scrub oak leading one frustrated geologist to write, "Where the steepness does not forbid the way, the chaparral everywhere disputes it!"   A large look at mountain structures, coupled with a detailed look at their component rocks, helps envision the geologic history of this bold terrain. Three distinct types of rocks, based on their origin, are recognized. Sedimentary rocks, the result of aging and death of mountains and life forms, are discussed in the following chapter. This chapter considers igneous (fire-formed) and metamorphic (changed-form) rocks which are generally associated with the birth and growth of mountains. Whether born from molten magma beneath the earth, cooled from volcanic eruptions, or emerged in changed form from intense heat and pressure, these are indeed the "Rocks of Fire."

DAWNROCK- Paleozoic Metasediments

Anza-Borrego's metamorphics are mainly marine sedimentary rock, metasediments, in shades of black and gray, chocolate and maroon. The metamorphic process consists of heat and pressure changing one type of rock into another, for example, turning shale into slate, sandstone into quartzite, and limestone into marble. These are the earliest or dawn rocks of the region. The younger igneous granitics are a series of medium to coarse-textured intrusive crystalline rocks which have intruded into the region from beneath the older, overlying metasediments, cooking, breaking up, and shouldering aside the latter.

San Ysidro Mountains looking west from San Felipe Wash. While the constituent rocks of these mountains are a hundred or more million years old, the current uplift of the range is relatively recent, perhaps 1 - 2 million years. The uplift is thus similar in time frame to the deposition of the Pliocene sediments visible in the middle ground. PR

It all began quietly enough about 500 million years ago - a time that well predated the celebrated reign of dinosaurs. In the dim past when these rocks were originally deposited, the area looked vastly different from today. There was no Borrego Valley, no hint of Coyote Mountain or the mud hills where the Borrego and Carrizo Badlands would be.

The area had been under the ocean's surface for the better part of 70 million years and perhaps longer. Its waters were hundreds of feet deep and stretched from horizon to horizon. Conditions were favorable for a full development of marine life, including corals, bryozoans, brachiopods, cephalopods, sponges and crinoids.

Somewhere to the east, extending from the present-day Gulf of Mexico northwestward into Utah, lay land, antecedent to the primordial supercontinent of Pangaea. Meaning "all land," Pangaea was a union of continents that existed during the Late Paleozoic Era. Shore-bound several hundred miles east of California, this land mass was surrounded by an ocean of unknown dimensions called Panthalassa, "all sea," the ancestral and now-shrinking Pacific Ocean.

From about 500 million years to about 120 million years ago, tens of thousands of feet of continentally-derived sediment was deposited oceanward from the western Pangaea shoreline. In Baja California, near El Marmol, San Marcos, and San Felipe, these Paleozoic beds have been found to be partially fossiliferous, yielding many crinoids, cup corals, bivalves, conodonts, fusulinids and bryozoa. It has been estimated that the deposits ultimately buried the Baja Peninsula and Alta, or Southern, California with carbonate sediments several miles thick.

Sometimes shallow, sometimes deep, the level of the sea repeatedly changed as new layers of rock were piled upon older ones. Each change in the environment - sea temperature, water depth, chemistry - would leave its mark as a distinct marker bed, first under clays and silt and beach sands, and later, as the sea water deepened, under carbonate muds. Gradually, in time, the accumulating weight and pressure, combined by chemical cement in the warm, transparent waters, consolidated the sediments into permanent rock (shale, limestone, and thinly layered quartz-rich sandstone). The wandering shoreline quietly distributed sediments which, ages in the future, would become the metamorphosed inclusions and roof pendants of the rising Peninsular Ranges of today.

The oldest rocks in the Anza-Borrego area include poorly fossiliferous sediments scattered throughout the Santa Rosa Mountains. A thick sedimentary section of layered carbonate rocks can be easily seen from the valley floor southwest of Villager Peak.

Nearby, metasedimentary outliers of the same age are equally exposed on the rock-ribbed lower slopes of the San Ysidro Mountains from Hellhole Canyon to Henderson Canyon. Also found in the Coyote Mountains, they are variously tilted and folded. Their haunting presence represents nearly 12,000 feet of tiered stratigraphic laminations including marble, slate, phyllite and hornblende, finely-banded schist and coarse-grained quartzitic rocks of vast antiquity.

Based on recently discovered fossil evidence, these rocks have been assigned an early Paleozoic (Ordovician to Mississippian) age of 350 - 500 MYA. Grouped with formations recognized in Baja, these rocks have close affinities to the Paleozoic metasedimentary rocks of the Desert Divide Group of the San Jacinto Mountains (including the Bull Canyon Formation and Ken Quartzite) plus marine sequences (Pogonip Group) of the southern Great Basin of eastern California and Nevada.

Along the western ramparts of Anza-Borrego, younger near-shore carbonate deposits are restricted to narrow perimeters in the Laguna Mountains with a dating of approximately 200-225 MYA. Known locally as Julian Schist, these younger metamorphic rocks consist of multi-layered quartzites, mica schists, and minor fossil-bearing limestones that obviously accumulated as a sedimentary wedge along the western continental shelf of the ancient coastline.

Although belemnites, bivalves, cup-corals, and other marine fossils were numerous during the Triassic-Jurassic periods, there is only fragmentary evidence of creatures large and small. The reason is the metamorphic process itself. Most remnants of life were either destroyed when the entombing rocks were ground into tectonic hash or changed beyond recognition by powerful compression forces. These forces, associated with the breakup of the Pangaea supercontinent, major plate collision, and subsequent batholithic emplacement, are the subject of the next section.

PLUTO'S MESSENGERS - Intrusive Granitics and Deeprock

Near the end of the Jurassic period, about 135 MYA, the westward moving North American plate and its continental cargo was colliding head-on with the eastward moving Farallon (East Pacific) plate with its oceanic cargo. Compression forces literally bulldozed North America up and over an unyielding heavier oceanic crust, subducting the sea floor with its sedimentary veneer downward and eastward at about a 45 degree angle beneath the continent's edge.

Trapped within the vise of subduction, the oceanic plate penetrated to a depth of 50 miles or more and slowly melted, consumed in defeat. Associated frictional heating, at temperature up to 1000 degrees C, produced large masses of molten magma.

In a series of intrusions, like casting plaster filling a mold, magmatic mate-

Pinyon Ridge, and most of the crest of the Peninsular Ranges, is dominated by huge, rounded granitic boulders, weathered remnants of the original intrusion of molten magma which cooled miles beneath the surface to become the Peninsular Batholith ("Deep Rock"). PR

rial slowly congealed into closely packed chambers called plutons, which rose under pressure towards the surface. Pluto, ancient god of the underworld, aptly lends his name to this process. The upward progress of the viscous rock in plutons metamorphosed and shouldered aside most of the older marine sediments of the upper crust.

Caught between converging crustal plates, the once-even bedding of the Julian Schist and earlier metasediments of the dawnrock were now wrinkled and mashed up like crushed newspaper. Where the overlying crust was weak, a battle line of volcanoes erupted on the surface, spurting fountains of red-hot andesitic lava or belching frothy sheet flows and ash along their periphery.

Each pluton, of different composition and age, took from ten to fifteen million years to cool under the crushing pressure of miles of country rock above. These infiltrating pulses or plumes thus chilled, hardened, and crystallized into the solid fabric of granitic rock collectively called batholith or "deep rock."

By late Cretaceous, about 70 MYA, the North American plate had overrun most of the Farallon plate beneath it. Several thousand miles of oceanic crust had been consumed and reconstituted at depth. This generated enough large granitic melt zones to ultimately coalesce into the underground basement mesh called the Peninsular batholith, the bedrock of our present Southern California mountain ranges.

While the batholith is the fusion of hundreds of separate plutonic plumes, it is not homogeneous. Each pluton brings its own history to the mix ranging from the dark-colored gabbroic "black granites" of Cuyamaca Peak to the light colored tonalites and granodiorites of Anza-Borrego's mountains. The general term "granitics" is used herein to describe any of these rocks of plutonic origin. Granite itself is one of many kinds of granitics, all of which are classified according to the relative mix of light colored minerals such as quartz and feldspar and dark colored minerals such as biotite mica, hornblende or pyroxene.

Dark-colored granitics represent the older generations of intrusion and are almost entirely confined to the western half of the batholith, on the gentle west slope of the Lagunas. Abundant quartz-rich rocks, saturated with silica through contamination   from the insulating continental crust, represent the younger generations and occur in the eastern, or Anza-Borrego, portion of the batholith. Within the parkland, light-colored tonalite (quartzdiorite) and granodiorite are by far the most abundant.

Field evidence, along with geochemical and petrographic characteristics, suggests that each plutonic intrusion occurred nearly nine miles below the earth's surface and each crystallized at different stages during a lengthy cooling history. Date samples of the Peninsular Batholith spread over an appreciable interval of the Cretaceous Period, from 105 to 65 million years ago, and indicate a systematic eastward decrease in ages of deformation and metamorphism. This is exactly what we would expect to find in the rocks if the sea floor had subducted easterly beneath the continent.

The Peninsular Batholith measures hundreds of miles in length, with a volume of rock so vast that it rivals the Sierra Nevada Batholith of central California. Both are contemporary features of the Nevadan Orogeny ("mountain genesis"), a paroxysm of mountain-building that is responsible for the great curvilinear chain of Mesozoic batholiths that contour western North America.

During the final stages of consolidation of the batholith, hot ascending gases and hydrothermal solutions accompanied many of the granitic intrusions. They forcefully infiltrated well-developed preexisting cracks and fissures, resulting in veins and seams of mineralization. The volatile solutions soon crystallized, forming exceptionally granular igneous dikes and pockets, called pegmatites.

Many of these pegmatites occur throughout the Anza-Borrego area, especially in the Box Canyon, Blair Valley and Grapevine Mountain regions of the park. Here, they can be viewed ranging from thin stringers to large dikes of light-colored quartz and feldspar. Many are remarkably persistent and occur as rows of subparallel dikes, while others may be discontinuous in extent. Mineral aggregates include quartz albite, muscovite and lepidolite micas, and tourmaline.

Large-scale mining of the gem-rich hillsides in the Pala, Mesa Grande and Rincon pegmatite districts (all outside of the park boundary), are produc-tive for their mineral wealth. Renowned the world over, gem-quality crystals of quartz, spodumene, garnet, topaz, beryl and vari-colored tourmaline are mined in "pegmatite pockets."

Gemstones are not the only precious minerals found here. Metals, including gold, were also emplaced from the depths in veins as the last of the granites cooled. Gold-bearing quartz ledges, discovered by transplanted miners prospecting for a new bonanza, touched off a sudden flurry of searching through-out the Laguna Mountains. This occurred after the Mother Lode rush in Northern California, and by the 1870s the Julian-Banner Mining District was teeming with

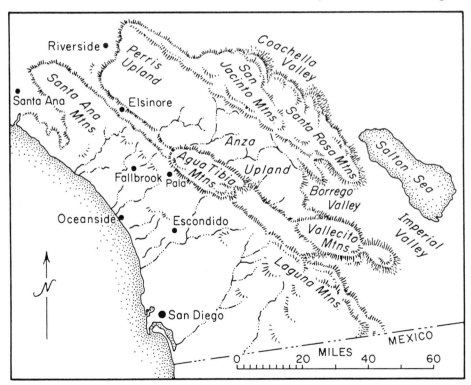

Map of Peninsular Ranges Province
*(From **Geology Field Guide** to Southern California by Robert P. Sharp, copyright 1975, reprinted by permission Kendall/Hunt Publishing Co.)*

hard-rock prospectors, all combing the hills and hoping to strike it rich. Valuable mineral deposits were recovered from several areas in metamorphic rock belonging to the Julian Schist. These rocks had been uplifted and exposed along the Elsinore Fault Zone, on the nearby slopes of Chariot and Banner Canyons. Here, lenticular gold-bearing quartz veins proved to be the most important mineral resource of the area before the turn of the century.

Today, although gold mineralization undoubtedly still exists in the hills near Julian, most gold mining operations are short-lived. It is now more profitable to quarry the granitic rock that once contained the gold. In San Diego County, granitic rock is used as dimension stone, crushed decorative gravels, building materials, gravestones and tombstones, and riprap for harbor jetties.

MOUNTAIN BUILDING - Mesozoic Uplift

Beginning at the close of the Mesozoic Era, about 70-80 million years ago, an episode of widespread warping and buckling of the earth's crust commenced across western North America. Known as the Laramide Orogeny, this mountain-building episode is responsible for the tectonic development of the Rocky Mountains from Canada to Mexico, continental uplift from California to the Mississippi upheaval of the Colorado Plateau, and establishment of the ancestral Sierra Nevada and Peninsular Range highlands.

The forces necessary to produce a new revolution in the landscape were part of a major compressive thrust system, reflecting the collision of a continental margin (North American Plate) with an underthrusting subduction zone (Pacific Plate) in Late Mesozoic and early Cenozoic time (60-80 MYA). Although the tectonic origins of this deformation remain obscure, many geologists believe this event was a continuation of the Nevadan Orogeny, referred to previously as the plutonic episode which resulted in the emplacement of the Sierra Nevadan and Peninsular Batholiths.

In the Anza-Borrego region the Laramide Orogeny coincided with waning metamorphism. It was a time of turmoil with large-scale folding, faulting, over-thrusting, volcanism, granitic emplacement and uplift. Occasioned by a speedup in plate motion, the ensuing structural deformation that accompanied this orogeny has left its mark not only in Anza-Borrego but over the entire Colorado Desert.

Throughout the park, widely scattered clues of a Late Mesozoic (65-75 MYA) overthrust fault system may be observed. Telltale signs consist of discontinuous, linear belts of mylonite in the Santa Rosa, Coyote, and San Ysidro Mountains that were originally continuous segments of the same body of rock. Locally known as the Borrego Springs Shear Zone, these mylonitic belts represent a zone of concentrated deformation, characterized by intense distortion of metasedimentary and host crystalline rock sequences.

They are part of the larger 62 mile-long Santa Rosa Cataclastic Zone which, in turn, forms the northern half of the regional Eastern Peninsular Ranges Cataclastic Zone. This is a major lineament of west-directed thrusting, folding and rock transport that extends southward into Baja California. Deciphering the evidence in these particular rocks has been a special focus of discussion because they involve a very complex process and provide valuable insight into major tectonic processes. In addition, they offer yet another set of relationships between rock structures locally and regionally in the Peninsular Ranges of the Californias.

Rocks termed mylonitic are a product of deep faulting, whereby intense grinding along shear zones at depth strain rock against rock, deforming and granulating individual mineral components embedded in them. Some minerals such as feldspar, amphibole and epidote demonstrate brittle responses. Bulk rock behavior, including metasedimentiary deposits, is ductile. In brief, the distorting forces of mylonization have stretched out the rock as in a plastic flow. These rocks are characterized by a highly-strained foliation and lineation which has reduced them to thin, strongly elongated stringers. Pressures sufficient to accomplish this generally occurred three to four miles below the earth's crust at temperatures above 250-300 degrees C.

Today, one can easily see these rocks along Montezuma Grade in road cuts just down from Crawford Overlook. Kneaded like dough, they carry the scars of cataclastic deformation, related to the crushing and tearing compressional stresses that produced considerable foreshortening of the crustal rocks in the Late Mesozoic. Rock displacements are known to exceed 12 miles in the Borrego area. Associated with the folding and faulting, massive earthquakes were generated that uplifted the ancestral Peninsular Range. This crustal unrest continued into the Cenozoic and abated about 50 million years ago.

For the first time in its history, Anza-Borrego found itself bowed upward above sea level with several hundred to several thousand feet of local relief.This uplift, forming a rugged highland, marks the time when the basement complex now became a new source area for sediments. Erosion's molding hand began unroofing the batholith, stripping away the overlying sedimentary and metamorphic rock and deeply scoring the granitics.

SHAPING OF THE LAND - Eocene Erosion

A widespread plain of low to moderate relief developed on the once mountainous terrain. Ancestors of today's western drainage systems transported large volumes of detritus downslope, forming a westward-thickening wedge of river-borne boulder fanglomerates to finer-grained coastal plain sediments. This continuous Late Cretaceous-Eocene (50-70 MYA) episode records a nonmarine to marine accretionary genesis.

The result was a broad continental apron of low flatlands lying between the eroding highlands to the east and the bordering bayfronts along the coast. Today, dramatic remnants of these deposits are exposed at Point Loma, La Jolla, and along the Torrey Pines sea cliffs. These create some of the most spectacular scenery along the San Diego coastline.

Locally, the tectonic setting of the ancestral Peninsula Range was gradually transformed from a region rife with activity into one of great erosion and stability. Unroofing of the Peninsular Batholith ushered in a long erosional phase, a tectonic lull, spanning 30 million years, into the Oligocene Epoch (23-37 MYA). With some exceptions, a major chunk of Anza-Borrego's early Cenozoic history was erased by erosion. Fortunately, there exists just enough field evidence and imprints on the topography to help geologists piece together the Eocene-Oligocene chapters of the Anza-Borrego story. Much remains to be deciphered.

To understand this extended period of erosion, we must briefly look back some 50 million years into the abyss of Eocene time. Then, Anza-Borrego was still united to mainland Mexico. (It would be another 40 million years before the opening of the Gulf of California would shift the area to the northwest.) The landscape was near sea level and was much nearer the equator than it is now, giving the area a hot, humid climate with rainfall exceeding 50 inches per year.

On San Diego's coastline, the fossil record shows this ideal environment supported a lush rainforest type of vegetative cover with mangrove and nutpalms.

In other words, the general scenario for much of Southern California somewhat resembled Central America of today. The subtropical scene remained unchanged for millions of years.

To the east, the rasp of erosional forces to which the mountains were subjected was enough to tear down many of them even as they rose. With the passage of time the relentless assault ground them into a low, featureless plain covering much of southern Arizona and northwestern Mexico (Sonora) including Anza-Borrego. This once extensive erosion surface remains a very durable feature. Remnants, broken and uplifted by later block-faulting, are an unusually persistent landmark. We can see evidence of this elevated, mature tableland while driving across Montezuma Valley, Shelter Valley, and Jacumba.

Across the smoothed-off ruins of the old mountains, semi-permanent Eocene drainage systems reached inland for hundreds of miles. Each produced enough runoff from Mexican highland sources to carry them to the Pacific Ocean. These through-flowing rivers, filled with rock debris from out of the region, permitted the deposition of an ever-growing accumulation of stream-washed silts, sands and gravels along lower elevations of the San Diego coastal margin.

The new coast, at that time, served as the apex of large deltas, receiving a heavily laden supply of gravels and sediment from meandering streams. The riverine material spread and repeatedly buried acres of beach flat in nearly horizontal layers, forming the foundation rock of what is today Poway, Kearny Mesa and Mission Valley. Defined by distinctive reddish meta-rhyolite to dacite porphyries and quartzitic gravels, these rounded stones have no local source in California. The source is in the mountains of Sonora, Mexico.

Locally termed Ballena or "Poway-type" gravels, only a handful of remnants still survive throughout the eastern portion of San Diego County. In the central portion of the park, poorly exposed outcrops have been reported in the rugged Vallecito Mountains south of Borrego Valley. Their presence in and around Bighorn Canyon and Mine Canyon is the only clue we have for interpreting the obscure early Cenozoic paleoenvironment of Anza-Borrego.

The flat valleys and meadows that straddle the Laguna and San Ysidro Mountain crest are remnant plains from the Miocene Period which rose a few hundred feet above sea level, before the uplift of the now mile-high Peninsular Ranges. CP

BLOCKS AND BASINS - Miocene Breakup

Abruptly, in Miocene time, the situation changed. A new orogenic (mountain building) trend along the west cost developed from the earlier Mesozoic compressional regime to one of extensional breakup of the earth's crust. It became a formative period, marked by great instability in the upper crust, that virtually eliminated the former tablelands and gradually began to establish our present high-relief terrain.

In terms of the terrain, geologists believe it was a real fester. Grand-scale faulting commenced with blocks of crust shifting about laterally or up and down, generating massive earthquakes that unleashed their fury throughout the region.

In order to maintain equilibrium, considerable vertical relief developed along great zones of weakness, with older granitic basement rock lifted to view. Raised blocks became mountainous terrain, the ancestral Pinyon-Vallecito-Fish Creek, the San Ysidro, and the Santa Rosa-San Jacinto Mountain Ranges; down-dropped blocks became the structural basins of Vallecito-Fish Creek and Borrego.

These events were accompanied by widespread, eastward-trending folds of regional scope and associated titanic faults of detachment that juxtaposed older rock units above younger units. Examples of these low-angle extensional landforms may be seen today throughout the rugged Santa Rosa Mountains, as well as nearby along the eastern edge of the Pinyon Ridge-Yaqui Pass alignment. This detachment fault extends from Tubb Canyon to the Narrows of the Vallecito Mountains along the southern margin of Borrego Valley.

Almost without exception, every structural configuration seen throughout southeastern California, western Utah and Nevada can be attributed to the evolving response of the earth's crust to extensional pressure. This response ultimately molded the landscape into the baffling yet distinctive basin-and-range features that characterize the Mojave and Colorado deserts of today. All in all, one might suggest that "all hell broke loose" in and around the Borrego Basin-Salton Trough about 20 million years ago.

VULCAN'S FIRES - Extrusive Volcanics

Imagine a setting of early eruptions, reeking of brimstone, marked by clusters of relatively small volcanic emissions. Medium sized outbursts of molten lava pour forth while steam and ash propel billowing mushroom clouds high into the sky. The magnitude of these forces were similar to the newsworthy eruptions that now occur on the big, young, and growing island of Hawaii. Similar volcanic rocks from about 15-20 million years ago are found in the southern part of the Anza-Borrego region and east into the Imperial Valley.

Granitic rocks, intruded and cooled in a plutonic or subsurface setting, have dominated the Anza-Borrego rock story. Metamorphic rocks, as cooked and eroded remnants of earlier marine sediments, have also been introduced. Now, late in geologic time, it's Vulcan's turn.

Pluto, ancient god of the underworld, is the namesake for intrusive igneous rocks which slowly solidify below the surface. Paralleling this is Vulcan, ancient god of fire, who is the namesake for extrusive (volcanic) igneous rocks which solidify rapidly on or above the earth's surface. While chemical composition may be almost identical, a rock will be an intrusive or extrusive depending upon its rate of cooling.

Intrusive granitics cool slowly, allowing time for individual minerals to form crystals, visible to the naked eye. These are the "salt and pepper" rocks referred to in a previous section of this chapter. Extrusive volcanics cool rapidly, without time for minerals to crystallize, and therefore appear generally uniform in composition.

Basalt is fine grained and dark colored on fresh surfaces and is the most common of the Salton Trough's volcanics. It is a rich blend of iron and magnesium, low in silica, and makes a very fluid rock. As a result, basalt usually forms the magma melt generated beneath spreading plate boundaries such as beneath the Imperial Valley.

Rhyolite, on the other hand, is viscous and light colored. When erupted it is rich in potassium and sodium with a high silica content. Obsidian is a black, glassy volcanic rock formed from high silica magma similar to rhyolite but is devoid of mineral crystals. Pumice refers to highly porous rock fragments blown from volcanic vents. These fragments are light in color and weight and filled with small gas cavities or vesicles.

The best place to see Anza-Borrego's only volcanic field is between Jojoba Wash and Mortero Wash along Hwy S-2, south of Bow Willow. Here, in the eerie stillness of the Volcanic Hills, basalt-capped landforms of dark lava flows punctuate the gentle landscape. About three square miles, including portions of nearby Rockhouse Canyon, were inundated by hot fluid streams of lava and ash in relatively thin sheets. Similar, though less accessible, thermal rock displays are located in Superstition Mountain, Fossil Canyon and Lava Gorge in the Coyote Mountains, and Table Mountain near Jacumba.

Volcanic rock in the Fish Creek Mountains is named the Alverson Formation. It is a contemporary stratigraphic unit with the fanglomerate (alluvial fan

Round Mountain, near Jacumba, is an expression of volcanism from the middle Miocene, in and near the southern end of the park, related to the initial breakup of the Pacific coast of the continent. LL

plus conglomerate) sedimentary rock of the Split Mountain Formation. Typical of most flows in the region, a sea of magma spewed out from source vents alternating with andesitic to dacitic ash flow tuffs, agglomerates, bombs called volcanoclastics, lava domes, and plugs. Individual beds range from six to 140 feet with a maximum measured thickness of 400 feet. Sediments beneath all this, the Red Rock Canyon Member of the Split Mountain Formation, were baked to a brick red by the heat of molten rock.

Much of the evidence of this volcanic activity has been eroded away. It is apparent that faulting broke apart the old fabric of the crust, from time to time, much like tiles laid over a cracking floor. Eruptive events, on one or more occasions, followed these surface ruptures and issued basaltic and andesitic flows over broad areas.

Scientists agree that the distribution of volcanic centers during the Miocene Epoch appears to be the evolving response to the onset of continental rifting of the proto-Gulf of California. Rift-related volcanism here marks the northern location of widespread activity that extended the entire length of what would become the Baja California peninsula.

The first pyrotechnics took place about 20 million years ago and continued sporadically for several million years. Related to the tectonic interactions of the North American and Pacific Plates, these volcanics were harbingers of a marine connection that wouldn't succeed in the Salton region for another 14 million years.

The best and most varied expressions of volcanism in the Salton Trough may be seen on the southeast shore of the Salton Sea, near the National Wildlife Refuge Headquarters. A short distance beyond the thermal pools (intermittently covered by the Salton Sea) are five small volcanic domes - Obsidian Butte, Rock Hill, Red Island 1 and 2, and Mullet Island.

Collectively known as the Salton Buttes, they are indicators of new, fresh volcanics that breached the surface, betraying the presence of a shallow subterranean spreading ridge. These Quaternary (last two million years) volcanic rocks are dense and heavy basalt accompanied by rhyolite, obsidian, and pumice. They are derived from parental, iron-rich magma that is identical in composition to rocks erupted from the East Pacific Rise throughout the Gulf of California. They are young and uneroded with the westernmost dome, Obsidian Butte, yielding a date of only 16 thousand years.

The plumes of steam from nearby geothermal wells, including the aptly named Vulcan Power Plant, are reminders that planetary forces of tectonics and weathering are far from finished with the regional landscape. The Anza-Borrego region remains in the powerful throes of creation.

Chapter 5

EROSION AND THE ROCKS OF WATER

NEPTUNE'S TURN - Sedimentary Rocks

If Pluto's chambers form granitic rocks and Vulcan's fires yield volcanic rocks, then it may be said that Neptune's waters produce sedimentary rocks, or "rocks of water." The role of Neptune, ancient god of the sea, must be broadly construed here. Sediments not only derive from marine deposition but also from delta, lake, stream deposits, and weathering. Examples of these include sandstone, shale, and conglomerates that are generally well layered fragments or "clasts" of preexisting igneous or metamorphic rock. Chemical precipitates such as gypsum and organic remnants such as limestone are other types of sedimentary rocks. King Neptune's claim to a major portion of the rock realm seems valid, since water is the change agent resulting in most sedimentaries.

The boulders of the highlands are examples of rock that is intermediary between its plutonic block origin and the grains of sand and sandstone that may be its destiny. The next section examines such rock.

WONDERLAND OF ROCKS - The Boulder Factories

If the only image of Anza-Borrego is flat desert, then her extraordinary boulder-strewn granitic highlands are a pleasant surprise. Indeed, save for those few approaching from the east, these stony sentinels welcome almost every visitor to the desert.

Even the most casual observer traveling down Devil's Canyon on Interstate 8 must be impressed by these ponderous boulders that dwarf the roadway north and south. In what has been called a Brobdingnagian landscape, referring to Gulliver's travels through the land of giants, the roadway cuts a winding course here through the mountain core. Rising from the desert floor to a height of 4,500 feet, a sizable portion of this lumpy and chaotic foundation - part of the In-Ko-Pah and Jacumba Mountains - forms the eastern escarpment of the Peninsular Ranges.

Looking farther north, one can see boulder outcrops in other areas of Anza-Borrego. Major rock gardens concentrated at Bow Willow, Mountain Palm Springs, Culp Valley and Sheep Canyon provide their own assortment of bulbous monoliths dotting the parkland.

How did these stones of fantasy evolve? While scrambling over boldly sculptured mountainsides on Sombrero Peak or Granite Mountain, we are apt to recognize granite as a hard, light-colored crystalline rock. A general examination shows it to be freckled with a distinctive salt-and-pepper appearance made of white and pink feldspars, dark hornblende, and shiny mica, all in a light grayish quartz matrix. The minerals are coarse-grained and can be easily seen by the unaided eye.

In some places, the rocks appear to have been shaped from the same mat-

Sedimentation and Folding

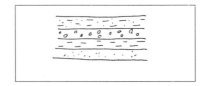

As sedimentary beds are deposited horizontally, the older beds on the bottom are inaccessible to the paleontologist. In the formation of an anticline, these beds are subjected to opposing forces as represented by the arrows. This action causes a bulging up of the land.

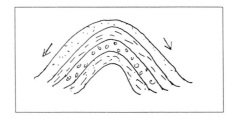

Looking at a cross-section of an anticline, the beds on opposite sides dip in opposite directions as indicated by the arrows.

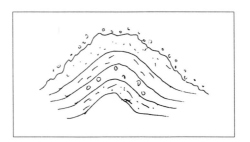

As soon as a landform is elevated above base level, erosion begins to take place.

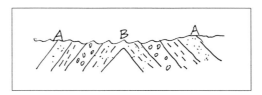

With continuing erosion, the anticline is finally levelled off exposing the older beds at the surface. It is now possible to walk from A to B and walk back in time. Fossils that were buried are now exposed at the surface.

Illustrations and text by George Miller, Environment Southwest, Summer 1985 crial. Yet they are not identical. Locally there are several different kinds of granitic rock that vary according to mineralogy, texture, color, and durability. These key variations are intimately related in determining how the rock will respond to the ravages of weather.

At one time, millions of years ago, this Peninsular granite originated as a molten, igneous body deep within the earth's crust. Slowly, dynamic pressures forced it to intrude into the older, overlying sediments that existed as crustal exposures. It then crystallized in place. Today, after millennia of uplift and erosion of its protective ground and plant cover, the granitic bedrock is gradually being uncovered on the surface.

Once exposed to groundwater and acids in solution, the massive and previously unfractured rock begins jointing and sheeting. Directly responsible for much of the rock's personality, these zones of weakness are vulnerable to attack by weathering agents. This persistent influence takes its toll as it rounds and subdues the angular and blocky stone. Weathering attacks not only the face, but also downwastes the edges and corners.

Weathering is the slow, but inevitable, disintegration and decomposition of rock. It is the process by which fresh rock is mechanically and chemically broken down, converted grain by grain into a coarse, gravelly residue called grus (decomposed granite). Depending upon the cohesive strength of the individual mineral grains, they will eventually become dissociated and the rock simply crumbles away. Joints are horizontal and vertical fractures along which the rock cracks, occasionally in intersecting sets. The ornate sculptures of the stone facade are determined by the lacework of its joint system.

Sheeting or exfoliation describes the cracking and peeling of rock along curved surfaces generally parallel to its surface. This process is best known for the spectacular domes in Yosemite National Park. Daily changes of temperature seasonally result in water freezing by night and thawing by day, and the rock itself expanding and contracting. As the flaking bedrock is slowly pried apart in ever-widening fissures, the erosive action of running water, snow, and ice quarry the stone into blocks and boulders, large and small.

Spheroidal weathering, related to flaking and sheeting, renders the strength and bulk of the rock more susceptible to erosion. Spheroidally weathered boulders will continue to erode until almost completely isolated from the parent bedrock. Ready to topple, they take on a variety of shapes and sizes: goblins, pillars, turrets and balanced rocks. The most picturesque formations have acquired names like Dos Cabezas (Two Heads) and Piedras Grandes (Big Boulders).

THE EROSION CYCLE - Highlands to Lowlands, and Again

The ruggedness and intricacy of Borrego's badlands correlate with episodes of mountain building. The higher the mountains rise, the more vigorously they are attacked by rain, snow, ice, wind, and the constant pull of gravity. Yielding slowly and steadily to the elements, the magnificent peaks, cliffs, and boulders of the western ranges pass away. They produce a huge amount of sediment that is carried into a few named and many more unnamed canyons and washes. Additional sediment finds its way onto great alluvial fans at the foot of the slopes and mouths of the canyons.

Such lowland sites are typical environments of deposition. Marine deposits or delta deposits are other examples of environments of deposition. Then the tectonic processes of mountain building may once again lift up these lowland environments to lofty plateaus or peaks. Thus nature's artistry continues to unfold in an erosion cycle that imperceptibly renews the landscape. Canyons and washes become again the conduits of deposition from highland to lowland.

CANYON CUTTING - Conduits of Destruction

The line of mountains that spread through the park are scarred from east to west by a network of parallel, deep, stream-cut canyons and arroyos. These V-shaped breaks in the mountain crest are formed by headward stream erosion into bedrock as the mountains are uplifted.

Some are visually dramatic and easy to see: Henderson, Borrego Palm, and Hellhole. Many others of equal interest are not so visible and are therefore lesser known: Rockhouse (both north and south), Rattlesnake, Salvador, and Cougar. Each owes its existence to the assault of water, removing rock debris from high ground and depositing it in low desert catchment basins.

Though best known, Borrego Palm Canyon remains a fascinating visit even for veteran canyoneers. Tucked between the monolithic walls of Indianhead and San Ysidro Peak, a one and a half mile maintained trail and then hard scrambling beyond leads into the gorge. Sheltered palm groves, cascading water and gurgling brook, and whorls of polished crystalline rock beckon the adventurous hiker.

Returning to the mouth of the canyon, one crosses the rugged and growing alluvial fan. This is an intermediate destination of the rock debris that weathered from the mountain mass before erosional transport to the fan. Unless countered by uplift, entire ranges will eventually be beveled down to a featureless plain by running water, that principal agent of erosion.

Unlike Borrego Palm Canyon, few others sustain a year-round stream. Most remain bone dry, draining occasional snow melt from the crest in easily forded trickles. These placid brooks seem incapable of carving through several thousand feet of rock. The calm can be deceptive because, when occasional rains strike the desert, they can arrive by the canyon full in short-lived summer cloudbursts that result in the infamous desert flash floods.

Such sudden and heavy rainstorms can be brutal to the desert landscape, unleashing a pelting rain which pounds on the lightly vegetated surfaces. Runoff funnels down every crack and crevice, purging side canyons of debris and rubble in rills, becoming rivulets that turn into muddy torrents. Powered by gravity down steep slopes, the narrow confines of the canyon act as a sluice for the rushing water. Its engorged bow wave moves at higher velocity as it careens basinward. Boulders diminish to cobbles, pebbles, sand, silt, and mud in a classic grading sequence. The smaller the fragment, the farther it may be carried onto a fan or into a basin.

INTO THE FAN AND SINK - Deposition Complete

When mountains are uplifting, relative to actively sinking basins in arid areas, alluvial fans debouching from canyons are particularly pronounced. In Borrego Valley major fans may be seen at the mouths of Coyote, Henderson, Borrego Palm, Hellhole, and Harper Canyons. These delta shaped outwash plains radiate from an apex where the stream channel emerges from the canyon.

Fans will grow with repeated outpourings, spreading so extensively that they may coalesce laterally along a mountain front. Such a merger is called a bajada or Spanish skirts. These continuous alluvial aprons, such as western Borrego Valley, can extend many miles and build an enormous wedge of sediment.

Canyon gradient, permeability of the fan apex, and amount of water are the important factors that determine grading of alluvium. Coarsest and thickest deposits occur near the apex including boulders, cobbles, and gravels. These are poorly sorted (multiple-size fragments), immature (not stable), and coarse-grained sediments. Sand, silt, and clay occur down-fan, representing sheet flood deposits distant from the canyon mouth apex.

As drainages become choked with alluvium and level out, streams breach their own levees to seek steeper gradients of less resistance. Shifting from side to side, they distribute the load like a windshield wiper. Obedient to hydrodynamic laws over millenia, flash floods tend to maintain fan symmetry through this shifting mechanism over time.

Alluvial fans, relating mountain canyon to desert basin, are important recorders of relative motion between subsiding basins and uplifting ranges. For example, the frayed eastern base of the San Ysidro Mountains is characterized by a range front half buried in its own erosional debris. A broad bajada of approximately uniform slope spreads from Henderson to Hellhole Canyon. Relative motion in west Borrego Valley is apparently less than across the valley, in the Santa Rosa-Clark Basin counterpart.

The Santa Rosa Mountains rear upward over 7000 feet above Clark Basin. Governed by the active San Jacinto Fault Zone, the Santa Rosa canyons reveal only short, steep, and isolated alluvial cones along their western bases. The lower ends of these cones are continually buried by playa sediments collecting in the actively subsiding basin of Clark Dry Lake. Uplift of the mountain front has been so recent that erosion has had little time to smooth it.

In other areas of the park, similar faults that parallel mountain ranges have elevated the lower fans, rejuvenating their channel gradients. Streams, entrenched into their earlier deposits, build new alluvial cones. Such features may be observed along the Tierra Blanca Mountains at Canebrake and along San Felipe Creek near Tamarisk Grove.

Flood by flood, deposition is the last chapter of the erosion cycle. Sediments eventually collect in low lying basins without external drainages - Borrego Sink, Clark Dry Lake, and the Salton Trough. These comparatively young structural depressions are filled with thousands of feet of inter-bedded silt and clay playa deposits. The amount depends on basin subsidence and the input of yet another natural cycle, that of water.

The "rocks of water," sedimentary deposits from many sources, tell the story of many desert landforms. The following sections discuss Split Mountain and the Vallecito-Fish Creek Basin as dramatic examples of various environments of deposition.

WRECKAGE OF TIME - Split Mountain Formation

Touch the canyon walls and you touch the dismantled bare bones, the telltale granites and the grus of the ancestral Fish Creek-Vallecito Mountains. The initial record of sedimentation within the Vallecito-Fish Creek Basin is obser ved at cliffside, concentrated in poorly sorted horizontal aprons of debris and loaded with large and small matrix-supported boulders. Appropriately named the Split Mountain Formation, it represents a textbook example of active alluvial fan and valley bottom deposition. Here the enormous force of moving water conveyed material directly from an upland source area onto a low basement surface with moderate relief.

To interpret the earth's story here, we must look back to a distant   past of cataclysmic mountain upheavals (orogeny) and highland destruction (erosion). Repeatedly, the area witnessed great tectonic disturbances because of Miocene strike and dip-slip movements along major fault   strands, related to basin and range crustal extension (5-15 MYA).

As the Fish Creek-Vallecito Mountains experienced local tectonic events along their fault-bounded eastern margin, the uplift steepened stream channel gradients. Their drainages began to incise themselves farther   back   into   the granitic core.   Crystalline bedrock shed angular gravels and veneers of coarse sediment as breccia downslope.

Infrequent, short duration, high intensity, torrential   floods carried this load basinward, delivering a thick wedge of clastic sediment onto an alluvial plain.   These rock layers, superposed vertically on one another through time, would eventually become the red cliffs and pink canyons of Split Mountain.

Because of the close proximity of distinct rock layers to their source area, geologists have been able   to   recognize two   informal, nonmarine depositional environments for the Split Mountain Formation. These include a lowermost braided-stream series named the Red Rock Canyon Member and the upper fan-glomerates of the Elephant Trees Member.

Braided streams flowing westerly   laid   down   porous   and permeable granular sandstones mulched with assorted gravel sheets and bars. This Red Rock Canyon Member chronicles an early tectonic setting and its subsequent erosion. It also contains a small percentage of Eocene age "Poway-type"   extra-regional cobbles and Miocene volcanic rocks.

Alluvial fans which comprise the west side of Borrego Valley issue from the steep canyons of Hellhole, Henderson, and Borrego Palm (pictured above). DL

Duration	Era	Million Years Ago	Epoch	Epoch	Geomagnetic Polarity Scale	No. American Land Mammal Ages	Dates in Vallecito and Carrizo Badlands
65 Million Years	CENOZOIC "Age of Mammals"	0	Holocene Pleistocene Pliocene Miocene..... Oligocene Eocene Paleocene	Pleistocene	Brunhes Normal	Rancholabrean	0.01 MYA Desert forms 0.18 MYA Ice Age peaks 0.50 MYA
							0.73 MYA Bishop Tuff
					Matuyama Reversed	Irvingtonian	0.94 MYA "Jaramillo Event" PALM SPRING FORMATION (locally derived Alluvial Fan-Floodplain deposits)
160 MM yrs.	MESOZOIC "Age of Dinosaurs"	65					
		225					1.9 MYA Hogback, VOB (2) "Olduvai Event"
				Pliocene	Gauss Normal	Blancan	3.1 MYA "Mammoth Event" DIABLO FORMATION (Colorado River delta)
345 Million Years	PALEOZOIC "Age of Lower Vertebrates"						
		570			Gilbert Reversed		3.8 MYA "Cochiti Event"
4 Billion Years	PRE-CAMBRIAN "Age of Invertebrates"					Hemphillian	IMPERIAL FORMATION (marine sediments, Gulf of California)
				Miocene			5.4 MYA
		4500				Clarendonian	6.6 MYA

GEOLOGIC TIME CORRELATION SCALE

Notes: (1) In the magnetic scale, black represents normal and white represents reversed polarity. "Events" are polarity events.
(2) See detail, page 159 for range 1.9 - 3.0 MYA.

Used by permission of George Miller, IVCM. Adapted from Environment Southwest, Summer 1985, SDNHM. Revised by P. Remeika and L. Lindsay, 1992

Related to uplift of the bounding Vallecito Mountain range, a thick bedded boulder sequence was laid down above the Red Rock Canyon Member. Informally named the Elephant Trees Member, this aggregate of thousands upon thousands of coarsely defined, angular "devil's marbles" is quite unique to the Split Mountain area. It forms the tall, picturesque east-facing battlement of the gorge. The matrix-supported boulder beds, deposited in a seemingly haphazard collage called fanglomerate, stand well above the adjacent plain. They represent the erosional deroofing of the nearby uplands.

The Elephant Trees Member is a local part of the vast fill that buried the eastern front of the young mountain range. Sedimentation occurred as debris flows and sheetflood deposits, grading from coarse-grained to fine-grained, all proportional to the slope of deposition.

Sheetfloods are defined as sediment-laden surges of water. Likewise, debris flows are dense, viscous combinations of mud, gravel, sand and water. Chock-full of protruding granitic boulders, both are a product of an eastward-thinning wedge of sediment that debouched from stream channels and spread out laterally, suggesting outbuilding, lobed alluvial fans and aprons that lean up against the Vallecito Mountains.

During the Miocene Epoch, about 20 million years ago, the relatively stationary depression in and around the Split Mountain area was managed by a dominant range-front fault margin along the Vallecito Mountain mass. The high-standing mountain front was characterized by a steep fault scarp similar to the western or Clark Valley side of the Santa Rosa Mountains. Earthquakes were frequent as the mountain block not only rose higher and higher but shifted northwest, assuming its present position and form.

Periods of local tectonism, structural deformation and resultant topographic relief were followed by long spans of erosion and deposition. Erosional debris shed east into the nearby depression, then ultimately coalesced into a broad alluvial apron. As a result, a thick blanket of fault-bounded fanglomerates, the Elephant Trees Member, now accounts for the notable scenery in the northern half of Split Mountain Gorge.

The incredible force necessary to move mountains also triggered local phenomena called landslides. The capstone rock within the Elephant Trees Member, midway through Split Mountain Gorge, is a locally prominent landslide deposit. The slide, known as The Lower Boulder Bed, directly overlies the Elephant Trees fanglomerate sequence, forming a prominent, greenish-gray cliff face 130 feet thick.

This massive, megabreccia represents a catastrophic mountain-front landslide. It apparently derived, in part, from the ancestral Fish Creek Mountains. It is an impressive feature to see, containing very large blocks of bedrock up to 15 feet in diameter that are poorly sorted in a jigsaw puzzle rock-soup. Riding on a friction-reducing air cushion, a section of mountainside broke loose and raced downslope, burying all in its path.

This landslide deposit is a classic example of the rapid movement of earth materials, probably generated by strong seismic events that rocked the area. It is another harbinger of geologic events associated with the initial opening of the Gulf of California in the late Miocene Epoch (6-10 MYA).

Marine sediments of the Imperial Formation start appearing between the Lower Boulder Bed landslide and the well known anticline of Split Mountain. Bear in mind that southerly travel into Split Mountain and westerly into the Vallecito-Fish Creek Badlands is a journey from older to younger strata. The sequence described so far has been: early terrestrial fanglomerates of the Split Mountain Formation (Red Rock Canyon and Elephant Trees members), Lower Boulder Bed landslide, and then marine sediments. Exiting Split Mountain to the south, fossil-containing layers of sediment reflect younger environments of deposition during the Pliocene Epoch of Anza-Borrego's geologic history.

AN ANCIENT SINK UPLIFTING - Vallecito-Fish Creek Basin

This basin developed in response to crustal thinning and subsidence, volcanism, and tremendous sedimentary deposition. This 150 square-mile structural depression is a fossil basin. Such a basin is, by definition, an extensive, low-lying area receiving sediments from adjacent highlands and containing relatively flat-lying rocks. Here the source of deposition is the Pinyon-Vallecito and Fish Creek Mountains to the north and northeast, and the Tierra Blanca and Coyote Mountains to the west and south.

The stack of predominantly sedimentary rock, measuring as much as 15,000 feet thick, chronicles the formative years of the paleobasin. Nearly tripling, in vertical sequence, the depth of the Grand Canyon, the sediments have been subjected to gradual uplifting. They have been thrust on edge 20-26 degrees down to the west into a remarkable stairway of rock, telling time's own story. It is the most structurally intact and stratigraphically complete Miocene-Pliocene - Pleistocene (1-8 MYA) rock section within the Salton Trough.

Marine sediments, typified by the Elephant Knees feature south of Split Mountain, developed in response to the Miocene-Pliocene (4-5 MYA) transgression of the northern Gulf of California. Features farther west shift from marine to brackish tidal and delta deposits which record the early history of the Colorado River delta system (3-4 MYA). Finally, the Sandstone Canyon area is dominated by Canebrake Conglomerate that is locally derived from the surrounding mountains.

By traveling westward from the stony depths of Split Mountain to Sandstone Canyon, one begins the journey through the pages of time. The remaining portion of the journey may be made southwest from the Diablo Dropoff to Highway S-2 in the Carrizo Corridor. Both of these trips are described in the field trip chapters. With a bonus for the trained eye at almost every turn, the stories told by this cavalcade of rocks are the chronicle of the ages.

Ranger George Leetch exploring Sandstone Canyon in upper Fish Creek. SP

The Peninsular Ranges, aptly referred to as the "Western Barrier" by park naturalist Mark Jorgensen, restrict winter-time westerly winds from delivering moisture from the Pacific Ocean to the deserts. LL

Chapter 6

THE DESERT CLIMATE

INTRODUCTION

The Anza-Borrego region may be classified as a unique tectonic laboratory for two basic reasons: (1) graphic evidence of two of the three types of tectonic plate encounters is seen almost everywhere. The first of these plate boundary actions is the divergence of the East Pacific Rise which is expressed as the Gulf of California with the Salton Trough at its apex. The second of these encounters is the slide-past boundary between the Pacific and North American tectonic plates, expressed by the three great fault zones of Southern California. (2) Anza-Borrego is a desert and, as in most deserts, it presents a scene unencumbered by cloaking vegetation. Thus the naked evidence of tectonic activity, as seen in the area's mountains, subsided valleys and faults, is immediately visible. The effects of plate tectonics as revealed here have been a major cause of change in Anza-Borrego's desert landscape.

However, another equally important cause of landscape change is erosion. Changes wrought by erosion are seen almost everywhere as alluvial fans, bajadas, and badlands. Since erosion is usually induced by water flow, and a paucity of vegetation is an effect induced by lack of water, desert erosion would appear to be an anomaly. Some of the erosive features seen in Anza-Borrego may have occurred during periods of earlier, wetter climates. However, erosion is still active and is not an anomaly. For that reason, a discussion of Anza-Borrego's climate and the changes in landscape it induces is included in this book.

CLIMATIC OVERVIEW

A weather station has been located near Borrego Springs for several years and from its measurements of temperature, precipitation, wind velocities, etc., a general indication of the climate of the area can be derived. The climate is typical of low Sonoran desert areas - warm, sunny days and cool nights in winter, and hot, dry summers. The average annual rainfall is low -- 6.7 inches. Monthly averages of temperature and precipitation, measured over the 30-year period from 1962 to 1991 are as follows:

Month	Average High Temperature Degrees F.	Average Low Temperature Degrees F.	Average Precipitation Inches
January	68.8	42.7	1.15
February	73.6	46.6	1.07
March	76.7	49.5	0.81
April	83.6	53.5	0.24
May	92.3	60.0	0.08

Month	Average High Temperature Degrees F.	Average Low Temperature Degrees F.	Average Precipitation Inches
June	102.0	67.9	0.02
July	107.2	75.3	0.35
August	106.0	74.8	0.67
September	100.2	69.4	0.46
October	90.3	60.6	0.31
November	77.6	50.2	0.69
December	69.0	43.2	0.87
			6.72 total

Desert rainfall does not necessarily have to reach cloudburst proportions to induce erosion, though cloudbursts occur in most deserts and Anza-Borrego is no exception. Vegetation, which provides protection of slopes and flat surfaces from the spattering effects of raindrops and from flood-like runoff, is sparse in desert places. Thus, many of the formidable flash floods which occur in Anza-Borrego have resulted from relatively light rains. The debris loaded runoffs which sometimes occur, deepen and widen Borrego's canyons and arroyos, depositing silt and rocks in basin areas and over alluvial fans. Therefore, over a period of time, enough rainfall occurs in Anza-Borrego that the readily identifiable effects of erosion can take place and may be seen.

Anza-Borrego's climatic profile is complicated by the fact that four life zones exist within the park. These are the Lower Sonoran, the Upper Sonoran, the Transition Zone, and the Canadian Zone. Each zone has its own specific climatic definition. This complex climatic picture may be clarified to some extent when the causes which produce these climates are considered.

The two phenomena which influence Borrego's climate the most are global airflow patterns and regional topography. As a result of global airflow, Anza-Borrego might be called a horse latitudes desert, a name which could be given to most of earth's deserts, and which accounts for many of Anza-Borrego's general climatic characteristics. Regional topography has not only produced a variety of life zones in Anza-Borrego, but other peculiarities as well, such as the rain shadow effect which greatly influences precipitation in Borrego Valley. In succeeding sections these two major climatic influences will be discussed.

DESERTS AND GLOBAL AIRFLOW PATTERNS

Areas called deserts comprise one seventh of the earth's land surfaces. Deserts are characterized by many common features among which are a lack of moisture, a paucity of vegetation, high surface temperatures, and high evaporation rates. Most of the world's deserts lie in bands of latitude of about 5 degrees and 30 degrees both north and south of the equator. These bands include the largest desert in the world, the Sahara of North Africa (3,500,000 square miles), the Gobi (500,000 square miles) in Mongolia and China, the Great Victoria (150,000 square miles) in Australia, the Chihuahuan (140,000 square miles) and Sonoran (70,000 square miles) of North America.

Deserts occur not by coincidence, but as a consequence of global airflow patterns directly traceable to earth's characteristics as a planet orbiting its parent star, the sun. Among earth's planetary characteristics are:

(1) Earth's surface heat is induced by radiant energy from the sun. The influence of heat received from earth's molten core is infinitesimal and is not considered.

(2) Earth rotates about its own axis, with a period of rotation of approximately 24 hours. Thus as earth rotates, the amount of sun's radiant energy received at most locations on earth's surface varies daily from a maximum at midday to a minimum at night. Because earth is a rotating spheroid, the periods of daylight and darkness vary in length as the poles are approached. These variations in surface heat are called daily variation patterns.

(3) Earth's rotational axis is tilted at an angle of about 23.5 degrees to its orbital plane. The orientation of this rotational axis is fixed in space (for all practical purposes). Thus as earth orbits the sun, the amount of sun's radiant energy received at particular locations on earth's surface varies depending on Earth's location on its orbital path. Therefore, radiant energy received at a surface location varies from a maximum during summer to a minimum during winter. These familiar variations in surface heat are called seasonal variation patterns.

(4) Earth orbits the sun with an orbital period of one year or 365.24 days, thus the seasonal heat cycle is repeated on a yearly basis.

(5) Earth's surface is enclosed in an envelope of gas (called air) composed of a mixture of oxygen, nitrogen and other gases; 71% of earth's surface area is water (oceans); 29% is land. Each in this combination of solid, liquid, and gas has its own thermodynamic properties. Each interacts with the others and responds in kind to the variations in radiant energy received from the sun.

(6) Earth's surface displays a random distribution of land and ocean areas.

These features of planet Earth produce formations of ocean, land, and air which vary in thermal content, produce variations in the moisture content of the air envelope, and produce ocean and air currents. These, in combination with the distribution of land masses, form the phenomenon called weather. One result is the formation of deserts in the regions just north and south of the equator.

Earth's equatorial zone lies within two parallels (or latitudes), the Tropic of Cancer (23.5 degrees north of the equator) and the Tropic of Capricorn (23.5 degrees south of the equator). In this zone, at some period of the year, the sun is directly overhead. Elsewhere the sun's rays never shine directly down from the zenith overhead. The equatorial zone is therefore the region of greatest heat.

The heated air in the equatorial zone rises and as it rises, cools. The ability of air to hold moisture varies proportionally with its temperature. Thus as the rising air cools, its ability to hold moisture decreases and its excess water falls, as the heavy rain experienced in the equatorial or tropical zone. The cooled air then flows northward and southward from the equatorial zone into either of two belts, or regions, in the neighborhood of 30 degrees north and 30 degrees south latitude. These zones are often referred to as the horse latitudes and are characterized by high atmospheric pressures and light, baffling winds. Journalist George Stimpson suggested that the zone was called horse latitudes possibly as a comparison between the zone's high pressure calms and winds and the actions of a restive horse. At any rate, in this region of 30 to 35 degrees latitude the cooled air descends and gains heat, enabling it to hold much more water. After descending, much of the air then flows back toward the equator absorbing moisture as it goes and the cycle is repeated. As a result, deserts develop in the horse latitude belt, continually dehydrated by warm, dry winds that evaporate any moisture present.

The pressure belt of descending air in the horse latitudes is sometimes referred to as the subtropical high, or the subtropical anticyclone. The subtropical anticyclone over the Pacific Ocean may be characterized as a system of huge elliptical swirls of air perhaps 2000 miles across at their widest points. The swirls, when they move near North America, generally tend to move in an easterly direction due to the direction of rotation of earth. During the summer as the swirl, or high, approaches the western coast of California, it tends to lie tangent to, and to some extent, overlaps the coast. As a result, California's summer months are dominated by this high pressure, dry air and the region assumes drought-like conditions.

During winter months the high pressure, storm-free swirl tends to decrease in size and moves seaward and toward the equator. The resulting low pressure area replacing it allows storms, which have originated in latitudes to the north, to cross the California coast, bringing rain and winter conditions.

As has been stated, the climate of this "horse latitude" Anza-Borrego Desert may be characterized, in general, by lack of moisture, a paucity of vegetation, high surface temperatures, and high evaporation rates. However, the climate of this desert, as with the other North American deserts, displays its own peculiarities brought about by topography and geographical location. Temperatures tend to decrease in magnitude with elevation and distance from the equator. Thus the low elevation (625 feet) and latitude (32.2 degrees north) of Borrego Springs would tend to induce higher temperatures than are experienced at Barstow in the Mojave Desert (2100 feet elevation, 33.8 degrees north).

Precipitation in Borrego Valley and other low lying areas, already light due to Anza-Borrego's location as a "horse latitudes" desert, is further limited by its surrounding mountain ranges, whose western slopes remove much of the moisture in the form of rain and snow from the incoming winter ocean air from the west. The now dry and cooler air flows down the eastern slopes of these mountains, warming as it goes, and evaporating any moisture in its path. This removal of incoming moisture from air flowing over the western slopes results in cool, dry air which flows down the eastern slopes. This flow of dry air and the resulting evaporation, or dehydration occurring over the surfaces it transits, produces what is called "the rain shadow effect." Such is the case at Borrego Valley which is located in the so-called rain shadow of its surrounding mountains.

REGIONAL TOPOGRAPHY

It is interesting to note that the climatic conditions at Anza-Borrego occur within a very few miles from the areas of vegetation and pleasant climates associated with the coastal maritime fringe in which San Diego is located. The maritime fringe and the mountains which border and separate it from the interior regions, is the first land along California's coast to be crossed by air coming off the sea. This proximity to the sea, and the sea's much larger heat storage capacity than that of land, tends to stabilize coastal air temperatures, thus producing much narrower variations in daily and seasonal temperature variation patterns than are experienced in the interior regions. Because Southern California's maritime fringe is separated from the interior regions by relatively high mountains, precipitation runoff, which occurs in the fringe, forms drainage streams which flow toward the ocean and not into the dry interior regions. Thus Anza-Borrego, and the rest of Southern California's dry interior, is deprived of any river or stream flow from the moist coastal areas, and becomes even drier.

About two-thirds of Anza-Borrego Desert State Park is mountainous. The

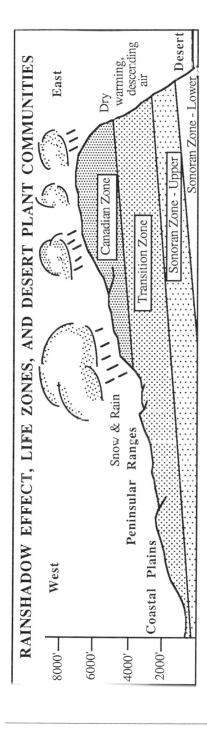

RAINSHADOW EFFECT, LIFE ZONES, AND DESERT PLANT COMMUNITIES

SAN DIEGO COUNTY PLANT COMMUNITIES IN ANZA-BORREGO REGION: (BASED ON P. A. MUNZ AND R. M. BEAUCHAMP)

CONIFEROUS FOREST 3500-6200'
Brecksnort Mtn. (Combs Peak to Sunrise Hwy (Jeffrey Pine, Ponderosa, Coulter, Canyon Live Oak, Black Oak, Bracken Fern)

GRASSLAND 3000-5000'
Cuyamaca Lake, Pena Spring, San Felipe Valley

OAK WOODLAND 3500-5000'
Montezuma Valley (Ranchita), Banner Canyon (Live Oak, Poison Oak, Squaw Bush)

PINYON-JUNIPER WOODLAND 3500-5000'
Culp Valley, Pinyon Mts., Smuggler (Scrub Oak, Mtn. Mahogany)

DESERT TRANSITION CHAPPARAL 1500-5000
Culp Valley, Oriflamme Canyon, Jacumba (White Sage, Manzanita, Toyon, Yucca)

ROCKY SLOPE (DESERT SUCCULENT SCRUB) 500-3500'
Cliffs, high washes, fans (Cacti, Agave, Brittlebush, Ocotillo, Jojoba)

DESERT WASH WOODLAND 0-1000'
(Smoke Tree, Catclaw, Tamarisk)

RIPARIAN (STREAMSIDE) WOODLAND
(Desert Willow, Cottonwood, Arroweed)

PALM OASIS 0-1000'
Sandy Desert (Creosote Scrub)

FRESHWATER MARSH 0-1000'
San Sebastian, Carrizo

DESERT (MESQUITE) DUNE 0-1000 ft.
Lower Borrego Valley

ALKALI SINK 0-2500'
Borrego Sink, Blair Valley

remaining third, which includes Borrego Valley and the eastern fringes of the park toward the Salton Sea, is typical low desert.   For example, the elevation of Borrego Springs is 625 feet. This elevation decreases gradually towards the Salton Sea area (some 235 feet below sea level).

The mountains which surround Borrego Valley are rugged and unique. The Santa Rosas to the northeast rise to 6,000 feet elevations and are among the steepest on the continent. The San Ysidros to the west are also high in elevation with steep eastern slopes, while several other ranges extend beyond Pinyon Ridge to the south. These north, south, and western ranges form a cul-de-sac in which Borrego Valley is located. All provide barriers against incoming moisture-laden air from the sea, thus producing the rain shadow in which the Borrego and other valleys dwell.   Conversely, summer winds and storms driving northward from the Gulf of California via the Salton Trough have a tendency to partially side-track into Borrego's cul-de-sac.

The non-mountainous third of ABDSP features valleys and basins typical of those found throughout the Sonoran Desert. Playas or dry lakes, also character-istic of the Sonoran Desert, are found in some of the park's basins such as Clark Basin and Blair Valley. Playas are formed by runoff from the mountains, which flows into the basins where the water stands until evaporated. Deposits of the various salts the water had accumulated remain. Alluvial fans are found at the mouths of most of Borrego's canyons and though they have been built-up over long periods of time, they are continuing to grow as a result of runoff. These cone shaped accumulations of sand and rock are deposited by the runoff from canyons which fan out when no longer restricted by canyon walls. When several alluvial fans overlap, the wide slope formed is called a bajada and can cover a consider-able portion of a valley or basin floor. Ravines and arroyos which carry the runoff into areas of lower elevation throughout Anza-Borrego are continually being abraded, widened, and deepened by rain-induced erosion.

LOCALIZED CLIMATES AND LIFE ZONES OF ANZA-BORREGO

The Anza-Borrego Desert is located about 50 miles from the Pacific Coast and stretches along the western edge of the Colorado Desert. The Colorado Desert, so named for the Colorado River flowing through it, is part of the Sonoran Desert which extends over southern Arizona, most of the Mexican state of Sonora, and over most of Baja California. Because of its lower elevation and its southerly geographical location, the Sonoran Desert generally experiences higher temperatures year around than do the higher elevation, northerly deserts of North America.

The Sonoran Desert experiences two rainy seasons, and as a result a wider diversity of plant and animal life exists than in the other North American deserts, which experience only one rainy season per year. In addition to the creosote bush and ocotillo found throughout the park, isolated stands of the rare Elephant Tree, native to the Baja regions of the Sonoran Desert, are found in Anza-Borrego.

Anza-Borrego, as a part of the Sonoran Desert, also experiences two rainy seasons. In summer the high pressure, tropical anticyclone off the California coast causes Pacific storm paths to move northward, and the eastward flow of moisture laden air diminishes over California, resulting in arid climatic conditions. At the same time, storms developed over the Gulf of Mexico low pressure region move north and westward due to the location of the Atlantic anticyclone. These storms bring the summer thunder showers and flash floods to the Sonoran region, some of which reach Anza-Borrego Desert State Park.

Additional summer rain enters the Colorado Desert area from Pacific Ocean storms which originate southwest of Baja California. Southerly winds from the Gulf of California drain off the moisture-laden air, carrying it up the negative elevations of the Salton Trough. Due to the topographic cul-de-sac which is the Borrego Valley, much of this moisture may be deposited against the eastern slopes of the surrounding mountains, bringing rain and flash floods to Borrego Valley and other of the park's canyons and bajadas. In winter, Pacific Ocean storms move eastward, bringing precipitation to the California coastal areas. Some of this, in spite of Borrego's high surrounding mountains, gets over the peaks with enough moisture to bring rain into the desert region.

Other rain from Pacific winter storms has entered the Borrego area via the Salton Trough route due to eccentricities in the location of the Pacific high (anticyclone). Periodically, patterns followed by the Pacific high have been thoroughly upset by the onset of the little understood El Niño. El Niño is characterized by a periodic heating of the equatorial Pacific Ocean surface which alters the direction and temperatures of ocean currents with related induced changes in global air flow patterns. As a result, radical increases in precipitation can occur in normally arid regions, and lack of precipitation can occur in normally wet regions. Such increases in precipitation levels have been felt in Anza-Borrego with resulting flood damage.

A popular concept used to correlate areas with similar vegetation was that of life zones in North America, developed by biologist C. Hart Merriam in the 1890s. Merriam observed the positive correlation of plant groupings with elevation and latitude (i.e. higher elevations have plants similar to more northerly latitudes). For example, the piney Transition zone high on the western ramparts of Anza-Borrego is similar to the lower foothills of the northern Sierra Nevada, while the Lower Sonoran zone of Borrego Valley is host to shrubs closely related to their Mexican kin in mountains far to the south.

These life zones may be designated by elevation, and are defined as regions where characteristic plants or animals are most often found. Common definitions are:

Lower Sonoran	Below sea level to 2000 feet Common trees and shrubs: creosote bush, mesquite, ocotillo, palo verde, brittlebush, cholla cactus, ironwood, desert willow, cottonwood, smoke tree.
Upper Sonoran	1500 to 3000 feet Common trees and shrubs: sage, juniper, pinyon pine, barrel cactus, prickly pear, yucca, sycamore, scrub oaks.
Transition	3000 to 5000 feet Common trees and shrubs: ponderosa pine, live oaks, Coulter pine, Jeffrey pine, juniper, Great Basin sagebrush.
Canadian	5000 to 10000 feet Common trees: sugar, and lodgepole pine, Douglas fir, aspen.

Life zones in Anza-Borrego, as functions of elevation, experience air temperature decreases as elevation increases. Very dry air can cool as much as 5.7 degrees Fahrenheit with each 1000 feet of elevation. As a result, there are several areas throughout the park which are located in the Upper Sonoran and Transition life zones which experience cooler temperatures, and on average, heavier rainfall than that seen in Borrego Valley which is in the Lower Sonoran zone. A seldom visited area of the park along Sunset Highway southeast of Julian features Transition zone coulter pine, ponderosa pine, sycamore, and oaks -- and temperatures which average 15 degrees cooler than Borrego Valley. A somewhat similar Transition zone area is seen around Ranchita, adjacent to the western boundary of Anza-Borrego Desert State Park

The Upper Sonoran life zone of Pinyon Ridge, the Pinyon Mountains, and the Jacumba Mountains provides a change in scenery and somewhat cooler temperatures than the basins. The major canyons throughout the park rapidly increase in elevation as they climb into the mountains. Some such as Coyote Canyon feature brooks or streams and are cooler than valley temperatures.

The Lower Sonoran climate shared by Borrego Springs and the eastern stretches of Anza-Borrego features summer storms which can produce heavy runoff from the mountains and flash floods. Some are particularly severe although decades may pass before a major flash flood occurs. Tropical Storm Kathleen produced such a major flood in September 1976. The rainfall in the vicinity of Mount Laguna measured ten inches in less than 24 hours with 4.8 inches falling in a three hour period. It was estimated that the runoff down Carrizo Creek

Summer-time hurricanes Kathleen (1976) and Doreen (1977) dealt deadly blows to transportation arteries in the Anza-Borrego region as they roared up the Gulf from the southeast. LL

exceeded 29,000 cubic feet of water per second which inundated Interstate 8, wrecked the nearby railroad, and wiped out part of the town of Ocotillo. Needless to say, when summer rains occur in Anza-Borrego, the otherwise dry creek beds and runoff channels are to be avoided.

The famed desert wildflower displays, such as occurred in the spring of 1992, result from the right combination of weather factors which include adequate and periodic winter rains, sufficient and properly timed sunshine, and lack of moisture-robbing, dry winds. These annual wildflower displays are in addition to the blooming of the perennials such as the red flowered ocotillo, which blooms when sufficient rainfall occurs. Other common perennials, which blossom and bud in accordance with rain received, include the ironwood, desert willow, cottonwood, smoke tree, and tamarisk. The tamarisk, a native of western Asia, is called salt cedar because it exudes a salt that forms encrustations on its branchlets.

The fan palm is the largest of the true desert trees in the park, and can attain a height of up to 80 feet. It is the only native palm in California and prefers canyons with their reliable water sources. Fan palms are also found on the open desert wherever a seepage has created an oasis. Borrego Palm Canyon, with its springs, is probably the most beautiful of the several palm-studded canyons and was the site first recommended for the establishment of a state park. Other areas which include palm trees are Mortero Canyon, Mountain Palm Springs, and various canyons feeding Coyote Canyon from the west.

SUMMARY

In summary, the 620,000 acre Anza-Borrego Desert State Park, the largest desert state park in the United States, offers many desert features not easily observed elsewhere. It is one of the foremost desert regions in the nation where the effects of plate tectonics, climatic erosion, and other geological processes are being preserved, are easily accessible, and may be readily studied and monitored.

As a state park, ABDSP has a well developed and maintained system of roads and trails. The easy access they provide to the various areas throughout the park have helped to make possible the hands-on geological experiences provided in the eight geology field trips which follow.

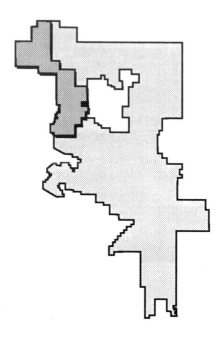

Rare glimpses of the peninsular bighorn sheep, namesake of Borrego, are available along the ridgelines above Montezuma grade. PR

PART II - GEOLOGY FIELD TRIPS

Chapter 1 - Northwestern Area

FIELD TRIP NO. 1

MONTEZUMA GRADE (Hwy S-22 West)

Length: 11.1 Miles (one way)

Road Conditions: Good. Paved Road

Season: All Year

Route Summary:
This tour starts at the visitor center and climbs west on Highway S-22, ascending Montezuma Grade in the San Ysidro Mountain range. This fault-controlled mountain front is the edge of a rising block of bedrock that is little modified by erosion. The route features many single and double road cuts which verify author-naturalist John McPhee's sage remark, "A road cut is to a geologist as a stethoscope is to a doctor." There are magnificent views of Borrego Valley and its surrounding Santa Rosa and Vallecito ranges, Borrego Badlands, Pinyon Ridge, and on a clear day, the shimmering Salton Sea in the distance.

General Description:
From the arid desert lowland along its base, the sheer-faced San Ysidro Mountains thrust abruptly to an average height of over one mile. High enough to wring moisture from storm clouds, this sierran-like barrier consists mainly of a powerfully-built **crystalline intrusive rock** of deep-seated origin. This granitic rock was forceably intruded under and into older **metasedimentary country rock** by a **tectonic** mountain-building episode 70-100 million of years ago.

While all the rocks are ancient, dating back into the abyss of geological time, the uplifted mountains are youthful. They are an unbroken profile of a block of the earth's crust while also the abrupt western boundary of the widening and sinking Salton Trough/Gulf of California structural depression.

Today the San Ysidro Mountains are crossed by only one paved road: Montezuma Grade. In less than 20 minutes, the 11-mile journey whisks visitors through a rare showcase of spectacular mountain scenery, steep-cliffed canyons, viewpoints and a jumbled terrain strewn with boulders which number in the tens of millions. Within this realm are life zones ranging from the Lower Sonoran at the visitor center to the verdant Canadian zone high atop Hot Springs Mountain (part of the Los Coyotes Indian Reservation). This is the highest peak in San Diego County. From a fine regatta of cacti to a forested tableland of pinyon pine and oak, this byway is a classic "palms to pines" experience. Spectacular views of

Borrego Valley and the surrounding mountains are seen along the grade which features frequent viewpoints and pull-outs.

County mile markers start at mile zero at the junction of S-2 and S-22 west of Ranchita, and increase to the east into the desert along S-22, reaching mile 11.6 at the new park boundary at the foot of Montezuma Grade.

Route Log:

0.0 Miles, Visitor Center, Between Mile Markers 17 and 18

Exhibits on natural history and cultural history, information, literature, publications and restroom facilities are available here.

The awesome eastern escarpment of the San Ysidro Mountain Range rises behind the visitor center. These mountains are among the most impressive of Anza-Borrego due to their steep rise at the western edge of Borrego Valley. Indianhead (elevation 3,960 feet) is the pronounced pinnacle on the northwest skyline. Towering above the Borrego Palm Canyon campground, it is made up of a metasedimentary rock sequence of gneiss, marble, quartzite, and amphibolite deposited about 470 MYA. All have been locally faulted, folded and sheared, and intruded by pegmatite about 70 MYA. The suite of rocks resembles those in the Santa Rosa Mountains.

Indianhead's metasedimentary layers represent the uplift of ancient Ordovician seabed, atop the emplacement of the Peninsular Batholith 70 - 100 MYA. Due to perspective, Indianhead appears as the highest peak of the mountain range. On the contrary, it is actually at the two-thirds mark, only one of many ridges, peaks and knolls that make up the mountain front. At its base is the Borrego Palm Canyon campground (elevation 800 feet). Between the two points there is a vertical difference of over 3,100 feet within a mile. This abrupt change in altitude causes rapid changes in climate and vegetation, mirrored by the steep ascent up Montezuma Grade.

0.2 Miles, Borrego Palm Canyon Campground Turnoff

0.4 Miles, S-22/Palm Canyon Drive Junction, Palm Canyon Resort

Turn right (south) onto S-22/Montezuma Valley Road, crossing the very prominent alluvial fan actively draining outward from Hellhole Canyon. The creosote-covered desert floor is veneered with granitic boulders and coarse debris, becoming finer-grained as it grades basinward. Gradually, these deposits are filling up the western half of Borrego Valley.

0.7 Miles, Hellhole Canyon Fault

At the first major bend in the highway, the Hellhole Canyon Fault is crossed. It is a local or second-order magnitude fault. **Left-lateral strike-slip** movement along this narrow fracture zone has thrust the Church Spur ridge, prominently seen on the left-hand side of the highway, several thousand feet into Borrego Valley. Evidence of the fault includes the low pressure ridge seen just east of the highway.

0.9 Miles, State Park Boundary

Entering Anza-Borrego Desert State Park (elevation 800 feet), Culp Valley Sector. This sector, consisting of nearly 75,000 acres, is composed of rugged mountainous topography of the San Ysidro Mountains and Pinyon Ridge. It is a formidable barrier of granitic monoliths. Cut laterally by many canyons, the ridgelines and bold peaks provide wilderness experiences that invite exploration and offer splendid vistas of both Borrego Valley and the Anza-Borrego Desert.

1.0 Miles, Hellhole Canyon View, Mile Marker 17

Straight ahead, the remote and rugged Hellhole Canyon is a major eastward-flowing drainage cut deep within the San Ysidro Mountain **escarpment**. There is no vehicular access into Hellhole Canyon. Along the eastern edge of the San Ysidro Mountains are many other such palm canyon oases in canyons including San Salvador, Sheep, and Borrego Palm. Most of these oases occur near fault zones that are still uplifting the mountains, providing a route for ground water to reach the surface. The palms are native California Fan Palms which are the largest of all fan palms. All told, there are over 100 palm groves in the Colorado Desert.

Majestic Washington Fan Palm Groves exploit near-surface water supplies in many of the east-draining canyons of the Peninsular Ranges as in this view of Borrego Palm Canyon. PR

1.3 Miles, Church Spur

This feature is named for the cluster of churches at its eastern end. The highway begins to climb a series of low hills (a fault **scarp**) onto the upthrown Church Spur block of the earth's crust. Exposed in the first series of double road-cuts are reddish-brown, angular-weathered **cataclastic** (fragmented) metamorphic rocks. These highly-deformed rocks were originally deposited as a thick marine sequence of layered sandstone, limestone and shale about 470 million years ago during the Ordovician Period. Since then they have been metamorphosed, altered by heat and pressure, into a sequence of quartzite, gneiss, phyllite, marble and schist. These rocks, with others exposed along the base of the San Ysidro Mountains, may be the oldest within Anza-Borrego Desert State Park. Similar formations may be seen in the Santa Rosas (Field Trip No. 2, Pegleg Monument), and Coyote Mountains (Field Trip No. 5).

2.0 Miles, Riding and Hiking Trail, Mile Marker 16

The ridge just uphill from Marker 16 is the end of this portion of the California Riding and Hiking Trail that descends to the desert floor from Culp Valley and beyond. Most of the route follows an old cattle trail between the mouth of Hellhole Canyon and Montezuma Valley atop the ridge line.

The sinuous stretch of Montezuma Grade was built in 1963. It contours up the steep eastern edge of the San Ysidro Mountains from Borrego Springs to Ranchita, ascending through three plant life zones, which are Lower Sonoran, Upper Sonoran, and Transition (including chaparral). The Lower Sonoran life zone of the desert floor is characterized by mesquite, cat claw, smoke tree, indigo, California fan palms and creosote bush. The creosote bush is the domi-nant plant cover over one-sixth of the North American continent. It was used, among other things, for medicinal purposes by the local Cahuilla Indians.

2.5 Miles, Metasediments, Mile Marker 15.5

Gravelly turnout on the left-hand side of the highway. Metasedimentary exposures of quartz, gneiss, and schist are the layered and interbedded tan and grey rocks seen in road cuts opposite the turnout. These rocks have been drag folded, thrust-faulted and deformed by Late Cretaceous forces associated with the waning stages of deep rock emplacement into this overlying **country rock** about 70 MYA. Discontinuous exposures of the Santa Rosa Formation extend from the San Jacinto Mountains in Riverside County southward to the Sierra de las Cucupas in Baja California, Mexico. This is the thin spine of primeval Paleozoic Era (Ordovician Period) marine metasediments noted in Chapter 1 dating about 470 MYA. Marker 15.5 begins the remarkable shift in rock structure which follows.

3.0 Miles, Plutonic Rocks, Mile Marker 15

Note the abrupt change in rock structure, or **lithology,** from the older, darker and finely layered metasediments to the younger, light-colored plutonic rocks of the Peninsular Batholith. (Don't confuse the dark of desert varnish on light colored plutonics with the metasediments which are dark all through.)

4.0 Miles, Breccia Inclusions, Mile Marker 14

Note vertical cliffs of highly-fractured, freshly-exposed granitic rock with dark-colored diorite breccia **inclusions** in the double road-cuts. Rock falls are common along this section of roadway.

To the left of the highway is Dry Canyon. It is an excellent example of how efficient erosive forces have combined to cut through the mountain's bed-rock, creating a spectacular chasm. The Dry Canyon creek bed is choked with granitic boulders and residue broken from the mountain peaks and swept down the canyon by seasonal flashfloods. Below, the canyon drains onto the desert floor, discharging its load of sediments onto the **apex** of a gravel fan and grading from coarse to fine proceeding basinward.

4.5 Miles, Dry Canyon, Mile Marker 13.5

The Upper Sonoran life zone is represented here on the rocky desert slopes by a plant assemblage including ocotillo, cholla, barrel cactus, and agave. There is also desert apricot, jojoba and brittlebush. Keep an eye out also for the elusive desert bighorn sheep that inhabit the rough eastern slopes of the San Ysidro Mountains. This bighorn (*Ovis canadensis cremnobates*) is a most remark-able animal. As a true wilderness monarch, it is well-endowed with telescopic vision, excellent hearing, strength, and is so sure-footed as to easily adapt to the treacherous terrain of hidden palm canyons and magnificent desert peaks.

5.0 Miles, Desert Varnish, Mile Marker 13

Many old boulder surfaces are liberally stained with a reddish-brown patina or desert varnish. This common phenomena occurs on natural, desert-rock landforms, baked onto them by many years of heat and sunlight. Note that fresh rock exposures lack desert varnish, appearing a natural light-gray in color.

This lineated, foliated rock in an uphill road cut between mile markers 12.5 and 13 is an example of mylonization whereby rocks are kneaded like dough 3-4 miles beneath the surface. BH

5.2 Miles, Mylonization

In double road cuts are examples of **foliated** and **lineated plutonic** rocks, reduced to thin strips or laminae, that have undergone **mylonization**. This is a complicated process that is incompletely understood, whereby the rocks here have been metamorphosed and deformed at depth. The overall zone of sheared rock exposed along Montezuma Grade is locally referred to as the Borrego Springs Shear Zone. It is a Late Mesozoic-Early Cenozoic tectonic byproduct of mountain-building 60-70 MYA. See also Field Trip No. 2, Pegleg Monument, for similar mylonization notes on Coyote Mountain.

DESERT VARNISH

Desert varnish is a common phenomenon on rocks of arid areas. Centuries of dry heat and day-long brightness bake a dark mineral coating onto exposed areas. Due to subtle differences in the coating's color, texture, shadow and lighting, well varnished surfaces take on a prominent dull luster that causes entire hillsides to glisten with its brilliance.

Darkly-coated surfaces occur on a variety of rock surfaces, particularly granitic and metasedimentary rock outcroppings. Excellent examples include many older alluvial and gravel fans which have a surface stain of a thin crust of manganese, iron oxide, clays, and trace elements. These may be a fraction of a millimeter thick, creating a patina the color of terra cotta, lavender-brown, or black. If the patination is rich in manganese oxides, it will develop a blackish color-coating. Where iron is more prevalent, the varnish hue will be a sunburnt orange tinge.

The deposition process is not precisely known. Although the components of desert varnish are almost entirely inorganic, the imperceptible growth of organic, acid-secreting lichens, bacteria, and other microorganisms seem to be part of the process. These organisms, acting together, concentrate the mineral-bearing solutions from the rock and its surrounding environment. In a complex cementation scheme, the microbial community glues the components to the rock surface in a uniform coating. In arid settings, it may take as long as 10,000 years to complete the process.

It is possible to determine the absolute age of varnished surfaces via radiometric measurement. Dating desert coatings can be a useful guide in determining past environmental changes as well as aging petroglyphs or other early human artifacts.

5.4 Miles, Crawford Overlook, Between Mile Markers 12.5 and 12

This overlook at 2,300 feet is without a doubt the most dramatic and most easily accessible viewpoint in the state park. The Anza-Borrego Desert here is a part of the Colorado Desert which, in turn, is a part of the larger Sonoran Desert of Mexico and Arizona. It is one of the hottest, lowest and loneliest deserts in North America.

The San Ysidro Mountain front is the edge of a rising block of bedrock that is little modified by erosion. It is a fault-controlled landform made up of a voluminous mass of Late Mesozoic plutonic rock known as the Ranchita Pluton

(70-100 MYA) and much older metasedimentary rocks (480 MYA) that are actively being uplifted.

To the north, in the distance, stand two elongated mountain ranges: the majestic northwest-southeast trending Santa Rosa Mountains reaching elevations above 8,000 feet, and closer at hand, the lesser ridgeline of Coyote Mountain. Both ranges are bounded by major faults, related to Cenozoic basin-and-range crustal deformation and extension of the earth's crust. Eastward sprawl the Borrego Badlands. Beyond on a clear day, the shimmering Salton Sea and Chocolate Mountains can be seen, 28 miles and 53 miles away, respectively. And to the south, trending diagonally toward the Vallecito Mountains, is Pinyon Ridge.

To the right and directly below, Culp and Tubb Canyons separate Pinyon Ridge from the San Ysidro Mountain block. They are narrow, extraordinarily steep and unbranching canyons that have steadfastly held their courses, etching deeper into the rising mountain range. Their V-shaped profile is typical of stream-eroded mountain canyons.

Today the leveling processes are just beginning to assert themselves. The mountain face is constantly changing as erosion continually battles with the rocks, slowly wearing them down. Along the base of the mountain range, weathering, mass wasting and deposition have removed an enormous amount of rock debris from high ground and deposited it in the low desert basin of Borrego Valley. As a result the fan-frayed mountain front lies literally buried in its own debris.

6.7 Miles, Big Spring Turnout (right), West of Mile Marker 11.5

Across the highway are the upper reaches of Culp Canyon and beyond, Tubb Canyon, which together drain Culp Valley. Tubb Canyon has a dependable supply of water at Big Spring which supports cat claw, mesquite, seepwillow and cottonwood. It serves as an important year-round watering hole for bighorn sheep and other wildlife.

At this location, you are leaving the Borrego Springs Shear Zone. The geology along the highway ahead is made up of widespread bouldery exposures of medium to coarse-grained granitic plutonic rocks of the Ranchita Pluton of the overall Peninsular Batholith. It originated as an igneous rock deep within the earth's crust during the Late Cretaceous Period of geological time, 70-100 MYA. For the most part, it contains distinctive medium to coarse-grained minerals that can be easlly identified. They include dark colored hornblende and mica, plus lighter-colored feldspar and quartz.

7.3 Miles, Old Culp Valley Road (left), Mile Marker 10.5

This historic side road leads approximately four miles west to the junction with Jasper Trail. Four-wheel drive is recommended. Boulder-strewn Culp Valley is an intermontane valley, 15 square miles in extent, alluviated by tributary drainage primarily from Montezuma Valley. This low relief surface has been developed on fault-bounded slices and blocks of roughly-textured lighter tonalitic and darker granodiorite plutonic rock. Both rock types are very similar to granite, being composed of the same minerals. They differ only in the proportion of quartz and feldspars. All may properly be referred to as granitics.

7.8 Miles, Thimble Peak

Thimble Peak, elevation 5,779 feet, is the high and rugged, conical peak on the northwestern skyline.

8.7 Miles, Culp Valley Campground (right), Between Mile Markers 9.5 and 9

Culp Valley is crisscrossed by many fractures in the rocks. Some of the nearby springs, such as Cottonwood Spring, Pena Spring, and Bubbling Spring are fault-controlled and issue forth along subsidiary fissures associated with the Hellhole Canyon Fault that is present a short distance to the north.

The rounded, spheroidally-weathered boulders of granitic rock are a feature distinctive of the Peninsular Range. The phenomena responsible for the many rocky outcrops is "jointing." These jointed cracks are parallel and perpendicular features that develop in the rock as it is exposed and weathered.

Spheroidal weathering is the chemical process whereby acidic rainwater, in an arid environment, attacks the rock's interlocking mineral crystals, especially feldspar, along joints. Through time, the blocks are chemically weathered, erosion gnawing not only at their face, but downwasting the edges and corners. Crumbling and falling apart, corners of granitic boulders tend to decompose at a faster rate than the sides and edges, thus rounding out their profile. They vary greatly in size and shape.

9.3 Miles, Pegmatite Dikes, West of Mile Marker 9

Double road-cuts of undecomposed granitic "core" rock. Look for small lighter-colored **pegmatite** and **aplite dikes** that form very thin stringers to fairly thick dikes coursing throughout the enclosing rocks. Light colored pegmatites are characteristically coarse to very coarse-grained intrusive rocks that accompanied episodes of igneous activity within the batholithic complex of later cooling stages during the Late Cretaceous Period of the Mesozoic Era, 65-75 MYA. Pegmatites are composed of granitic rocks with albite (a plagioclase feldspar), muscovite, mica, potash, feldspar, and quartz being the more common minerals. Pegmatites intrude almost explosively into cracks in the older rock bodies when decreasing heat and pressure allow these cracks to form.

10.0 Miles, Chaparral Plant Community, Mile Marker 8

Chaparral is a densely-spaced, wood-scrub botanical community with over 150 species of plants. Examples here include Mojave yucca, bushy toyon, manzanita, mountain lilac, ceanothus, scrub oak, laurel sumac, buckwheat, chamise and red shank. They all grow as a stunted elfin forest, about 3-8 feet above the ground. Many plants have an extensive root system and are resistant to fire.

11.3 Miles, Jasper Trail Junction (left), West of Mile Marker 7

Access to the old Culp Valley Road and Grapevine Canyon. This jeep trail is quite rugged. Four-wheel drive is mandatory.

11.6 Miles, Park Boundary, East of Mile Marker 6

Mountain crest (elevation 4,275 feet above sea level). Leaving Anza-Borrego Desert State Park at its western boundary. To the north, on the skyline, is the pine-clad, sawtoothed ceiling of the San Ysidro Mountains, part of the Los Coyotes Indian Reservation. County Highway S-22 continues ahead another 6.4 miles to the T-intersection with County Highway S-2, crossing the mature erosion surface and oak-grown canopy of Montezuma Valley.

Church Spur (upper right middle ground) has been offset east, out from the mountain mass, along the left-lateral Hellhole Canyon fault in this view from the Culp Valley overlook. SB

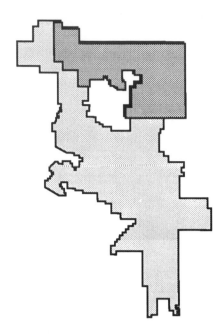

The prominent "swiss cheese" Truckhaven Rocks, north of Hwy S-22, are Canebrake Conglomerate derived from the eroding highlands of the rising Santa Rosa Mountains and tilted to the south. PR

Chapter 2 - Northeastern Area

FIELD TRIP NO. 2

BORREGO/SALTON SEAWAY (Hwy S-22 East)

Length: 21.3 Miles (one way)

Road Conditions: Good. Paved Road

Season: October through May

Route Summary:

This tour begins at the visitor center, one mile west of Mile Marker 18. It proceeds eastward, generally following the historic route taken by Alfred Armstrong "Doc" Beaty's Truckhaven Trail to the Imperial County boundary at Mile Marker 39. The ABDNHA "Erosion Road" brochure, available at the visitor center, describes highlights of the route.

General Description:

Across a spacious beige desert setting, bereft of tourist amenities, the Borrego/Salton Seaway traverses a vast realm of unspoiled natural scenery. To the north are the titanic ramparts of the Santa Rosa Mountains, thrust upward on a grandiose scale with the greatest vertical relief of any range in the state park. To the south is a wizard's hideaway known as the Borrego Badlands, a parched, eroded landscape which houses many treasures of natural history.

The feel of the land between and beyond is at once immense and unreal, sepulchral enough to evoke Colin Fletcher's *The Man Who Walked Through Time* or Edward Abbey's *Desert Solitaire*. Vistas are sweeping and distances deceiving.

It is a dynamic landscape where spectacular examples of geological forces beckon the inquisitive desert visitor to take time to explore this remote and rugged corner of Anza-Borrego Desert State Park.

Route Log:

0.0 Miles, Visitor Center (parking lot exit)

Proceed east toward Borrego Springs, descending the gradual slope of the large Hellhole Canyon alluvial fan.

2.0 Miles, Christmas Circle (east exit), Mile Marker 19

2.4 Miles, DiGiorgio Road

The noticeable dip in the road marks the channel for floodwater seasonally flowing from Borrego Palm Canyon to the Borrego Sink. During exceptionally wet winters, a good stream of water often surfaces here.

3.4 Miles, Borrego Springs Elementary School (stop sign)

Borrego Valley, actually a sink or basin, is a structural depression that has undergone significant down-faulting along its eastern margin (Coyote Creek **Fault**) in relation to the bounding mountain ranges that have been uplifted to heights above 5,000 feet.   Erosional retreat of the bold eastern **escarpment** of the San Ysidros has also played an active role. The valley floor, which appears to be flat, actually ranges in elevation from 400 to 1,200 feet.

Borrego Valley is surrounded on three sides by magnificent fault block mountain ranges. To the north, the Santa Rosas tower over the shorter, elongated ridgeline of Coyote Mountain. Both ranges trend in a northwesterly direction. To the west are the San Ysidro Mountains (Field Trip No. 1) and to the south, Pinyon Ridge (Field Trip No. 3) and the Vallecito Mountains (Field Trip No. 4).

To the left (northwest) of Coyote Mountain is Coyote Canyon. Seasonal streams such as Coyote Creek, Borrego Palm Canyon and San Felipe Creek supply most of the recharge to the natural ground-water reservoirs in the valley. Most of the surface water inflow to these reservations occurs as runoff during the winter season.

Font's Point (elevation 1,294 feet.) is the high point of the Borrego Badlands which are being warped and uplifted as a result of right-lateral motion in the San Jacinto Fault Zone. LL

4.6 Miles, Borrego Springs Airport Entrance, West of Mile Marker 22

Recent subsurface gravity measurements near here indicate that the thickness of alluvium fill of Borrego Valley is between 2,000 - 2,500 feet deep and may be as much as 10,000 feet along its eastern edge, adjacent to the active Coyote Creek Fault.

6.0 Miles, Pegleg Road/Palm Canyon Road Junction, Mile Marker 23

Access to the community dump, Dump Wash, Anza Trail, San Felipe Wash and the **tectonically** subsiding Borrego Sink. Southward, the mesquite-engulfed Borrego Sink is the lowest structural feature in the area at elevation 468 feet. Consequently, the sink receives the greatest percentage of surface water streamflow and groundwater inflow entering the Borrego Valley aquifer. Continue curving north on S-22.

To the west is the great western mountain barrier protecting Borrego Valley. The San Ysidro Mountain Range rises abruptly nearly a vertical mile from the valley floor. San Ysidro Peak, at 6,147 feet above sea level, is the highpoint punctuating this skyline.

6.5 Miles, Font's Point View

To the east, the highly eroded Borrego Badlands are predominantly composed of late Pliocene and Pleistocene (0.2 - 3 MYA) Borrego **Formation** underlying Ocotillo Formation, all of which are capped by Font's Point Sandstone. The beds are here described in ascending order from older to younger. The pinkish-brown **lacustrine** (lakebed) Borrego Formation consists of shallow-water claystones (older than 1.2 MYA) with minor interbedding of sandstones derived from the ancestral Colorado River delta (approximately 3 MYA). Atop these beds, the grayish Ocotillo is a locally-derived, poorly-bedded formation and coarse-grained sandstone representing **fluvial** (alluvial fan-floodplain) deposits. These deposits spread out into the Borrego Basin during the Middle to Late Pleistocene (0.4 - 1.2 MYA). Salmon-colored Font's Point Sandstone overlies these beds, representing a semi-arid environment of deposition during the Late Pleistocene (less than 0.4 MYA) The slightly upwarped and deformed array of distant hills is known to paleontologists as "Mammoth Cove," dominated by the well-known promontory of Font's Point at elevation 1,294 feet.

7.0 Miles, Coyote Creek Fault, Mile Marker 24

Along this three-mile stretch of roadway, Pegleg Road crosses the active Coyote Creek Fault. This fault represents the major western branch of the San Jacinto Fault Zone which, in turn, may be the most active system in California. On April 9, 1968 the Borrego Mountain Earthquake (magnitude 6.4 on the Richter Scale) hit Anza-Borrego. It was the largest earthquake to occur in California in more than 15 years. The main **epicenter** was located in the southern Borrego Badlands near Third Wash. Ground rupture occurred along 31 miles of the Coyote Creek Fault. This earthquake was caused by **right-lateral** displacement. (See Trip No. 5, Ocotillo Wells, for additional discussion of this quake.)

In conjunction with the Clark Fault (eastern branch of the San Jacinto Fault Zone), both form an active, **right-stepping en echelon pair** that, through time, represent major local tectonic mountain-building processes. As a result, this part of the Anza-Borrego Desert is one of the most seismically active regions of the far larger Salton Trough-Gulf of California structural depression.

8.0 Miles, Coyote Mountain, Mile Marker 25

.   Directly ahead, Coyote Mountain (elevation 3,192 feet) is a fractured block of granitic **intrusions** and **metasedimentary basement rock** that has been recently uplifted along the Coyote Creek Fault on the mountain's western side. Note that the southwestern end of Coyote Mountain is made up of several terraced landslide blocks. Also note the shear, nearly vertical western slope of Coyote Mountain. Along this range-front fault-line, many **faceted spurs** in the bedrock may be seen, these **facets** being evidence of fault effects.

8.6 Miles, Pegleg Road/ Henderson Canyon Junction, Between Mile Markers 25 and 26

The Pegleg Historical Marker is a few hundred yards northeast of this junction. (Mileage to the marker is not included here.)

Thomas L. Smith, alias "Pegleg Smith" was a mountain man and desert rat. Legends regarding his lost gold mine abound throughout the desert southwest. At this location there is an interesting cairn of rock piled high to commemorate him. "Let him who seeks Pegleg Smith's gold add 10 rocks to this monument," a sign reads. As a result, a variety of rock samples from the Salton Trough area make up this unique monument: tonalite, marble, pegmatite, travertine, petrified wood, tufa, pumice, quartzite, gypsum and sandstone concretions.

Behind the monument, Mesozoic crystalline granitics of the Peninsular Range **Batholith** (70-100 MYA) and older metasedimentary **roof pendants** (470 MYA) make up the southern half of Coyote Mountain. They have been deformed by **mylonization**, whereby the rock fabric has undergone a period of intense shearing and stretching associated with large-scale faulting and mountain-building. They are similar to rocks exposed along Montezuma Grade, noted at Field Trip No. 1, Mile 5.2.

During Anza-Borrego's geological past, there have been several important episodes of mountain building. The most recent episode coincides with the opening of the Gulf of California and the rifting apart of Baja California from the Mexican mainland during the Pliocene and Pleistocene Epochs (0.1 - 5 MYA). It is still continuing today.

9.3 Miles, Rockhouse Canyon and Clark Dry Lake Turnoff Between Mile Markers 26 and 27

To the north is the large structural depression of Clark Valley, averaging 600 feet above sea level. Field observations and recent geophysical data strongly suggest that Clark Valley is a **pull-apart basin** in a classic right lateral and right step sense. The dry lake bed, or playa, lies between two branches of the northwest-striking, right-slipping San Jacinto Fault Zone. The void of the dry lake bed formed as a direct result of oblique crustal extension or thinning of the earth's surface. This was produced as the Clark Fault transferred motion, or stepped, from one fault strand (Clark Fault) to another (Coyote Creek Fault). Such a closed-in basin, characterized by interior drainage, is referred to as a **graben**. It continues to subside and is bordered by some remarkably recent fault features now dominating the relief of this area.

The San Jacinto Fault Zone is a well-defined master break of the earth's crust. Beginning on the north side of the San Gabriel Mountains, it has a known length of approximately 180 miles, extending southward where it converges with and eventually joins the San Andreas Fault Zone. This is in conjunction with sea-floor spreading activity that is presently and appreciably widening the northern Gulf of California.

This through-going fault zone consists of many smaller faults that network between the major zones of displacement. Evidence of recent faulting in the Borrego area include topographic expressions that are sharp and clear and are accompanied by crushed zones of crystalline basement rock, aligned canyons and arroyos, offset streams, fault-line and eroded fault escarpments that can be traced for miles, linear topographic trends and fault-line valleys, earthquake epicenter swarms, alignment of hot springs and sag ponds with springs of permanent water, and numerous recorded earthquakes.

As a rule, large-scale movements in this area, such as the Borrego Mountain Earthquake, have been **right-lateral, strike-slip**. There is also much evidence for vertical displacement. Large earthquakes, registering M6 and over on the **Richter Scale**, occur in the San Jacinto Fault Zone on an average every eight years.

10.0 Miles, Clark Valley View, Mile Marker 27

Continuing eastward, the highway traverses unconsolidated, cross-stratified Quaternary sand deposits which may be remnants of Clark Valley's early drainage system when it drained to the south and east, prior to the uplift of the Borrego Badlands.

Clark Basin is backed by the precipitous Santa Rosa Mountains rising along the right-lateral Clark Fault, a major component of the San Jacinto Fault Zone. Clark Basin and its bounding mountains, Coyote and the Santa Rosas, is a classic example of horst and graben "range and basin" topography. PR

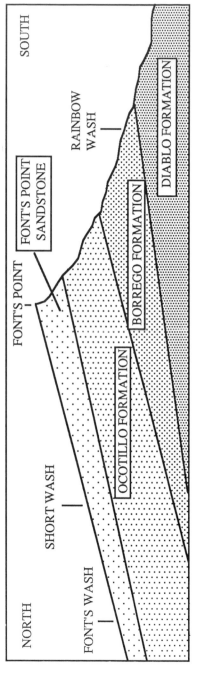

STRATIGRAPHY OF THE WESTERN BORREGO BADLANDS

GENERALIZED CROSS-SECTION OF THE LOCAL ROCK
COLUMN EXPOSED WEST OF FONT'S POINT (MAMMOTH COVE)

10.8 Miles, Truckhaven Trail Crossing, Park Boundary, Mile Marker 28

At this location, the Borrego/Salton Seaway twice crosses the pathway of the old Truckhaven Trail. To the east is an excellent, unobstructed panorama of the uplifted Santa Rosa Mountain block and its classic alluvial fan front. Geologically, the Santa Rosa Mountains mark the eastern boundary of the geomorphic Peninsular Range Province. The range is composed of an ancient metasedimentary rock sequence, including marble, biotite schist, quartzite, gneiss and amphibolite with younger **plutonic intrusions** of quartz diorite, granodiorite and pegmatite (70 - 100 MYA). These various metasediments form the prominent bands and layers visible high in the Santa Rosas and were deposited in Ordovician times, 470 MYA.

The entire basin-and-range model of Clark Valley, sandwiched between Coyote Mountain on the west and the Santa Rosa Mountains on the east, represents a dynamic **horst and graben** transfiguration of the earth's crust. Reflecting the recency of earth movements, the desert is actively splitting open, coming apart, pulled, and thinned. There are few foothills. Fault scarps are everywhere. Earthquakes, frighteningly persistent, abound. This type of topography is what is seen during active mountain building episodes. This is a lively land, indeed.

11.4 Miles, Inspiration Wash

Ranger Jim Meier reported two feet of water crossing the highway here during Hurricanes Kathleen (1976) and Doreen (1977).

12.3 Miles, Font's Point Wash, Between Mile Markers 29 and 30

During the Pleistocene Epoch (0.5-2 MYA), normal valley stream drainages, either seasonal or year-round, flowed from Coyote Canyon, Clark Valley, and Borrego Basin in a southeasterly direction towards the Salton Trough structural depression. Today, the presence of the Borrego Badlands implies that uplift of the central portion of this area has been occurring. It is a unique, dynamic interplay of sedimentation, erosion, and **tectonics**. Each Influences the other. The tectonic uplift has made the landscape more susceptible to erosional processes. In response, Font's Wash, Inspiration Wash, and their tributaries, represent an adjustment to rock structures. Seemingly against the grain of gravity, they flow northward into the dry lake bed of Clark Valley while the Coyote Canyon drainage makes an end run right around the uplifted Borrego Badlands and continues to the southeast via the San Felipe drainage system.

13.0 Miles, Santa Rosa Overlook (south), Mile Marker 30

The flat-lying desert floor is characterized by plant life of the Lower Sonoran life zone, including the very hardy creosote bush, cholla cactus, and burroweed.

The margin between Clark Valley and the Santa Rosa Mountains is discretely marked by the Clark Fault, which lies beneath the younger alluvial fill of Clark's Dry Lake. Geological relationships along this reach of the Santa Rosa Mountain front suggest that eastward tilting of the basin has occurred and continues to occur.

Note the steep profile of the nearby immature **alluvial fans** as compared with older, mature fans developed along distant western slopes of the Santa Rosa Mountains to the north, behind Clark Well. Their steepness strongly reflects recent mountain building. In addition, the coarseness of the rock material composing them produces fan surfaces that are rough and irregular with an abundance of large boulders. This is another indication of an actively subsiding basin in relation to an uplifting mountain front. Both old and young fans are cut by little fault **scarps** running through them. Also note the many **faceted** spurs developed in the bedrock. Lastly, the older fan materials are covered with a modest coating of **desert varnish.**

The interpretive panel here notes Cal Tech geologist Robert Sharp's observation that the San Jacinto Fault Zone is the most active fault in California.

13.8 Miles, Blowsand Turnout (north), Mile Marker 31

"Erosion Road" (1976) referred to this point as "Blowsand Turnout" while the 1989 edition calls it "Toro Peak Viewpoint." As the roadway crosses a small dry wash it enters a subtle, elongated structural graben, or valley, bounded on both side by prominent northwest-southeast trending fault scarps. These features can be traced with certainty as far as Palo Verde Wash. On the left, located between the highway and the Santa Rosa Mountains, is a series of low-lying, rolling hills known collectively as Lute Ridge. Although it is not obvious from this vantage point, the northeastern edge of Lute Ridge is a classic, textbook **strike-slip fault scarp**, altogether extending two miles in length, along the Clark Fault. It represents the largest known fault scarp on the North American continent existing in unconsolidated sediments.

Lute Ridge is a pressure condition, continuing to be domed up, resulting in quite obvious and not so obvious unconformities throughout the area. The irregular, hummocky topography is deeply dissected. It is made up of late Pleistocene (0.1-0.5 MYA) to Holocene alluvial fan material derived from the Rattlesnake Canyon area. There are six additional scarplets visible on the southern slopes of Lute Ridge. This is an example of **right lateral, left stepping** fault activity resulting in a **pressure ridge.**

14.8 Miles, Thimble Trail, West of Mile Marker 32

This is the junction with Thimble Trail on the right (south) and the old Truckhaven Trail on the left (north). To the north on the eastern edge of the prominent ridgeline is the foreboding chasm of Rattlesnake Canyon. There are two well-developed alluvial fans located adjacent to it on the right, along the southern base of the Santa Rosa Mountains. If you look closely above the creosote-lined desert floor, there is a prominent fault scarp visible, chopping off both alluvial fans at their apex or upper ends. In this vicinity, the existence of multiple fault-scarps marks the trace of the Clark Fault. There is over 100 feet of lateral displacement on the alluvial fans. Higher on the mountain, tortured, twisted layers of light colored marble are remnants of Ordovician marine sediments, 470 MYA.

15.7 Miles, Palo Verde Wash Road, West of Mile Marker 33

To the northwest, diagonally across the highway, the prominent light greenish-colored mudhills, immediately seen, are **pressure ridges** that have been squeezed up, marking the trace of the Clark Fault. The unconsolidated sediments, clays and cobbled sandstones are representative of the late Pliocene Borrego Formation 1-2 MYA.

Beyond to the northeast, the light-colored foothills and slopes along the southern end of the Santa Rosa Mountains include the Early Pliocene Canebrake

Conglomerate (4 - 5 MYA) overlain by the younger, Middle Pleistocene Ocotillo Formation (0.5 - 1 MYA). Both sedimentary rock formations are made up of locally-derived fragments of granitic **intrusives** and **metasediments** that are typical of Anza-Borrego basement rock. Their presence in the stratigraphic record indicates periods of active mountain building and erosion, with deposition of sedimentary formations (alluvial fans and floodplains) that extended out onto the low-lying Borrego Basin.

Along the southern end of the Santa Rosa Mountains, the Canebrake Conglomerate has been overthrust over basement rocks from east to west, as a result of a reactivated Miocene-aged detachment fault (15 - 20 MYA) that may extend many miles northward to the San Jacinto Mountains. There is evidence that this nearly horizontal detachment fault was reactivated during the Middle and Late Pleistocene Epoch (0.1 - 1 MYA).

16.8 Miles, Clark Fault, West of Mile Marker 34

After the gentle ascent from Palo Verde Wash (mile marker 33), three **normal fault-scarp** remnants cross the roadway in a northwest-southeast direction. This location is near the epicenter of the 1954 Santa Rosa Mountains earthquake which measured 6.2 on the Richter scale.

At this point the Clark Fault (easternmost of the San Jacinto Fault Zone) **side-steps** right (southeast), away from the Truckhaven Rocks which lie ahead to the northeast and are described below. Southeast, throughout the Borrego Badlands and beyond the San Felipe Hills, the Clark Fault can only be recognized by such features as folds, surface tears, and separate splay faults that mark differential movement between basement rock and cover sediments.

17.4 Miles, Borrego Badlands Overlook, Between Mile Markers 34 and 35

Turn right (southeast) onto a short loop of road which is described in *Weekender's Guide* as "Smoketree Overlook." This surprising, and unmarked, vantage point overlooks Palo Verde Wash and the Vista del Malpais area of the Borrego Badlands. The non-marine sedimentary sequence to the right (west), in the vicinity of Short Wash and Fault Wash, and ascending from older to newer, is similar to that featured at Font's Point View above (between mile markers 23 and 24). It includes pinkish-brown **lacustrine** Borrego Formation, grayish **fluvial** Ocotillo Formation, and salmon-colored Font's Point Sandstone of semi-arid alluvial origin. These slightly deformed badland deposits, representing an aggregate thickness of several thousand feet, are soft, fragile, and easily weathered.

In these beds, paleontologists describe the "Borrego Local Fauna" in terms of the North American Land Mammal Age Scale (see Geologic Time Correlation Chart by George Miller). The middle to late Irvingtonian (0.6 - 1.0 MYA) and possibly early Rancholabrean (0.03 - 0.6 MYA) Ages are represented by significant fossil discoveries including the Columbian and Imperial mammoth, saber-tooth cat, American lion, ground sloth, bear, camel, horse, and deer. This Borrego Local Fauna is one of the most important Irvingtonian Age fossil collections in Southern California.

Cross-references to slightly older fossil fauna include: Trip No. 4A (Sandstone Canyon, "Layer Cake Local Fauna," Hemphillian-Blancan); Trip No. 5 (June Wash and Vallecito Badlands, "Vallecito Creek Local Fauna," Blancan-Irvingtonian); Trip No. 5A (General Description of the Vallecito Badlands, "Vallecito Local Fauna," Blancan-Irvingtonian).

Borrego Mountain lies south in the middle ground near Ocotillo Wells, while beyond are the Vallecito-Fish Creek Mountain Ranges and, on a clear day, the brooding presence of Superstition Mountain on the far horizon.

17.5 Miles, Smoketree Wash
This excellent badlands wash walk is described in *Weekender's Guide.*

17.7 Miles, Coachwhip Canyon (left, north), Ella Wash (right, south)
Both may be driven for about two miles on primitive roads.

17.8 Miles, Arroyo Salado Turnoff (right, south), West of Mile Marker 35
The popular badlands primitive campground is one half mile southeast.

18.5 Miles, Truckhaven Rocks (left, north), East of Mile Marker 35
These are the prominent, tilted "swiss cheese" slabs to the north, one beautiful mile up Arroyo Salado. These rocks belong to the Canebrake Conglomerate, a thick sandstone unit of early Pliocene age (4 -5 MYA). It is the oldest locally derived Cenozoic (Modern Era) sedimentary rock sequence in the Borrego Badlands. It was deposited basinward from the fan/floodplain outwash deposits. Subtle changes in particle size and bedding are quite evident throughout its exposures. About five sedimentary environments are recognized ranging from coarse, bouldery fanglomerates high in the section to lower (distal), non-pebbly, finer grained channel sandstones.

The Borrego Formation of lakebed origin is prominent in this view west from Vista Del Malpais (View of the Badlands). PR

19.2 Miles, Calcite Scenic Overlook (left, north), East of Mile Marker 36

"Erosion Road" brochures have variously called this superb overlook "Earth Movements" (1970), "Sediments in Motion" (1976), "Faults, Water, and Wind" (1989). The current name abbreviates the *Weekender's* version. A short walk from the parking area overlooks North Fork of Arroyo Salado.

Eroded slickrock sandstone country unrolls to the north with 2,700 feet "Traveler's Peak" as the high point on the northern horizon. This name was recalled by former state park ranger Art Morley. Hidden behind Traveler's Peak is 3,500 feet "Pyramid Peak," identified by the Lindsays and Schad (see bibliography) to describe crosscountry routes in the Santa Rosas. This intricately carved landscape is noted for its magnificent upthrown slabs and buttresses of blocky, orange-tinted sandstones, creased by a labyrinth of narrow, vertical-walled deep gorges and rugged slot canyons.

Since crossing over the Clark Fault, the Truckhaven Rocks have maintained a noticeable rotational dip around the southern end of the Santa Rosa Mountains. This is directly owing to stress complexities along the eastern margin of the San Jacinto Fault Zone. At this location the strata dip in a southerly direction. Previously, at the Arroyo Salado Primitive Campground, the sandstones dip more to the southwest. This large structural feature, referred to as the Truckhaven Anticline, is a direct result of rapid deposition of sediments superimposed on an area of active tectonism. As a result of the many faults that cross hatch the area, the rocks have been buckled, twisted and secondarily eroded into fantastic shapes by the earth movements.

19.7 Miles, North Fork Arroyo Salado

The Diablo Formation (new term) is notable for its rich bounty of petrified wood. The fossil wood uncovered here was derived from three temperate hardwood species of trees. The principal species that composed over 70% of the forest cover was ancestral forms of California Laurel, (*Umbellularia salicifolia*). The second most abundant form was a mixture of trees from the Willow Family (*Salicaceae*) containing both Cottonwood (*Populus*) and Willow (*Salix*). The abundant species was ancestral forms of California Walnut (*Juglans pseudomorpha*). Living relatives of these three native tree types still abound throughout California. This unique assemblage reflects a temperate climate with marine influences from the Gulf of California and predominantly winter rainfall in this region during the Early Pliocene Epoch, about four million years ago.

20.0 Miles, "Blake's Ravines," Mile Marker 37

The flat-topped mesa that characterizes much of the immediate area is all that remains of an extensive **pedimented** tableland that existed here during the Late Pleistocene Epoch. Finger remnants have been heavily dissected between today's entrenched desert washes, including the deep tributaries of Palm Wash, Arroyo Salado and Tule Wash. This eroded landscape, from here to Highway 86, is named for William Phipps Blake. He visited this area in 1853 as a geologist with a government Railroad Survey Party (Parker/Leetch, 1979).

Most mesa surfaces are capped with a bouldery residue of various-sized rocks derived from nearby source areas. These mosaics are probably produced by selective erosional processes that remove finer surface material, leaving behind heavier, coarser rock materials known collectively as desert pavement.

20.2 Miles, Cannonball Wash and the Diablo Formation

The Diablo Formation (new term) is easily identified in these roadcuts and cliffsides by its reddish brown and pale orange coloration. It has distinctive thick **marker beds** of **quartz-arenite** sandstone. These sandstone bodies form conspicuous strike ridges that yield an abundance of iron-bearing sandstone **concretions**, hence the name "Cannonball Wash."

These Diablo sandstones, generally considered members of the Palm Spring Formation, are herein treated as a separate formation. This is because of the Diablo's extensive exposure and separate identity in the Anza-Borrego region as well as its very separate origin as ancestral Colorado River delta deposits. These deposits are quite distinct from the locally derived alluvium from surrounding mountains that is Palm Spring Formation and which occurs only in the Vallecito Badlands in the southern park area. (See Appendix abstract for further discussion of the Diablo Formation- new term.)

Diablo sandstones in the Borrego Badlands are older than those in the southern park. This is because the landmass of Borrego (part of Peninsular California) moves northwest relative to the mouth of the Colorado River near Yuma. About 3 - 4 MYA, the ancestral Colorado first began dumping its sediments into the Borrego Basin. As the area moved northwest, away from the mouth of the Colorado, the Vallecito-Fish Creek Badlands was the later recipient of delta sediment (about 2 - 3 MYA). Not surprisingly, today's sediments at the mouth of the river near Yuma are very similar to the Diablo sediments in the Anza-Borrego region. See Trip No. 4A (Camel's Head Wash) for a discussion of the Diablo Formation in the Fish Creek and Vallecito Badlands.

21.0 Miles, Salton View, Mile Marker 38

This 1970 "Erosion Road" term became "The Inland Sea Viewpoint" in the 1976 edition. Both refer to the sweeping view of the Salton Sea to the east. In 1905 the Colorado River was accidentally diverted from its normal channel into the irrigation canals of the Imperial Valley. For two years, river waters flowed unimpeded into the area. As a result, the Salton Sea - a man-made feature - is the largest lake in California. It is 33 miles long by 13 miles wide, covering over 400 square miles. Its present water surface lies about 235 feet below sea level.

The Salton Trough-Gulf of California depression is a true **rift** valley, an elongated, down-dropped block of the earth's crust that separates two major plate tectonic boundaries. It is also splitting apart, causing Baja California to raft away from mainland Mexico along segments of the San Andreas Fault Zone. This is all controlled by deep-seated **plate tectonic** movements, as one plate (Pacific Plate) gradually moves northwestward adjacent to the North American Plate, which is slowly moving southwestward. Both are separated by the San Andreas Fault Zone. This vast area of instability, including the Imperial and Coachella Valleys, is marked or characterized by **wrench tectonics, crustal spreading centers,** detachment faulting, seismic activity, volcanism, and geothermal activity with hydrothermal activity. It occupies the largest area (over 2,000 square miles) of continental land below sea level in the Western Hemisphere with the Salton Sea at its lowest part.

21.2 Miles, Calcite Mine Trail

Intersection with the Calcite Mine Trail to the north and the old Truckhaven Trail to the southwest.

The Calcite Mine jeep road is a narrow, rough and dangerous trail, extending 1.9 miles from the highway. Four-wheel drive is mandatory although hiking is recommended. The height of mining activity was during the early years of World War II. Optical-grade calcite crystals, a calcium carbonate mineral, were intended for use in bomb-sights and anti-aircraft weaponry due to its excellent double-refraction property. Today the abandoned mine area is honeycombed with many vertical, trench-mining slots and shafts cut into the sides of hills.

All calcite veining within the immediate area originated as a hydrothermal feature with mineralization that filled cross shears produced in the hard sandstones along major east-west, **strike-slip faults.**

Directly to the north, running parallel with the Borrego/Salton Seaway, is the south fork of Palm Wash. The colorful rock stripes of its canyon walls, banded in soft shades of yellow, reddish-brown and olive-green, belong to fine-grained sandstones and clays of the Diablo Formation.

Park Administrative Officer Fred Jee notes that reddish sediments typically reflect shallow, swampy, mucky deposition environments with rapid oxidation of iron minerals, whereas greenish or grayish sediments reflect deeper, calmer pond or lake environments. The Diablo sandstone of Colorado River delta origin, can be seen interfingering with the much coarser, local slope-derived Canebrake Conglomerate sandstones in many of the side washes and highway road-cuts along this portion of S-22. Within the upper reaches of Palm Wash, the Diablo sandstone has yielded large camelid footprints, trace fossils, and abundant petrified woods.

21.3 Miles, Park Boundary

Microwave Tower. This location marks Anza-Borrego Desert State Park's easternmost boundary. Ahead is the Imperial County Line and the Bureau of Land Management's California Desert Conservation Area. The Borrego/Salton Seaway continues eastward another eight miles to its intersection with State Highway 86 at Salton City.

Vertical rock strata in Coachwhip Canyon, between Mile Markers 34 and 35, north of Hwy S-22. PR

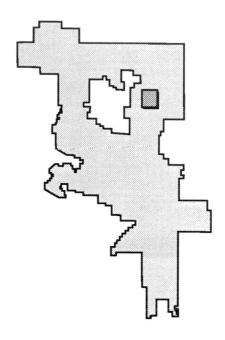

Wash in Borrego Formation (lakebed origin) below Font's Point. AY

FIELD TRIP NO. 2A

FONT'S POINT (Primitive Road)

Length:	4.1 Miles (one way)
Road Conditons:	Dirt Road subject to wash-outs. Check with visitor center before proceeding. Four-wheel drive recommended
Season:	October through May

Route Summary:

This Field Trip turns off from the Borrego/Salton Seaway portion of Highway S-22 (Tour No. 2) between Mile Markers 29 & 30 and proceeds along sandy washes, a four-wheel drive roadway to Font's Point. The views of Borrego Badlands from Font's Point are outstanding as is the geology of the area.

General Description:

Font's Point, at 1,294 feet above sea level, provides a spectacular view of the Borrego Badlands. Standing at the very edge of this receding cliff, the viewpoint exposes a wealth of Pliocene and Pleistocene earth history. Gazing down into the depths of Rainbow Wash and Hills of the Moon Wash, one looks back through several million years of local geologic time. Layered sediments preserve petrified environments of deposition.

Route Log:

0.0 Miles, Font's Point Wash/S-22 Junction

0.8 Miles, Inspiration Wash Member

The first series of hillsides on the left (east) are consolidated sandstones, red and greenish-colored mudstones and claystones of the Inspiration Wash Member of the Ocotillo Formation. They represent a mixed lakebed and riverine environment that periodically existed within the Borrego Basin during the glacial-interglacial Ice Ages. The ages of these sediments were recently assigned a **paleomagnetic** date of less than 500,000 years in age.

The Inspiration Wash Member is the youngest fossil bearing rock unit in the Borrego Badlands. Over the past several years, paleontologists have unearthed the fossil remains of now-extinct horse, camel, deer, ground sloth, Columbian and Imperial mammoth and camelid footprints from nearby localities. This brief and partial faunal list is characteristic of the Irvingtonian and early Rancholabrean Land Mammal **Epoch** (0.3-1.9 MYA).

1.8 Miles, Short Wash Junction (left, east)

Continue straight ahead and then veer to the right, following the established roadway as it leaves the main wash and enters a tributary arroyo.

2.4 Miles, Mammoth Cove Sandstone

Folded exposures of the Mammoth Cove Sandstone Member of the Ocotillo **Formation** can now be seen in the shallow roadcuts and along subdued hills. This sandstone is characteristically a gray-colored, pebbly to bouldery granitic conglomerate and sandstone unit that grades laterally and basinward into the lakebeds of the Borrego Formation. At this location the Mammoth Cove Sandstone underlies the Inspiration Wash Member. Nearby, their vari-colored formational contact has been paleomagnetically dated at about 700,000 years in age.

Folding and small **en echelon strike-slip faults** are common in the Borrego Badlands. Overlying rock sediments are folded in response to faulting in underlying basement rocks. **Right-lateral, strike-slip** movements of the Coyote Creek Fault, accompanied by **left-lateral slippage** on the nearby Inspiration Point Fault (clearly seen in the Mammoth Cove area west of Inspiration Wash), has rotated this block of the Borrego Badlands. Seasonal drainages along the Inspiration Point Fault are locally offset to the left by fault movements.

3.7 Miles, Loop Drive Junction (one way)

Veer to the left, continuing uphill. The dirt roadway has been graded directly on weathered exposures of the Font's Point Sandstone Member.

4.1 Miles, Font's Point Parking Area

The approach to Font's Point has been through a rather flat, subdued landscape of ocotillo and creosote bush. Now, suddenly at the brink, the park visitor confronts one of the most sublime spectacles in all of Anza-Borrego.

Font's Point (elevation 1,294 feet) is the climactic overlook of the Borrego Badlands. Beyond, on the southern horizon, are the Fish Creek, Vallecito, and Pinyon Mountains. The low mound of hills east of the Fish Creek Mountains is Superstition Hills. On November 23 and November 24, 1987, major twin earthquakes, measuring 6.2 and 6.6 respectively, hit along the Superstition Hills Fault. As a result, there were many rockfalls throughout the Borrego Badlands. One of two remaining palm trees at Five Palms toppled over and old cracks atop Font's Point were noticeably enlarged. During the Borrego Mountain Earthquake of 1968, over six feet of rock at the tip of Font's Point were pried loose and tumbled down the cliffside. An additional five feet of cliffside at the southeastern tip collapsed during the Landers earthquake of 1992.

The twin buttes of Borrego Mountain form a natural barrier along the San Felipe Wash drainage. San Felipe Wash can be easily traced from its confluence with Borrego Sink Wash, following the approximate trace of the Coyote Creek Fault. To the east are the shimmering waters of the Salton Sea. To the north stand the impressive Santa Rosa Mountains and Coyote Mountain, separated by the enclosed basin depression of Clark's Dry Lake. And on the western horizon is the mile-high San Ysidro Mountain Range.

The Late Pleistocene Font's Point Sandstone and Inspiration Wash Member of the Ocotillo Conglomerate (0.4 MYA) form the stratum sediments exposed in the receding cliffside of Font's Point. Below, the Mammoth Cove Sandstone Member mantles and interfingers with reddish-colored mudstones and claystones of the Borrego Formation (1 - 2 MYA). Mammoth Cove Sandstone Member sediments are easy to recognize due to their gray-buff appearance and locally-derived granule to boulder conglomerates. These terrestrial sediments, varying from unsolidated to semi-consolidated, were laid down as alluvial fan or floodplain deposition into the Borregan lake environment. Then a milder climate than today produced lush prairielands. A wide variety of Ice Age mammals, now extinct, flourished in the area, including saber-toothed cat, zebra, bear, lion, sloth and mammoth.

The older and lower Pliocene Borrego Formation represents an extensive impoundment of freshwater, lakebed sediments that are exposed in the Borrego Badlands and throughout the San Felipe Hills area to the east. These fine-grained muds, silts, clays and sands are derived from the Colorado River drainage. The yet older Diablo Formation, underlying the Borrego Formation, outcrops along the entrances to Rainbow Wash, Hills of the Moon Wash and Third Wash, in the distance, north of San Felipe Wash. It appears as dark red, tilted sediments from here. See Field Trip No. 2 (Salton View) for discussion on the Colorado River origin of the Diablo Formation. See Field Trip No. 4 (Borrego Mountain, West Butte) for notes on the Diablo shoved by granitic intrusions on the west side of Borrego Mountain.

As shadows move down into the arroyos, the scene changes in a constant drama. Erosion continues to eat down through the rising banded sequence of fossil bearing sediments. As a result, the once nondescript Borrego Basin has slowly become today's spectacular, intricately carved Borrego Badlands landscape.

View from Font's Point across the Borrego Formation above Rainbow Wash with West Butte of Borrego Mountain in the middle background across the San Felipe Wash (which is also the general trace of the Coyote Creek Fault). PR

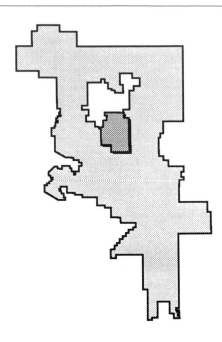

Tamarisk Grove is the only developed campground in the central portion of the vast state park and features the Cactus Loop Trail (shown here) and the Yaqui Well Nature Trail. LL

Chapter 3 - Central Area

FIELD TRIP NO. 3

YAQUI PASS (Hwy S-3)

Length: 12.0 Miles (one way)

Road Conditons: Good. Paved road

Season: October through June

Route Summary:

Tour No. 3 crosses Pinyon Ridge via Yaqui Pass, traveling along Hwy S-3 to Hwy 78. Pinyon Ridge provides a geologic window into the distant past, representing a cross-sectional overview of Anza-Borrego's regional tectonic framework. Mile markers start at mile 0.0 at the Hwy S-3/78 intersection, near Tamarisk Campground, and increase to the north to mile 12 at Christmas Circle.

General Description:

Jutting out from the San Ysidro Mountains to the west, Pinyon Ridge is a rugged desert mountain backbone that overlooks much of Borrego Valley. Maintaining an unbroken profile for seven miles, this elongated segment of the earth's crust is raised along faults and displays steep slopes on its north and south-facing sides. Traversed by a lonely two-lane road through Yaqui Pass, it is characterized throughout by **crystalline basement rock** outcroppings, and rocky plateaus that are home to bighorn sheep and mule deer populations.

Pinyon Ridge features a complicated Mesozoic compressional margin which is the same type of geology as in the San Ysidro mountains but not as pronounced. In some areas it is **overprinted**, or overlain, by sediments forceably shoved over bedrock by late Tertiary **detachment** faulting, 10-20 MTA. All told, the geologic history of the area is unique to this side of the San Andreas Fault. Fault geometries, ages of fault displacements, and topographic expressions relate closely to the overall structural development of the southwestern United States.

Route Log:

0.0 Miles, Christmas Circle, Mile Marker 12 (south exit)

Picnic tables and restroom facilities are available here. Drive south on Borrego Springs Road, County Hwy S-3.

0.4 Miles, Church Spur

On the right, and to the rear of the mission-styled St. Barnabas Episcopal Church, is the east end of "Church Spur." **Metasedimentary** rocks in the central and west part and **batholithic** rocks on the east edge of Church

Spur have been thrust several thousand feet into Borrego Valley along the **left lateral** Hellhole Canyon Fault. Coming into view behind Church Spur, Montezuma Grade can be seen snaking up the San Ysidro Mountain front, known geologically as the Borrego Springs Shear Zone.

2.0 Miles, Yaqui Meadows, Mile Marker 10

Double road-cuts slice through unconsolidated Quaternary fluvial and wind deposited **alluvium** originating along the western flanks of the Tubb Canyon drainage. This is the beginning of Yaqui Meadows, a gentle slope characterized by the creosote bush, ocotillo, cholla cacti and smoke tree of the Lower Sonoran life zone.

3.3 Miles, Glorietta Canyon Turnoff

This unmarked three-mile dirt road leads right (south) into Yaqui Meadows. Glorietta Canyon has been deeply etched along a portion of the Yaqui Ridge **Detachment Fault** of Mid Tertiary Age (10-20 MYA). This fault marks a major tectonic feature of the immediate landscape, eroded and **exhumed** along the mountain front of Pinyon Ridge.

5.0 Miles, Borrego Valley Road Intersection, Mile Marker 7

Curve right (south) on County Hwy S-3 onto Yaqui Pass Road. The highway climbs the southern flanks of Borrego Valley towards Yaqui Pass and Tamarisk Grove. Famed La Casa del Zorro resort hotel is on the left.

6.4 Miles, Ram's Hill

Entrance to Borrego Medical Center and the 3,200-acre Ram's Hill resort community on the left. Between Yaqui Meadows to the west and Cactus Valley to the east, the slopes of Yaqui Ridge represent an extensive **pediment** wherein basement rock occurs at shallow depth, hidden from view beneath a thin covering of gravelly and sandy alluvium. Field data and well logs indicate that this is basement rock and unconsolidated mid Tertiary **megabreccia** (10 - 20 MYA).

8.3 Miles, Park Boundary, (elevation 1,215 feet)

Enter Tamarisk Grove patrol sector, consisting of about 75,000 acres including Mescal Bajada, part of Pinyon Ridge, and all of the Grapevine Mountain section of the Anza-Borrego Desert State Wilderness Area. The area is a realm of outstanding wilderness value, bounded by many ravines, deep canyons, elevated tablelands and mountain peaks in a landscape dominated by granitic rock. It represents a transitional segment of the Peninsular Ranges geomorphic province where it meets the Salton Trough and the Colorado Desert. The sector extends from the desert floor at 780 feet up to ridgelines above 3,200 feet.

Directly ahead is the prominent, dome-shaped knoll, called Ship Rock (elevation 1,616 feet) for survey marker "Ship." It is a remnant feature of **detach-ment faultings,** preserved astride the Yaqui Ridge Detachment Fault.

8.5 Miles, Ship Rock, Mile Marker 3.5

The Yaqui Ridge **Detachment Fault** is a low-angle **thrust fault**, whereby one side (the younger plate) was upthrown and overlies an older, lower plate.

To unravel the complex geologic structure of this feature, we must examine the uplifted, eroded and exhumed topography along the southern (uphill) slope of Ship Rock. A calibrated eye is needed to actually see the fault contact between lower and upper plates. The older lower portion of Ship Rock consists of very light-colored, creamy, **gneissic granodiorite** that forms the local basement exposures of Yaqui Ridge. The upper portion of Ship Rock is made up of darker and younger unconsolidated **megabreccia** that may be equivalent to the Miocene Split Mountain Formation of the Borrego Mountain area. The fault contact is marked by a very thin band of intensely-sheared, crumbly, dark brown rock. It is displayed along a northwest-southeast trending alignment, diagonally crossing the paved roadway.

Overall, this detachment fault extends from east of the The Narrows (Vallecito Mountains), northwestward along Yaqui Meadows and the northeast base of Pinyon Ridge to the San Ysidro Mountains. It establishes Mid-Tertiary faulting in the area 10-20 MYA, synchronous with episodes of volcanism in and around the proto-Gulf of California. This detachment fault further represents the westernmost extension of classic, well-documented **detachment fault** complexes developed in Eastern California, Arizona and Mexico.

9.5 Miles, Desert Varnish, Mile Marker 2.5

For the most part Late Mesozoic (70 - 80 MYA) **plutonic** rocks make up the lower plate of the detachment fault and also form the bouldery countryside along both sides of the highway. Note that most of the exposed rock surfaces are coated with **desert varnish**. Light colored pegmatite dikes appear in the darker and older matrix granitic rocks.

View north into Borrego Valley across the Yaqui Meadows pediment, a retreating ridge erosional surface on bedrock which is thinly veneered with sand and gravel.
LL

9.9 Miles, Yaqui Pass Primitive Campground (elevation 1,680 feet)

Mechanical or chemical weathering has, through a short period of time, deposited a thin, loosely-consolidated mantle of decomposed granite (**grus**) atop Yaqui Pass. This coarse, gravel and sand residue, weathered a distinctive pinkish-brown, represents a locally-derived groundmass of mineral grains and rock fragments transported downslope by gravity and running water. It is similar in composition and age to the Font's Point sandstone of the Borrego Badlands. Eons of time are required, however, to consolidate these granitic fragments into a sedimentary rock, such as sandstone.

10.0 Miles, Kenyon Trail, Mile Marker 2

Just south of the summit at 1,750 feet is the Bill Kenyon Overlook Trail on the left, named for former park superintendent William Kenyon. It is a 0.5 mile hike that provides sweeping views of Mescal Bajada, the Vallecito Mountains including Sunset Mountain, and the bulk of the Pinyon Mountains directly to the south. Here in the Lower Sonoran Life Zone, the sun-baked hillsides are covered by thorny stands of agave, barrel cacti, ocotillo and cholla cacti.

10.5 Miles, Mescal Bajada Overlook (left), Mile Marker 1.5

Good exposures of granitic, **plutonic** rock are seen with light-colored **pegmatite** veins coursing throughout in road cuts (right). Some of this rock has undergone **mylonization.** The steepness of slope and shape along the south-facing edge of Pinyon Ridge is determined by Middle Pleistocene to Recent faulting. As the roadway descends the mountain front note the straight valley alignment of San Felipe Creek below. This is controlled by recent movements along the uplifted mountain block of Pinyon Ridge. Running parallel north of State Highway 78, the San Felipe Fault extends 16 miles from Buena Vista Creek (near Ranchita) down Grapevine Canyon to The Narrows.

11.0 Miles, San Felipe Fault, Mile Marker 1

Directly ahead, the roadway crosses a fractured portion of bedrock along the San Felipe Fault. Close at hand, exposed to view in road-cuts and terrace edges, remnant valley fill from the ancestral San Felipe Creek has been uplifted. These layered Late Pleistocene (0.1 - 0.2 MYA) riverine clays and sandstones are overlain by unconsolidated gravels derived from local bedrock sources. Interbedded iron laden sands are also visible here.

11.7 Miles, Tamarisk Grove Campground, West of Mile Marker 0.5

Nestled against the base of Pinyon Ridge along the San Felipe Fault, this developed campground offers car-camping facilities and interpretive, self-guided nature trails. Restroom facilities, showers, ramadas, picnic tables, and water are available. Publications are sold at the ranger station. The prominent fault escarpment can be seen directly north of the campground.

11.9 Miles, San Felipe Creek

One mile nature trail to Yaqui Well begins on the north side of the wash. On the right is the dirt road to Yaqui Well Primitive Campground. Drive-in campsites are available.

12.0 Miles, Highway 78

T-intersection with State Highway 78 marks the end of Highway S-3.

The monument at Kenyon Overlook surveys the San Felipe Wash, one of the three great drainages in the Anza-Borrego region (along with Carrizo and Coyote Creeks). DL

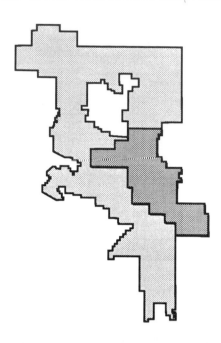

Metamorphic rock overlying granitic rock in Nude Wash, warped into a small anticline. LL

Chapter 4 - Central and Southeastern Area

FIELD TRIP NO. 4

SAN FELIPE CORRIDOR (Hwy 78)

Length: 23.5 Miles (one way)

Road Conditons: Good. Paved road

Season: October through May

Route Summary:
Field Trip No. 4 proceeds eastward on Highway 78 from its Hwy S-3 intersection (Field Trip No. 3) near Tamarisk Grove campground and continues to Ocotillo Wells. The route then follows Split Mountain Road to road-end at the United States Gypsum Mine gate. This area, over the past few million years and especially in the vicinity of Fish Creek Wash, has given birth to some of Anza-Borrego's most spectacular geological exhibits - the notable Coyote Creek **Fault**, **anticlinal folds**, marine fossils, ice age vertebrates and awesome Split Mountain itself.

General Description:
Beginning at the rocky defile of San Felipe Creek Narrows and ending at the narrow abyss of Split Mountain, the Vallecito Mountains wilderness totally dominates the surrounding desert landscape. Situated in the east-central midriff of the state park, the isolated bulk of Sunset Mountain and the Vallecito Mountain Range are immense strongholds of rough-hewn granitics and its decomposed by-products. Sunset Mountain itself seems small in comparison to the nearby highlands along the park's western barrier. Yet from atop this summit are absorbing panoramas that stretch in all directions, from the Laguna Mountains on the west to beyond the Salton Sea and Chocolate Mountains on the east.

Split Mountain is one of the most heavily studied geological features in all of Southern California. The three-mile long canyon abruptly defines a unique boulder-strewn layer cake of colorful fanglomerates, landslide deposits, gypsum beds, marine sediments and abundant fossil "reefs" that punctuate the soft mudhills landscape of the Carrizo and Fish Creek badlands.

Route Log:

0.0 Miles, Highway 78/S-3 Intersection Near Tamarisk Grove
Proceed eastbound towards Ocotillo Wells. Near-vertical road-cuts on the right-hand (south) side of the highway expose angular granitic rocks of the Peninsular **Batholith**. These basement rocks represent an old landslide block and are veneered by a deeply-weathered, unstable bouldery residue. Rockfalls are

a common occurrence along this particular section of highway.

For the next couple of miles, the highway crosses over the gentle, rolling countryside of the Mescal Bajada. Mescal Bajada is actually a well-developed **pediment** carved on the Pinyon Mountains bedrock. It is not a true **bajada,** which is a landform of coalescing **alluvial fans,** also known as "Spanish skirts."

Covered by coarse sand and gravel, the surface of erosion was accomplished by mechanical weathering, **rill wash** and **slope wash** as the steep northern face of the upraised Pinyon Mountain block was worn backward, retreating slowly at the expense of the landmass behind it. Although it looks fairly flat and level, the surface of the Mescal Bajada is trenched by Chuckwalla (Mile 2.0), Mine (Mile 2.8), Nolina and Pinyon (Mile 4.2) Washes.

Draining northward, each of these desert washes seasonally carries eroded material downward to the eastward-flowing San Felipe Creek. Along watercourses where stream flow replenishes soil moisture, drought-tolerant ocotillo, cacti, creosote bush and stiletto leaves of the agave are adapted to the arid environment of the Lower Sonoran life zone.

The light-colored hillocks of granitic bedrock bordering the highway on the right (south) are named Round Granite Hills (elevation 1,502 feet). These are **inselbergs**, residual hills surrounded by low lying surfaces of erosion.

4.7 Miles, Quartz Vein Wash and Narrows Earth Trail

At the large, left curve in the road is the Narrows Earth Trail parking area. Just beyond, the road up Quartz Vein Wash departs on the right (south). **Metasedimentary** bedrock and granitic **cataclastic rocks** of the Peninsular **Batholith** have been upthrown along major **faults**, most notably the Yaqui Ridge **Detachment Fault** and shear zone of Mid-Tertiary Age (10 - 20 MYA) and the younger San Felipe Fault that cuts through Quartz Vein Wash. The main fault trace of the San Felipe Fault originates in the Vallecito Mountains ahead to the east and forks here along the northern flanks of Sunset Mountain. It continues in a straight line along the southern base of Pinyon Ridge. See Field Trip No. 3 for San Felipe Fault exposure just above Tamarisk Grove.

A short 0.5 mile self-guided nature trail is located in Powder Dump Wash, just west of Quartz Vein Wash. It has been developed to help park visitors to understand, by visual example and in basic text, the complex geology exposed at The Narrows. A self guiding ABDNHA brochure is available at the visitor center.

5.0 Miles, San Felipe Narrows, (elevation 1068 feet)

Exposed along the steep, flood-carved gorge walls is **plutonic** bedrock which extends to an undetermined depth. These rock outcrops have been breached by the **superposed**, intermittent San Felipe Creek. During uplift of the area, the creek has steadfastly maintained its course, superposing or cutting down through the mountain mass, exposing a cross-section profile of Pinyon Ridge. See Field Trip No. 2 (Font's Point Wash) for a similar example of tectonic uplift vs. erosion in the sedimentary environment.

5.7 Miles, Nude Wash (right, south)

Turnout is east of the electrical power substation. Hike a short distance back up the small gorge south of the cul-de-sac. Here the exhumed, eroded surface of the Yaqui Ridge Detachment Fault can be examined close-at-hand. Here, the **detachment fault** consists of several zones of sub-parallel, well-defined breaks. See Field Trip No. 3, (Ship Rock) for a discussion of this detachment fault on Yaqui Ridge.

6.9 Miles, San Felipe Creek at Old Kane Springs Road

Along much of its 50-mile length, the general course of San Felipe Creek is controlled by faulting. Thus also are the highways in the Anza-Borrego region which generally follow major fault zones. Fault-produced effects of the San Felipe drainage are visible along this highway.

During the Pleistocene Epoch, some authorities believe that San Felipe Creek may have flowed into the Salton Trough through Little Borrego Valley (now beheaded) ahead (east) and to the right. As a result of uplift in the Borrego Mountain area and possible basin depression north of Borrego Mountain, the San Felipe drainage was redirected ahead and to the left. The stream was revitalized at Texas Dip into the geomorphic low east of Borrego Sink, controlled by movement

Grossmont College geology class inspecting fault trace along Narrows Earth Trail. HF

on the Coyote Creek Fault of the great San Jacinto Fault Zone. From there, San Felipe Wash today follows the main trace of the Coyote Creek Fault southeastward as far as the playa of Benson Dry Lake and beyond to San Sebastian Marsh.

8.7 Miles, Borrego Springs Road and Texas Dip

Junction with Borrego Springs Road. A detour 0.2 miles left up Borrego Springs Road shows where San Felipe Creek has entrenched itself in mile-wide Texas Dip below a wedge of sedimentary deposits laid down atop an older **pediment** surface of Cactus Valley. Field Trip continues (east) on Hwy 78.

10.2 Miles, Buttes Pass Turnoff

The road left (north) leads to Borrego Mountain (West Butte), Buttes Canyon, and Hawk Canyon.

Earth movements, both lateral **strike-slip** and vertical **dip-slip** components which are associated with the Coyote Creek Fault, have shoved Borrego Mountain (West Butte) northwestward. This has buckled and canted a well-layered Miocene-Pliocene sedimentary sequence near Borrego Mountain Wash like a ship's bowwake. This sequence is primarily Diablo Formation (Colorado River delta deposit) and earlier Split Mountain Formation (alluvial fan conglomerate).

10.4 Miles, Cactus Garden and Harper Canyon Turnoff

To the right (south) are the rugged Vallecito Mountains dominated by Sunset Mountain (elevation 3,657 feet) with the Harper Canyon entrance to the left (east). Home to a remnant herd of bighorn sheep, the imposing Vallecito Mountains are composed of quartz diorite, quartz monzonite and diorite plutonic rock of the Peninsular **Batholith**. Remnant alluvial fan deposits (Canebrake **Conglom-erate** of Early Pliocene Age, 4-5 MYA) form the low mountain flanks west (right) of Harper Canyon.

Today you can also see **desert geologic processes** superimposed on features developed during the cooler and moister Pleistocene Epoch. The Harper Canyon alluvial fan (a desert process) reaches out from the Vallecito Mountains and merges with the adjacent valley fill of Little Borrego Valley. Nearby, it partly covers an eroded mountain **pediment**, a beveled surface, carved on the bedrock itself.

12.4 Miles, Borrego Mountain (East Butte) and OWSVRA

The highway now leaves Anza-Borrego Desert State Park and enters the 38,000 acre Ocotillo Wells State Vehicular Recreation Area. On the left (north), Borrego Mountain (East Butte) represents a fractured sliver of crystalline basement rock (about 70 MYA) that has been uplifted above the San Felipe plain along the Coyote Creek Fault. Goat Trail/Blow Sand Canyon turnoff (left, north) is just beyond (east).

13.4 Miles, Ocotillo Wells Ranger Station (left, north)

14.4 Miles, "The Mesa" Camping Area at "Main Street"

The sandhill on the side of East Butte, behind and to the left of the camping area, results from its position in the lee of the prevailing northwesterly winds. Similar but far more pronounced sand formations may be found on

Superstition Mountain about 20 miles southeast. The Superstition area is accessible via Wheeler Road, northwest of Seeley.

15.4 Miles, Ocotillo Wells/Split Mountain Road Junction (right) (elevation 163 feet)

Benson Dry Lake and the Ocotillo Wells County Airport are on the left. The small desert town of Ocotillo Wells is a year-round haven for off-highway vehicle enthusiasts. Make a right turn onto paved Split Mountain Road, continuing southbound toward the Fish Creek Mountains in the distance.

Ocotillo Wells is known for appreciable ground breakage formed during the 1968 Borrego Mountain Earthquake. The Coyote Creek Fault crosses Highway 78 at 0.2 miles east of Burro Bend Cafe and trends southeast along the western margin of the Ocotillo Badlands. Overall 38 cm. (15 inches) of **right-lateral** horizontal **slip** occurred along 31 miles of the Coyote Creek Fault. Post earthquake aftershock and **microseismicity** (feeble earth tremors) nearly doubled the original ground displacement. Here, in the Ocotillo Wells area, up to 23 cm. (9 inches) of vertical slippage was also recorded. Several homes and buildings were severely damaged.

The geological and seismological data indicate that the Coyote Creek Fault is the main locus of earthquake activity within the San Jacinto Fault Zone. Historically, the fault zone is one of the most seismically active and most intensely studied features in Southern California, periodically yielding large-format earthquakes at the Richter Scale magnitude 6.0 level or greater. The zone consists of networked segments, splays and strands that show surface evidence of recent

Blow Sand Hill on East Butte is a favorite climb for dune buggies. MC

fault displacement. Today many seismologists believe that some strain release in the San Andreas Fault Zone has now shifted to the San Jacinto Fault Zone, making Anza-Borrego an area of special interest and concern. See Field Trip No. 2 (Coyote Creek, Clark Valley) for related discussions on this important fault.

16.3 Miles, Ocotillo Badlands

The sandy hills on the left (east) belong to the Ocotillo Badlands. The Ocotillo Badlands are bounded on two sides by **left-stepping en echelon** segments of the Coyote Creek Fault that have upwarped and deformed Pliocene-Pleistocene sediments (1-3 MYA) correlated to the older and lower Borrego Formation and the younger and higher Ocotillo Conglomerate. See Field Trip No. 2A, Font's Point, and Field Trip No. 2 (Borrego Badlands Overlook) for similar exposures.

The main entrance into the Ocotillo Badlands is located 2.0 miles east of Ocotillo Wells on State Highway 78, just to the east of the Los Puertocitos Historical Marker.

18.0 Miles, Old Kane Springs Road

First major curve in the roadway, to the left connecting with the Old Kane Springs Road coming in on the right.

19.4 Miles

Second major bend in the roadway to the right. Eastward, Kane Springs Road leads to Highway 86, and passes close by San Sebastian Marsh. Here, during the 1968 Borrego Mountain Earthquake, a USGS report notes that the electrical power substation's large transformers were "shifted about, shearing anchor bolts and breaking the X-bracing."

Southward, the roadway crosses the low-lying desert floor of Lower Borrego Valley. Halfhill Lake (dry playa) on the left (east) may represent a **sag pond** developed along the southerly alignment of the Coyote Creek Fault. Lower Borrego Valley could very well represent the ancestral San Felipe Creek drainage, which may have flowed southeastward through here into the Salton Trough (ancient Lake Cahuilla) during the Pleistocene **Epoch**. (See Mile 6.9 above for a related comment.)

21.1 Miles, Park Boundary

Entering Fish Creek patrol sector which comprises much of the Fish Creek Mountains, eastern portions of the Vallecito Mountains and all of the Fish Creek Badlands are found within the Carrizo Badlands section of the Anza-Borrego State Wilderness Area. Overall, this sector encompasses about 85,000 acres. It is a remote and little explored piece of the Colorado Desert that yields great paleontological, geological and botanical treasures. Fossil evidence of marine shellfish and land-based vertebrates of unequaled scientific value are plentiful throughout the tilted reefs, highly eroded mudhills, deep gorges and gravelly mesas of this region.

21.3 Miles, Alma Wash and Elephant Trees

On the right (west) is the Elephant Trees Discovery Trail turnoff. The roadway leads 0.9 miles up the gradual contours of the Alma Wash alluvial fan. Alma Wash contains the largest drainages along the rocky eastern barrier of the Vallecito Mountains.

Standing apart, the remarkable, shaggy-barked elephant trees (*Bursera microphylla*) sparsely dot the bouldery, alluvial fan countryside. Higher up-canyon, more abundant specimens are noted to "roam" in such numbers as to obstruct the landscape. Until recently, Alma Wash represented the northernmost known stand of native elephant trees in North America. This honor now belongs to the Clark Lake grove 20 miles north and discovered by park naturalist Mark Jorgenson in 1987.

21.6 Miles, Fish Creek Alluvial Fan

23.4 Miles, Strontium Mine
The low, light colored hill on the right (west), with an abandoned derelict structure on its south side, marks the site of an old celestite (strontium sulfate) mining operation. Locally known as the Roberts and Peeler deposit, this exposure of intercrystallized gypsum and celestite was one of only three deposits in California that was mined for strontium minerals. The mine workings consisted of shallow cuts and trenches.

23.5 Miles, Split Mountain
Fish Creek Wash is an **antecedent water gap** that separates **gneissic**, marble and granitic rocks of the Fish Creek Mountains (left, east) from the **plutonic intrusives** of the Vallecito Mountains (right, west). This major watercourse drains all of the Fish Creek Badlands along the south-facing portion

San Sebastian Marsh, elevation minus 30 feet, is the confluence of three major drainages: Carrizo, San Felipe/Coyote Creek, and Fish Creek. The year-round running water here supports a great variety of wildlife and plants. LL

of the Vallecito Mountains plus the southeastern flanks of the Pinyon Mountains, including Sandstone Canyon, Mud Palisades and the Hapaha Flat areas of the state park.

Split Mountain, to the right, is a mere ribbon of near-vertical canyon walls. Reddish-colored cliffsides portray extensive outcrops of the Split Mountain Formation, a non-marine Miocene **fanglomerate** sequence (alluvial fan conglomerate, 15 - 23 MYA), that is dramatically exposed within the gorge. Several miles beyond, the wash climbs out of the gorge and into an open topographic setting of mudhills (marine deposits of the Imperial Formation of late Miocene and Early Pliocene Age, 4 - 6 MYA) belonging to the Fish Creek Badlands differential erosion of Fish Creek Wash and tributary drainages.

23.6 Miles, Gypsum Mine and Lake Cahuilla Shoreline

Straight ahead, across Fish Creek Wash, the pavement soon ends at the closed gate to the United States Gypsum Mine which began here in 1946. Today this is the largest gypsum mine in the United States.

On both sides of the **strike** valley ahead and to the right, light-colored, frosty-looking exposures of this Fish Creek Gypsum can be seen. Brought to the surface by local faulting and folding associated with the Coyote Creek Fault, the gypsum beds may constitute the oldest and lowermost beds in the marine Imperial Formation (5 - 6 MYA).

The maintained, dirt "Trestle Road," so named on the state park map, runs southeast from this point along the narrow gauge railroad towards the trestle over Carrizo Wash. A growling little diesel locomotive freights ore daily over this line 25 miles to the processing plant at Plaster City.

The dirt road, on state park land in Imperial County, passes the park boundary after one mile.

About two miles to the east, high-stand shoreline remnants of ancient Lake Cahuilla may be found at an elevation of 45 feet above sea level. During the Late Pleistocene to Holocene epochs, many freshwater lakes repeatedly occupied the low-lying Salton Trough structural depression. Early lakebed sediments have been dated at nearly 40,000 years old. Younger lakes existed during the last few thousand years and may be as recent as 400 years old. Collectively they are known as ancient Lake Cahuilla (named by geologist William Blake in the nineteenth century).

At its maximum extent, Lake Cahuilla was about 100 miles long by 35 miles wide. It derived most of its water from distributary drainages of the Colorado River during periods of high water flow, coinciding with interglacial epochs of the Ice Ages.

On the west side of the Salton Trough, wave action left behind a wide variety of fossil shoreline features. These include barrier beaches, recessional shorelines, highwater marks, spits and **tombolos** (a bar of land connecting island to mainland). Prominent highwater shoreline marks can be seen along the eastern and northern base of the Fish Creek Mountains. While little known, they rival the prominent marks seen at Travertine Rock on the Riverside-Imperial County Line along State Highway 86 (visible for miles along the eastern base of the Santa Rosa Mountains). In places, small gastropods and pelecypod fossil shellfish, derived from soft, weakly consolidated Lake Cahuilla sediments, litter the desert floor below the water lines.

The U.S. Gypsum Mine narrow gauge railroad freights ore daily in an operation reminiscent of hundreds of specialized railroads in the history of the west. LL

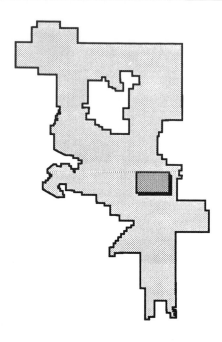

Geology students observe bold cliffs of the Split Mountain fanglomerates in the position in shadows in right center of the aerial view. (See Page No. 130.) SB

FIELD TRIP NO. 4A

FISH CREEK BADLANDS
(Primitive Road)

Length:	9.8 Miles (one way)
Road Conditons:	Primitive Road subject to wash-outs. Check with visitor center before proceeding. Four-wheel drive mandatory south and west of Split Mountain, recommended for total route
Season:	October through May

Route Summary:
This field trip turns off from the Split Mountain Road (Field Trip No. 4) and proceeds along a four-wheel drive roadway up Fish Creek Wash to Sandstone Canyon. The roadway leads approximately 4.9 miles through a narrow defile and out into the Carrizo Badlands (at the intersection with the North Fork of Fish Creek Wash). Road conditions along Fish Creek Wash are subject to seasonal changes. Check visitor center for the latest updates.

General Description:
This rocky chasm with its vertical walls provides excellent viewing of the Split Mountain Formation. Nearly 2,500 feet thick, the formation has been subdivided into the lower Red Rock Canyon Member and the upper Elephant Trees Member. The Split Mountain **Formation** is dramatically exposed in the gorge exposed between vertical canyon walls. The area abounds in marine fossils and violent evidence of **tectonic** activity. Traveling southwest through the gorge is a journey from older to newer events in geologic time. The sequence is terrestrial, then marine and Colorado delta, and finally alluvial deposits. The strata generally dip westerly.

Route Log:

0.0 Miles, Junction of Fish Creek Wash and Split Mountain Road
Proceed west (right) towards Split Mountain Gorge, 8.1 miles south of Ocotillo Wells.

1.5 Miles, Fish Creek Primitive Campground (left)

1.7 Miles, Enter Split Mountain Gorge
This rocky chasm displays many features that are characteristic of desert watercourses. These include undercut banks, vertical canyon walls and boulder-

Aerial view south through Split Mountain up through the "pages of time" from about 8 MYA in terrestrial fanglomerates in mid-picture to about 4 MYA in the marine sediments towards the top. The entrenched meander in the middle leads upstream to a linear stretch controlled by the left-lateral Split Mountain Fault. Fish Creek Primitive Campground is center lower edge. CP

choked tributaries shaped by rampaging flash floods. Seasonally, the gorge funnels torrents of floodwater, filling Fish Creek Wash from bank to bank, across Split Mountain Road.

2.1 Miles, Split Mountain Formation

On both sides of the roadway, vertical canyon walls expose the entire thickness of a remarkable sequence of land-laid, **braided-stream** sandstones, **fanglomerates** and mudflow deposits named the Split Mountain Formation. Nearly 2,500 feet thick, the formation has been subdivided into the lower and older Red Rock Canyon Member and the upper Elephant Trees Member.

2.2 Miles, Red Rock Canyon Member

On the right-hand side of the roadway, the reddish-colored sandstones at the base of the cliffs represent the Red Rock Canyon Member. This is a genetically distinct rock unit, consisting of coarse to granular massive sandstones derived from local source areas of the ancestral Fish Creek and Vallecito Mountain ranges. It is a braided-stream **facies** within the Split Mountain Formation with little conglomerate rock. A sharp left turn follows an entrenched meander through the cliffs.

2.5 Miles, Fault Offset

Beyond the entrenched meander is a remarkably straight segment of Fish Creek Wash. The wash is actually following the trace of the Split Mountain Fault. Up-canyon, for the next 1.3 miles, note that there is a sharp contrast in **stratigraphic** units on either side of the gorge. Rock assemblages that were side by side along the Split Mountain Fault have been left-laterally offset over 1,000 feet. Note how the red walls here on the left closely resemble their mates on the right at Mile 2.7.

3.0 Miles, Elephant Trees Member

Note the excellent, cross-sectional exposures belonging to the Elephant Trees Member of the Split Mountain Formation. Within the Split Mountain area they occur as reddish-colored boulder **fanglomerates**. There are various bedding types throughout the sequence, ranging from massive, matrix-supported boulder to cobble **conglomerates** to lesser debris-flows and sheet-flood deposits reflective of **alluvial fan** deposition. These environments of deposition occurred along the actively uplifting Vallecito Mountains during the Miocene Epoch, about 15-20 million years ago in a probable dry climate.

3.3 Miles, The Lower Boulder Bed Landslide

Atop the hillside on the left, extending away and downslope to the canyon floor, is a thick olive-gray, ledge-forming deposit. It caps the west-facing cliffs along here, overlying the red fanglomerate beds of the Elephant Trees Member of the Split Mountain Formation. This Lower Boulder Bed, approximately 150 feet thick, represents one of two local but massive landslide **megabreccia** units in the gorge deposited by catastrophic origin. It occurred in a terrestrial environment whereas the more recent Upper Boulder Bed, deeper in the canyon, occurred in a marine environment. (See below at Mile 4.6.)

Note the immense blocks of earth and smaller boulders that now litter the canyon floor. Many of these came crashing down from the heights during the Borrego Mountain earthquake of 1968, recorded so dramatically by ranger

George Leetch's eye-witness account, on tape recorder and camera, and now playing at the visitor center.

3.5 Miles, Fish Creek Gypsum Atop Landslide
On the left skyline above the chaotic boulders of the landslide is a thin wedge of marine mudstones with light colored **lensing** gypsum beds. Named the Fish Creek Gypsum, they mark the lowest and oldest unequivocal marine deposit in the Vallecito-Fish Creek Basin and may be the oldest marine unit exposed in the Salton Trough. They are, in turn, overlain by a thick olive-green **turbidite** sequence of marine sandstones, clearly visible on the right side of the jumbled landslide, known as the Lycium Member of the Imperial Formation. It consists of about 225 feet of medium-bedded, coarse-grained sandstones that have yielded foraminifera fossils (protozoans with shells) of Late Miocene Age (5-10 MYA).

3.7 Miles, The Upper Boulder Bed Landslide
On the right at wash level is a fault-offset jumble of Lower Boulder Bed in contact with more west dipping Split Mountain Formation beds below. On the right (west) skyline is the beginning of yet another massive slide, the Upper Boulder Bed. This plunges left and down towards the canyon floor to encounter the anticline noted below. Note the clear distinction between the older, terrestrial fanglomerates of the Split Mountain Formation with abundant boulders and cobbles versus the younger, marine sandstone of the Imperial Formation with few embedded rocks.

Light and frosty gypsum beds, evaporates of early marine origin, cap the Lower Boulder Bed landslide at Mile 3.3 in Split Mountain. SB

3.8 Miles, The Anticline and Split Mountain Fault
On the right at wash level, is the spectacular and oft photographed **anticlinal fold** involving bedded marine **turbidite** sandstones of the Lycium Member squeezed tightly and deformed against down-thrown landslide **breccia** of the Upper Boulder Bed deposit. Just around the right corner, the Split Mountain Fault can be seen in the canyon wall as it crosses the upper flank of the Split Mountain anticline. An interpretive panel (left) tells part of the fascinating story revealed here.

All told, the **stratigraphy** of the Fish Creek area is exposed to view as part of the broad erosionally-breached Split Mountain upwarp. The sediments have been folded and faulted due to a close proximity between the nearby San Jacinto Fault Zone (historically one of California's most active seismic zones) to the east and the Elsinore Fault Zone to the west. Local faulting has taken more toll, disrupting the continuity of the land and, providing a convenient avenue by which the Fish Creek drainage could easily establish itself.

4.0 Miles, The Lycium Ledges
The bend in the canyon marks the narrowest confines of Split Mountain Gorge. Conspicuously exposed are alternating, ledge-forming sandstone beds of the Lycium Member of the marine Imperial Formation gently dipping to the west. The gorge itself separates the plutonic, intrusive Vallecito Mountains on the right (west) from the Fish Creek Mountains (granitics with some metasediments) on the left (east). Due to the steepness of the cliffsides, rockfalls are very common along this stretch of Fish Creek Wash.

4.1 Miles Exit Split Mountain at "The Pillars"
The Upper Boulder Bed is a massive, chaotic-looking landslide **breccia** that forms the prominent, resistant knob of rocks on the left and caps much of the slope on the right of the wash. The Upper Boulder Bed is similar in outcrop appearance, texture and scale to the Lower Boulder Bed, except that the upper took place in a marine environment on the shore or beneath the Late Miocene-Early Pliocene sea. It is overlain by a continuation of **turbidite** sandstones of the Imperial Formation's Lycium Member. Both landslides probably represent catastrophic events resulting from earthquake activity 5-10 MYA that disrupted the region during the initial opening of the Gulf of California.

4.4 Miles, North Fork of Fish Creek Junction (right, west)
North Fork offers access to the interesting, deeply dissected Fish Creek Badlands on the right. Canyons such as Oyster Shell Wash, Lycium Wash and Mollusk Wash below the southern base of the Vallecito Mountains preserve a rich concentration of ripple marks, mudcracks, worm burrows and tracings, and shell-hash, reminiscent of a shallow-water, beach intertidal zone. These fossils, found within the silent floors of departed seas (Imperial Formation) have been paleomagnetically dated at over four million years old (Early Pliocene Epoch).

The Imperial Formation has been named for exposures extending from the Coyote Mountains up to the Fish Creek Badlands. Briefly, they consist of a richly fossiliferous sequence of fine-grained claystones and **calcareous** sandstones. These were deposited into the tectonically unstable Salton Trough during Late Miocene-Early Pliocene times before the Colorado River delta effectively dammed off the Salton Basin from the Gulf.

4.7 Miles, Mudhills Wash (left) and Interpretive Panel

The low mudhills consist of deeply-weathered clays and silts of the Mudhills Member of the Imperial Formation. It is a massive claystone bed, about 1,800 feet thick, reflective of an inner shelf-intertidal environment during the Early Pliocene Epoch 4-5 MYA. The Mudhills Member grades upward into the Deguyños Member that makes up much of the prominent hogback ridge of Elephant Knees, clearly visible to the south above Mudhills Wash.

5.0 Miles, Deguyños Member

For the next 1.5 miles, the wash passes through yellowish sandstones and yellow-gray silts and clays of the Deguyños Member of the Imperial Formation. About 900 feet thick, this unit features noticeable **rhythmite** bedding suggestive of an alternating sequence of rock ladders carved into the cliffside. One superimposed upon another, these thin beds systematically increase or decrease in thickness throughout the exposures.

Rolling hillsides underlain by the Deguyños Member are often deeply-weathered, featuring a mud-cracked, "popcorn-ball" surface texture occasionally sprinkled with reflective selenite particles, a form of gypsum.

7.0 Miles, Loop Wash (eastern end) Junction (right, north)

Throughout the Fish Creek Badlands and the distant Carrizo Badlands to the left, the upper half of the marine Deguynos Member of the Imperial Formation consists of continuous, resistant sandstone beds that are oftentimes associated with fossil oyster coquinas or "reefs." These coquina beds are composed of thou-

Fossil bearing coquina shell beds form a caprock in marine Imperial Formation sediments in the Carrizo Badlands. PR

sands upon thousands of oyster shell fragments in varying concentrations, with lesser amounts of scallops, barnacles and clams. Obvious species include *Ostrea vespertina, Pecten deserti. Turritella imperialis* and the larger *Ostrea heermanni.* To the north, in the heartland of the Fish Creek Badlands, many sand dollars, gastropods and additional mollusks of an intertidal beach zone have also been found. The Deguyños Member, in this vicinity, has been assigned a paleomagnetic date of 3.8 million years old.

7.5 Miles, Camels Head Wash (left, south)

Notice that up-section, the yellowish-green claystones of the Deguyños Member of the marine Imperial Formation have been replaced in a complex transitional sequence of reddish-brown claystones and pale-orange sandstones (tributary-channel deposits) of the overlying Diablo Formation (new term). This section of transitional **strata** is named the Camels Head Member of the Imperial Formation. Local evidence of petrified wood, fossil vertebrate bones and shellfish heaped in great abundance mark this area along Fish Creek Wash where the ancestral Colorado River met the sea. Many large fossil footprints of the Pliocene camel *Megatylopus*, measuring up to eight inches long, have been found within these sediments above and below beds of marine oyster fossils. See Field Trip No. 2 (Cannonball Wash) for discussion on the ancestral Colorado in the Borrego Bad-lands in an earlier time than what is seen here. Much of Trip No. 5A (Vallecito Badlands) discusses the Diablo Formation in this area.

The Layer Cake feature, found at Mile 10.7 in Fish Creek, displays stripes of Pliocene delta and lagoon sandstones and mudstones. LL

9.0 Miles, Loop Wash (western end) Junction (right, north)
The open geologic setting to the north is part of "Blackwood Basin" as it is known to local paleontologists Here, the Diablo Formation completely divides the columnar succession of strata between the marine Imperial Formation (Early Pliocene) and the adjacent, overlying Palm Spring Formation of the Vallecito Badlands (Early to Middle Pleistocene).
The Diablo Formation is easily discernible by its reddish-brown coloration and by the distinctive marker beds of quartz **arenite** sandstone. These beds outcrop as conspicuous **strike** ridges and yield an abundance of iron-based sandstone concretions, petrified wood, and shellfish.

9.8 Miles, Diablo Dropoff Wash (left, south)
This is one-way from the other direction. A one-mile hike leads to the base of the Diablo Dropoff, which is a highlight of Field Trip No. 5A.

10.2 Miles, Ancient River Deposits
Beneath the corrugated mesa top, the tilted strata expose a long series of old river **meander** belts including channel sandstone, **point bar** deposits, natural levees, and **overbank** deposits. These sands and silts of the Lower Pliocene (3 - 4 MYA) Diablo Formation represent an overburden of sediment from the ancestral Colorado River. Bands of massive quartz arenite sandstone in channel deposits contrast with thin reddish-brown claystone deposits from overbank spills during high water periods.

10.4 Miles, West Mesa Fault
Evidence of this fault can be seen across the wash. On the right, **left-lateral strike-slip** movements have locally displaced the reddish-brown overbank claystone against a weathered exposure of quartz arenite channel sandstone.

10.7 Miles, Layer Cake
This prominent erosional remnant is a stack of thinly-bedded, fine-grained deposits. The massive, fine-grained sandstone Diablo layers are punctuated by softer, olive-green claystones and lagoonal muds of the Olla Member of the Canebrake Conglomerate. These fine sediments slowly settled out of suspension, separating the thicker sandy layers. Layer Cake has paleomagnetic date signature of 3.3 MYA.

12.0 Miles, Olla Member
As the established roadway veers right, increasingly thicker, olive-green claystones and grayish fluvial (riverine) sandstones of the Olla Member become more prominent. Boundaries between interbedded layers are not sharply defined. Instead, they are gradational, thin slices of time subtly blending into the stratigraphic column above and below.

12.4 Miles, Diablo and Olla Beds
Ahead, the vertical canyon walls to the west are composed of these two different rock groups. The upper half is the pale orange, blocky Diablo channel sandstones while the lower half is the gray-colored, fluvial Olla siltstone and sandstone with minor biotite-rich, olive-green claystone stringers. Note that the Olla Member is prominently coarsening and thickening up-canyon. These two sturdy sandstone types are responsible for the higher-relief slick rock topography of the area and spectacular slot canyons such as Sandstone Canyon.

12.9 Miles, Sandstone Canyon

The entrance to this magnificent canyon is carved into massive, distal sandstone of the Olla Member (Canebrake Conglomerate). The difference between the Diablo and Olla now becomes more clear. Olla sediments are locally shed from the Canebrake Conglomerate on the mountain mass to the north while Diablo sediments are derived from far to the east via the ancestral Colorado River. This marks an extensive basin-margin alluvial fan complex on the northwest periphery of the Pliocene delta plain. Sedimentary structures at this site include **cross-stratification, ripple marks,** and mudcracks, all of which suggest a **braided stream** interpretation for the Olla Member in this vicinity during regressive phases of the Colorado River.

Nearby, petrified sabal palm fronds mark the first occurrence of fossil leaf material in Anza-Borrego. They came from cross-stratified channel sandstones between Diablo and Olla contacts.

Paleontologists have recognized the "Layer Cake Local Fauna" as a local representation of the Blancan North American Land Mammal Age (1.9 - 3.6 MYA). Although incomplete, this is the oldest Blancan assemblage currently recognized in California. Deposits in and around Sandstone Canyon offer one of the richest concentrations of Lower Pliocene (3.6 - 5.4 MYA) fossil vertebrates in North America. Examples include extinct, rabbit-like mammals such as *Hypolagus* "pre-hare" and *Pewelagus*. These ancestral rabbits occupy a crucial position in the evolutionary ladder of modern rabbits and hares.

Cross-references to related fossil fauna include: Trip No. 2 (Borrego Badlands, "Borrego Local Fauna," Irvingtonian-Rancholabrean); Trip No. 5 (June Wash and Vallecito Badlands, "Vallecito Creek Local Fauna," Blancan-Irvingtonian); Trip No. 5A (General Description of the Vallecito Badlands, "Vallecito Creek Local Fauna," Blancan-Irvingtonian).

In addition, rare camelid trackways have recently been found in Sandstone Canyon and Olla Wash. Unrecognized for years, the recent discovery and survival of these normally ephemeral traces is unique, capturing for us a frozen moment of time from the Lower Pliocene. The weathered footprints are tentatively identified as belonging to the North American camelopine *Megatylopus*, an ungainly beast with a heavy stature. The size of the footprints measure eight inches long by nearly five inches wide indicating an animal in staid maturity. They are much larger than *Camelops* tracks from Middle Mesa in the Vallecito Badlands and rival in size camelid prints from sites in the Mojave Desert.

Megatylopus is one of Anza-Borrego's oldest known terrestrial vertebrates. It is known to have existed only during the Lower Pliocene (Hemphillian-Blancan) in other locations of the southwestern United States and Mexico (3.0 - 5.4 MYA).

Sandstone Canyon marks the end of the Split Mountain/Fish Creek field trip. Further exploration of the Fish Creek Badlands can be very rewarding. Fish Creek Wash continues northward, leading up to Olla Wash and its tributaries, the slickrock countryside of upper Blackwood Basin, and finally to Hapaha Flat located between the Pinyon and Vallecito Mountains. Route is one-way down (this way) at Harper Flat.

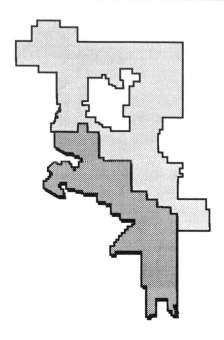

Fossil sand dollars are found in the Imperial Formation, Coyote Mountains. JL

Chapter 5 - Southern Area

FIELD TRIP NO. 5

CARRIZO CORRIDOR (Hwy S-2)

Length: 46.2 Miles (one way)

Road Conditons: Good. Paved road

Season: October through May

Route Summary:

This tour proceeds west on Hwy 78 from Tamarisk Grove, near the Hwy S-3/78 intersection, to Hwy S-2 at Scissors Crossing. It then proceeds southeast on Hwy S-2 to the Imperial County Boundary. The ABDNHA/ABDSP brochure "Southern Emigrant Trail" describes highlights of this route. Mileage markers on County Hwy S-2 start at zero at the junction of S-2 and Hwy 79 near Warner Springs and reach 17 at Scissors Crossing (east). The Imperial County boundary is Mile Marker 56.

General Description:

Plant communities in the famous Carrizo Corridor range from high desert juniper and chaparral at Blair Valley to low desert cholla, barrel and ocotillo at Bow Willow. In between is lonely country, an outdoor laboratory of vast desert mountain ranges and valley landscapes produced as a direct result of faulting. This faulting continues to play a dynamic role in delineating and determining the natural bounds of this mountainous, mysterious, high-and-low desert region.

The Tierra Blanca, Jacumba, and Laguna Mountains soar to rain-shadow heights to the west, while the Vallecito-Fish Creek Basin displays a terrestrial sea of erosion on the east. The area crossed by Vallecito, Bow Willow, and Carrizo Creeks offers solitude in hidden palm canyons, and scenic dirt roads that pierce the stark beauty of this least visited area of the state park.

Over 100 years ago, the area was variously called the Jornada del Muerto "Journey of Death," Overland Mail, Gateway to California, Southern Emigrant Trail, or Sonora Road. Then and now, the narrow passage of the Carrizo Corridor remains a rich pathway and an integral part of the story of the west. Its many mysteries and evidence of its history abound. Rusting relics, wagon-wheel ruts, historic inscriptions, adobe ruins, and tales of lost gold are still to be found along this southern portal to Anza-Borrego.

Route Log:

0.0 Miles, Tamarisk Grove Campground Entrance

0.3 Miles, Junction of Highways 78/S-3

Proceed west on State Highway 78/S-3. On the left (south), the obvious angular mixture of **crystalline** rocks, varying from boulder size to large mega-blocks, form a landslide deposit along the highway roadcut. In this vicinity, some geologists believe that these rocks represent by-products from a collapsed block of the earth's crust that detached and slumped downward into the western Salton Trough during the initial opening of the Gulf of California in Miocene time (5 - 15 MYA). (See Dr. Phillip's comments in Chapter 1.)

1.2 Miles, Lizard Canyon Trail

On the right (north), beyond the green vegetation marking Yaqui Well Primitive Campground, the upper and lower sections of each alluvial fan are dissected by erosion. This dissection is caused by continuing uplift of Pinyon Ridge along the San Felipe Fault, which has steepened gradients, causing entrenchment of new arroyos into the older fan surfaces. The fault line can be followed through Yaqui Well.

1.9 Miles, Kenyon Cove Turnout

On the left, the Blue Spring Fault separates the lighter-colored granitics (on the east) from the reddish-brown gneissic, metasedimentary rocks on the west. To the right (north), along the south-facing slopes of Pinyon Ridge, major segments of the steep mountain front have broken loose in the form of landslides. The triggering mechanism may have been movements associated with two strands of the San Felipe Fault which cut across Pinyon Ridge at this location, following Grapevine Canyon northward through Ranchita and Warner Springs to Aguanga (Agua Caliente Fault Zone). The alluvial fans draining southward from Pinyon Ridge form a "classic" mescal bajada unlike the named feature east of Tamarisk Grove.

3.2 Miles, Grapevine Canyon Turnoff (right)

3.6 Miles, Enter Sentenac Canyon

This canyon separates Grapevine Mountain on the north from the Pinyon Mountains on the south. **Migmatite** (mixed rocks consisting of complexly folded **metasedimentary schists** and granitic rocks) may be seen in road cuts throughout the narrow confines of Sentenac Canyon.

7.0 Miles, Scisssors Crossing (east), Mile Marker 17

7.3 Miles, Scissors Crossing (west)

Turn left (south) on County Highway S-2. For the next 40 miles, this highway segment, paved in 1955, closely follows the fascinating historic migrations of gold seeking argonauts, frontiersmen, and soldiers, plus stagecoach routes and way stations of the San Antonio-San Diego Mail Line (1857-61) and Butterfield Overland Mail (1858-61).

9.0 Miles, Mile Marker 19, Earthquake Valley

Shelter Valley is the small desert community situated within the fault-controlled intermontane **swale** of Earthquake Valley (elevation 2,300 feet above sea level). It takes its name from seismic events along the Earthquake Valley Fault, part of the major Elsinore Fault Zone. This fault can be traced with certainty from Warner Springs southward along the eastern side of San Felipe Valley (Grapevine Mountain) into the Pinyon Mountains. It is still active. On December 3, 1991, it generated a M4.2 earthquake centered in San Felipe Valley.

Intense decompositon of Earthquake Valley's underlying **crystalline** bedrock at shallow depth has, much like the other northwest-trending high desert **etchbasins** of Blair Valley, Mason Valley and Vallecito Valley, greatly reduced the bedrock to a relatively flat meadow surface. The brooding massif of Granite Mountain looms above Earthquake Valley to the west.

11.4 Miles, Pinyon Mountain Turnoff (left, east)

This marks the entrance to Anza-Borrego Desert State Park, Blair Valley Sector. This patrol sector encompasses over 115,000 acres, including much of the Granite Mountain, Whale Peak and Agua Caliente sections of the Anza-Borrego Desert State Wilderness Areas. This isolated region exhibits a wide diversity of geologic phenomena, ranging from old basement rocks of the Peninsular **Batholith** to fossiliferous Ice Age deposits that represent some of the finest exposures of badlands topography in all of North America.

Sentenac Canyon hosts a year-round stream which sinks into the sands of San Felipe Wash at Grapevine Canyon. LL

12.3 Miles, Little Blair Valley Turnoff (left, east), Southeast of Mile Marker 22

An ancient landslide is visible on the right (west) side of highway.

12.9 Miles, Blair Valley Entrance (left, east), Just Before Mile Marker 23

Foot and Walker Grade entrance to Blair Valley Primitive Campground is on the left. For the next several miles the local terrain of Granite Mountain (elevation 5,633 feet above sea level) is made up of granitic rock of granodiorite and light colored tonalite of the La Posta **Pluton**. There are also numerous light colored pegmatite **dikes**, and scattered screens of prebatholithic **metasedimentary** rock that together form the conspicuous, striped rock countryside along both sides of the highway. The stripes are especially visible on Granite Mountain to the right (northwest).

15.7 Miles, Box Canyon Historical Monument, Between Mile Markers 25 and 26

A short walk leads to the Box Canyon Overlook. Here, remnants of two historic roads are still visible, etched into the cliffside. The upper one is the oldest, representing a portion of the first wagon road in Southern California. It was built in 1847 by the Mormon Battalion as it traveled westward from Council Bluffs, Iowa to reinforce a small contingent of men from the Army of the West. The lower road was built in 1857 by Warren Hall as part of the southern route for the famed Butterfield Overland Mail.

The colorfully-striped beds of **prebatholithic** sedimentary rock exposed here are, for the most part, schists and quartzites similar to the **metasedimentary** Julian Schist, that were laid down as shales, muds and sandstones in a shallow-water, marine environment. The Julian Schist ranges in age from Late Paleozoic (about 250 million years ago) to Early Mesozoic (about 180 million years ago), and locally resembles metasedimentary rocks in the Laguna and Cuyamaca Mountains. These screens of old-age **country rock** have been **intruded** by light colored **dikes** associated with emplacement of granitic **magma** into the area during the Late Mesozoic, about 80-95 MYA.

16.8 Miles, Enter Mason Valley, Between Mile Markers 26 and 27

This valley is a northwest-trending structural **graben** situated between the uplifted Pinyon Mountains to the east and the deeply-scored Laguna Mountains **Escarpment** (Oriflamme Mountain) to the west. This escarpment has a maximum relief of about 4,500 feet. It is marked by numerous faults that delineate the western edge of the Mason Valley **graben**. Oriflamme Mountain (elevation 4,351 feet) represents an intermediate fault-bounded **bench** between the Laguna Mountains crest (averaging 6,000 feet above sea level) and the desert floor. Its mountain slopes are dotted with scrub oak, mountain mahogany and ceanothus.

The valley itself is a part of the active Elsinore Fault Zone, a major northwest-**striking** lineament of faults that trend parallel to the San Jacinto Fault Zone. It extends for more than 120 miles north to the Los Angeles Basin where it splits into the Chino Fault and Whittier Fault. The destructive magnitude 6.1 earthquake that jolted the Los Angeles Basin on October 1,1987, was centered on this Whittier-Narrows Fault. It extends southward to the Mexican Boundary near Ocotillo and beyond.

The Elsinore Fault can be accurately traced from the north end of Mason Valley through Rodriguez Canyon and Banner Canyons. This section is typical of the physiographic expression of the Elsinore Fault Zone. High-angle fault features include linear canyons, steep mountain walls, aligned benches, slump blocks and vegetation stripes that mark the fault trace. Also, Volcan Mountain on the east side of Banner Canyon, has been noticeably elevated about 1,000 feet above corresponding surfaces of the mountain community of Julian.

South of Banner Canyon, the Elsinore Fault becomes broader in Rodriguez Canyon, dramatically widening from about 10 feet to over 200 feet. This gouge zone consists of broken and shattered blocks of Triassic-aged (200-225 MYA) **prebatholithic** screens of Julian Schist and **brecciated** crystalline rocks and pegmatite dikes that have been offset, in a right-lateral sense, approximately 8,000 feet. Traveling southward, Elsinore Fault approximates the course followed by the power pole-line across Mason Valley.

16.9 Miles, Oriflamme Canyon Road (right, west) Between Mile Markers 26 and 27

Nearby, the historic San Diego Trail followed a well-worn Indian pathway up Oriflamme Canyon to Cuyamaca Valley. During the mid-1860s, this intersection also serviced the Old Mulkins Road from Cuyamaca Valley to Fort Yuma. It was constructed above the old San Diego Trail between Oriflamme Mountain and Chariot Mountain, via a portion of the modern-day Mason Valley Truck Trail.

17.0 Miles, Rainbow Canyon Parking Area, Mile Marker 27

Rainbow Canyon, favorite of desert naturalist Pat Flanagan, is a one-half

Blair Valley is a shallow sink, etched into the underlying granitic bedrock at shallow depth. LL

mile walk east down the highway and then north into the mountain. Its narrow defile slices into spectacular swirls and stripes of metamorphic bedrock, laced by pegmatite intrusions. A steep and difficult ascent over highly patterned ledges leads to an open bowl, ringed by granitic knobs. A scramble to the saddle at its east end reveals Ghost Mountain and the southern end of Blair Valley. One way hiking distance from Highway S-2 to Ghost Mountain roadhead, via Rainbow Canyon, is about four miles.

19.1 Miles, Butterfield Ranch, Just Southeast of Mile Marker 29

The R.V. Park on the right offers camping facilities and amenities, including gasoline, restaurant, and a general store for today's traveler passing along the historic Carrizo Corridor.

20.2 Miles, Campbell Grade Overlook, Southeast of Mile Marker 30

Campbell Grade marks the south end of Mason Valley. Known historically as La Puerta Grade, this small rocky pass preserves a view of a segment of the Butterfield Overland Mail route as it switchbacks up the mountainside. In the distance, the original route is plainly visible coursing across Vallecito Valley, heading towards the Vallecito Stage Station. Nearby are interesting and varied inscriptions carved in boulders along the route dating back to 1849.

Along the Elsinore Fault, Campbell Grade represents a unique anomaly, for here bedrock structures are continually exposed across the fault trace. There is no indication of **strike-slip** displacement. **Intrusive** rocks (La Posta **Pluton**) and **prebatholithic** rocks similar to those in Box Canyon form this bedrock **spur** connecting the Pinyon Mountains on the left with Sawtooth Range on the right. The spur is breached by Vallecito Creek.

Although minor faults are clearly visible in road-cuts along the highway grade, the main fault branch may actually be located north of the gorge cut by Vallecito Creek. Field studies have shown that the Elsinore Fault separates into two subordinate fault branches near here. Geologists infer a northern branch, which trends eastward through Vallecito Valley, Squaw Canyon and Agua Caliente County Park, and a southern branch, which runs diagonally through the Tierra Blanca Mountains, passing across the Inner Pasture and Indian Valley.

20.9 Miles, Rancho Vallecito (right, south)

To the left, range-bounding **normal faults** occur along the base of the Pinyon Mountains. These faults are expressed by multiple **benches** and scarplets in the crystalline rock that run parallel to the desert floor.

On the right of the highway, the scenery is dominated by the conical-shaped Troutman Mountain (elevation 2,080 feet), lesser knobs of granitic rock, and the Sawtooth Mountains, part of the Bureau of Land Management's 35,000 acre Sawtooth Wilderness Study Area. Separated by The Potrero, the mountain features consist of light-colored granitic rock of the La Posta Pluton.

A major fault zone, referred to as the Laguna Mountains **Escarpment,** crosses the upper reaches of The Potrero, Storm and Cottonwood Canyons northward to Mason Valley. Southward, it continues across the western headwaters of Canebrake, Indian and Bow Willow Canyons, extending beyond the eastern limits of the In-Ko-Pah tablelands. Fault traces are essentially parallel and are marked by vegetation lineaments, springs and seeps, northwest-trending side canyons, benches, fault-scarps and aligned saddles.

In the distance, the awesome and magnificent western barrier skyline of the Laguna Mountains is dominated by Monument Peak, towering 6,221 feet above sea level.

23.0 Miles, Vallecito Creek Crossing

Ahead is the historic, unmarked road of the Butterfield Overland Mail.

23.9 Miles, Enter Vallecito County Park, Mile Marker 34

To the left (north), the hummocky landscape that makes up the south side of Ghost Mountain represents a rock avalanche, active during the Pleistocene Epoch (1 - 2 MYA). The rock composition is mostly granitic quartz-diorite with lesser pre-batholithic metasediments.

24.8 Miles, Vallecito Stage Station (right, south)

On the right stands the restored Vallecito Stage Station. Located along the southwest toe of the Smuggler Canyon alluvial fan, the Vallecito Stage Station stands as a a reminder of how travelers pushed the American frontier to the Pacific Ocean. Originally built by James Ruler Lassator in 1852, the sod house and way station served travelers and soldiers over the Southern Emigrant Trail for many years. It was the first permanent settlement in Vallecito Valley and became a famous stopover point for weary desert travelers after surviving the dreaded stagecoach crossing of the Colorado Desert. By 1861, the War Between the States soon caused a discontinuation of the southern mail route and the eventual abandonment of this public way station.

The Butterfield stage route is still visible from Campbell Grade with the Vallecito station in the far middle distance. LL

26.5 Miles, Bisnaga Alta Wash (left, north), Southeast of Mile Marker 36

Exposed in the cactus-studded arroyos, road-cuts and intervening hillsides, the Canebrake Conglomerate is a grayish-tan, poorly-bedded pebble to bouldery conglomerate eroded from the Pinyon-Vallecito Mountain highlands to the north and northeast. Various-sized boulders are of predominantly granitic composition with metasedimentary fragments.

In the Tierra Blanca Mountains (Squaw Canyon area) on the right, the Canebrake Conglomerate overlies, and is faulted directly against crystalline bedrock along the Elsinore Fault (northern branch). Straight ahead and throughout the northernmost periphery of the Vallecito Badlands, the Canebrake Congolomerate grades laterally and basinward into the stream and lakebed sediments of the Pliocene-Pleistocene Palm Spring Formation (2 - 4 MYA).

27.0 Miles, Enter Carrizo Valley, Mile Marker 37

This valley represents a structural **graben**, not caused by erosion, that has been down-faulted in relation to the uplifting Tierra Blanca Mountains to the west and the Pinyon Mountains to the northeast. The low rounded mound on the skyline directly south of the Pinyon Mountains is Mount Diablo (elevation 2,410 feet) made up of Canebrake Conglomerate at the faulted saddle between June Wash and Sandstone Canyon.

28.1 Miles, Agua Caliente County Park, Southeast of Mile Marker 38

This park offers surprising tourist amenities such as bathing pools, indoor jacuzzi, mineral baths, and camping facilities. Here, movements along the Elsinore Fault (northern branch) are directly responsible for the upwelling of mineral-rich hot springs. Groundwater, heated at depth, upwells to the surface via cracks in the bedrock, reaching as high as 98 degrees F.

Moderate seismic activity, such as the 1973 Aqua Caliente Springs Earthquake (magnitude 4.8 on the Richter scale) has yielded data on the release of crustal strain. This data has allowed seismologists to estimate that the maximum probable earthquake on the Elsinore Fault may be on the order of magnitude 6.9 to 7.0 in this vicinity, with an approximate 100 year recurrence interval.

28.9 Miles, Tierra Blanca Mountains (right, southwest)

The Tierra Blanca Mountain Frontal Fault, one of the principal fractures of the Elsinore Fault Zone, bounds these highlands. It is a controlling factor in shaping the local topography. In Carrizo Valley, geologic mapping and paleo-magnetic studies indicate that the amount of right-lateral movement along the frontal fault in this vicinity may be at least 4.2 miles.

Along the highway in the Aqua Caliente Springs area, hydrothermally altered and fractured granitic rocks are easily weathered and eroded. These light colored rocks are thus exposed here as the residue of tectonic exuberance.

30.5 Miles, Fault Scarp

Directly ahead is a remnant fault **scarp** of the frontal fault that truncates an older gravelly fan surface now elevated above the present-day alluvial surface. This impressive topographic bench is probably related to the big M7.0 Laguna Salada earthquake of 1892 which, to date, represents San Diego County's strongest seismic event. Locally, many new channels and arroyos have incised this older surface to the level of the down-thrown (eastern) side of the fault. Most of it is now concealed by modern alluvium. Where it is exposed, the fault scarp measures between 10 - 15 feet in height.

31.4 Miles, June Wash and Vallecito Badlands (left, northeast)

The Elsinore Fault separates the sedimentary Vallecito Badlands from the plutonic tonalitic bedrock of the Tierra Blanca ("white rock") Mountains along its western margin. The high content of whitish quartz in tonalite prompted the naming of these mountains. Together with the Carrizo and Fish Creek Badlands, the Vallecito-Fish Creek Basin comprises the southwestern part of the Salton Trough structural depression, the landward extension of the Gulf of California.

The Vallecito-Fish Creek Basin represents an area of considerable sedimentation and tectonic activity, both past and present. It is surrounded by mountains on all four margins. To the north are the Pinyon-Vallecito Mountains; to the east, the Fish Creek Mountains; to the south, the Coyote Mountains; and to the west, the Tierra Blanca Mountains. The basin itself has been rotated about 35 degrees clockwise due to mountain-building forces in the last two million years. In addition to rotation, the northern Fish Creek margin has been elevated while the southwestern margin along Vallecito Creek has subsided. The Vallecito Badlands represent a sedimentary section about 9,000 feet thick with the younger, locally derived Palm Spring Formation overlying the older ancestral Colorado River delta deposits of the Diablo Formation (new term).

The Palm Spring Formation consists of interbedded sandstone, claystone, gravel conglomerate, and freshwater marl (an earth mixture of clay and calcium carbonate). This formation is of interest because it straddles the Pliocene-Pleistocene boundary at 1.9 MYA. The Palm Spring Formation is particularly important because of its well-documented megavertebrate and microvertebrate fossils, one of the richest Blancan (1.9 - 3.6 MYA) and Irvingtonian (0.9 - 1.9 MYA) fossil faunas in North America. Megafauna have included camel, sloth, mastodon, and horse ancestors.

Cross-reference to related fossil fauna include: Trip No. 2 (Borrego Badlands, "Borrego Local Fauna," Irvingtonian Rancholabrean); Trip No. 4A (Sandstone Canyon, "Layer Cake Local Fauna," Hemphillian-Blancan); and Trip No. 5A (Arroyo Tapiado, "Vallecito Creek Local Fauna," Blancan-Irvingtonian).

32.6 Miles, Canebrake Entrance (right, southwest)

This is the mailbox-lined north entrance to the small desert community. This community is built directly on the large alluvial fan draining from the mouth of Canebrake Canyon. This reach of the Tierra Blanca Mountain front is made up of tonalite, a granitic rock that weathers large fragments of broken rock. The Canebrake alluvial fan surface is therefore rough, corrugated and composed of large boulders throughout its extent.

33.0 Miles, Vallecito Creek/Palm Spring Turnoff (left, northeast)
Mile Marker 43

Entrance to Vallecito Creek. A large splinter-fault splays off the main branch of the Elsinore Fault, following the stream bed of Vallecito Creek. It cuts through Pliocene-Pleistocene sediments, extending southeasterly into the Carrizo Badlands below Carrizo Mountain (elevation 2,408 feet).

Vallecito Creek marks the beginning of the Bow Willow Sector. This patrol sector encompasses nearly 100,000 acres along the southern portal of Anza-

Borrego, including all of the Carrizo Canyon-Sombrero Peak, Carrizo Badlands and Jacumba Mountains State Wilderness Areas. It is one of the most scenic and dramatic areas in the state park, well endowed with important archeological sites, elephant trees, hidden palm groves, a wide variety of wildlife that live throughout the great variance in elevation (over 4,000 feet), and a diverse list of plant species found across the region's great horizontal and vertical span.

Vallecito Creek also marks the continuation of the Carrizo Corridor. The old pathway of the Butterfield Overland Mail can still be followed discontinuously, leading eastward to "lost " way stations at Palm Spring, Carrizo, Hall's Well and Alamo Mocho. Its tortuous *Jornada Del Muerto* ("Journey of Death") went through the Carrizo Gap between the Fish Creek and Coyote Mountains, then across the Colorado Desert to Fort Yuma.

33.9 Miles, Canebrake, South Entrance (right, southwest), Mile Marker 44
The Canebrake Ranger Station is 0.2 miles up this road on the left.

34.2 Miles, Tierra Blanca Mountains
As the highway straightens, the sheer east face of the Tierra Blanca Mountains (elevation 1,800 feet) can be seen. It represents a youthful fault scarp that is locally characterized by two wineglass canyons: Canebrake Canyon and Indian Gorge, carved into the mountain core. The wineglass image derives from the vertical viewpoint. The base of each wineglass canyon is distinguished by an alluvial fan along the foot of the mountain range, the stem is the narrow cut through the mountain front, and the bowl is the open, intermontane uplands. These uplands are the Inner Pasture in Canebrake Canyon, and the north-and-south fork, palm-lined headwater tributaries of Indian Valley. If traveling in the late afternoon, the shadowed scarp of the Tierra Blanca Mountain Frontal Fault can be seen cutting across the base of the mountain front. Here, the Elsinore Fault is essentially vertical, extending down to a depth of at least 1.8 miles. A similar amount of depth may be likely along the precipitous western front of the Coyote Mountains near the entrance to Canyon Sin Nombre.

35.2 Miles, Indian Gorge Alluvial Fan Southeast of Mile Marker 45
Good view of the cone-shaped Indian Gorge alluvial fan, extending outward from Indian Gorge onto the desert floor. Note that the Tierra Blanca Mountain Frontal Fault marks the eastern edge of bedrock here. The fault scarp is clearly visible as a prominent lineament, extending from the community of Canebrake southward into Sweeney Canyon. It is probably no more than a 100 years old, generated by earth movements triggered by the Laguna Salada earthquake of 1892. Northward, between Canebrake and Aqua Caliente Springs, unequivocal evidence of recent fault scarplets are approximately three feet high. These cut modern alluvial fans and washes and are an extension of continuing tectonic activity in this most active geological corridor.

36.1 Miles, Indian Gorge (right, southwest), Mile Marker 46
North Fork and south fork of Indian Valley lie beyond the narrow gorge.

36.2 Miles, Bow Willow Creek Turnoff (left, southeast)
The highway sign inaccurately portrays this roadway as belonging to the Great Southern Overland Stage Route of 1849. Beginning in 1857, stagecoach

traffic faithfully followed the Carrizo Corridor along Vallecito Creek (2.5 miles to the east), and never passed by way of Bow Willow Creek.

37.0 Miles, Mountain Palm Springs (right, southwest), Mile Marker 47

Beyond the primitive campground lies unlimited exploration and personal discovery. The Pygmy Grove of native California fan palms is easily seen from the primitive campground to the west and the north grove to the north. Rocky arroyos lead to additional hidden palm oases. There are many native elephant trees also scattered about.

At Mountain Palm Springs, subparallel fractures from the southern branch of the Elsinore Fault merge with the Tierra Blanca Mountain Frontal Fault. As a result, the crystalline granitic bedrock (brecciated leuco-tonalite) is so highly broken apart around the trailhead parking area that it resembles **sedimentary rock.**

37.3 Miles, Bow Willow Alluvial Fan, Mile Marker 48

For the next 0.7 miles, the highway crosses the large Bow Willow alluvial fan. To the right, on the western skyline above the McCain Valley plateau, stands conical-shaped Sombrero Peak (elevation 4,229 feet above sea level). Boulder-strewn and rugged, this prominent landmark is made up of light-colored tonalitic rock of the large La Posta **Pluton.**

Swirled gneiss and schist, pre-dating the batholitic intrusion, lend color and vari-ety to the rocks of Box Canyon. HF

38.2 Miles, Bow Willow Primitive Campground (right, southwest), Between Mile Markers 48 and 49

During the summer of 1983, the original campground was inundated by disastrous floodwaters rushing out of Bow Willow Canyon. It is surprising to learn that facilities including picnic tables, ramadas, fire rings, stoves and food storage lockers remain buried nearly 10 feet beneath the present-day fan surface. Today, newly-built campsites have been relocated nearby on higher ground that consists of black amphibolite metasedimentary rock and light-colored tonalite of the La Posta Pluton.

38.4 Miles, Carrizo Creek

During the summer of 1983, raging floodwaters gushing out of Carrizo Gorge and Rockhouse Canyon swept away the paved highway here, closing the road to through-going traffic for several months. Debris from the Jacumba and In-Ko-Pah Mountains was scattered from Carrizo Palms eastward through the Carrizo Impact Area to San Sebastian Marsh. In July 1990, photographer Jim Zuehl captured a spectacular half-hour flash flood sequence on video at this location. This video has been included in the Park Volunteer training program.

In road cuts along both sides of Carrizo Creek, **pediment** fan and alluvial outwash deposits of Mesa Conglomerate can be seen, capping older sediments. For the most part, these sediments consist of fine to coarse-grained sandstones and conglomeratic lenses that were laid down as discontinuous valley fill during the Late Pleistocene Epoch (0.5 - 0.1 MYA). Nearby, a mammoth tooth fossil has been found within sediments comparable to Mesa Conglomerate.

39.0 Miles, Entering Sweeney Canyon, Mile Marker 49

Sweeney Canyon lies directly on **strike** with the Tierra Blanca Mountain Frontal Fault, described above between Mile Markers 44 and 45. The main trace of the Elsinore Fault Zone is located east of here, bringing Palm Spring Formation (Hueso Member) into fault contact with older Canebrake Conglomerate. On the right of the highway, metasedimentary rocks of the Jacumba Mountains have been upthrown and exposed. As the highway climbs switchbacks to the mesa top, layered strata of locally derived, gray Canebrake Conglomerate and the reddish-brown Diablo Formation, of river delta origin, have been complexly faulted.

41.4 Miles, Carrizo Badlands Overlook, Beyond (southeast of) Mile Marker 51

This quarter-mile long turnout leads to an interpretive panel which offers a sweeping view of the entire Vallecito-Fish Creek Basin and the Carrizo Badlands with Canyon Sin Nombre opening out below. During the Pliocene-Pleistocene Epochs (1 - 5 MYA), the area was a low-lying basin which had been collapsing along bounding fault margins at a faster rate than debris, shed from the local uplands, could accumulate. During the last two million years of the current mountain-building episode, the basin has undergone major faulting, folding, uplift, widespread erosion of basin sediments, and even clockwise rotation. (See discussion above at June Wash related to basin development and fossil ages.)

A series of related environments evolved in the region including alluvial fan, delta, lakebed, and fluvial (riverine). Fossil remains of camel, sloth, mastodon, and horse ancestors indicate continuous deposition of sediments.

The Carrizo Badlands Overlook is made up of Pliocene Canebrake Conglomerate capped by residual Late Pleistocene Mesa Conglomerate (0.5 - 0.1

MYA). Eastward, in the near distance, the dark-colored backbone of the Coyote Mountains is composed of a complex assemblage of old metasedimentary rock, including quartz-feldspar schists, mica schists, phyllite, biotite-bearing quartzite, calcareous quartzite and marble of the Palezoic Era, Ordovician Period (about 500 million years old). In the low topographic **graben** of Canyon Sin Nombre, between the overlook and the Coyote Mountains, cuts the main trace of the Elsinore Fault system (Coyote Mountains Frontal Fault). See Field Trip No. 1 (Montezuma Grade) and Field Trip No. 2 (Santa Rosa Mountains) for discussions on related Ordovician metasediments in the central and north sections of the park.

The fault extends the entire length of the Coyote Mountains along its southwestern side. Locally, it is a **reverse fault** that has elevated the metasedimentary rocks (500 MYA) up and over Pliocene-aged (2 - 4 MYA) deposits of the Diablo Formation. This can only be explained by compression that may have accompanied or followed horizontal fault movements. Within Canyon Sin Nombre, the relatively young Diablo Formation overlies the ancient metasedi-mentary rock sequence depositionally or is directly faulted against it. Overall, geologists postulate at least 3.2 miles of right-lateral offset along the Coyote Mountains Frontal Fault.

43.7 Miles, Dolomite Mine View (left), Southeast of Mile Marker 53

The Dolomite Mine is clearly visible as light colored scars along the western slopes of the Coyote Mountains. The mine, now abandoned, once yielded

Carrizo Badlands Overlook reveals the right-lateral Elsinore Fault trace generally along the light colored wash of Canyon Sin Nombre in the middle ground. Dark colored ancient metamorphics of the Coyote Mountains (right) have been brought into fault contact with young Diablo sediments in the center. LL

dolomite which was trucked eight miles south to the rail siding at Dos Cabezas station. The mine was worked intermittently, producing road building materials, agricultural lime, and decorative stone on a small scale. Dolomite is a cousin to limestone but here it is usually harder, containing more concentrations of magnesium than limestone.

45.0 Miles, Enter Volcanic Hills, Mile Marker 55

To the right, located between Jojoba Wash and Mortero Wash, is the hummocky, multi-hued landscape of the Volcanic Hills, Anza-Borrego's major volcanic field. Imagine, during the Early to Middle Miocene Epoch (15 - 23 MYA), and perhaps later, numerous volcanic cauldrons erupting dark clouds of ash while belching out flows of molten rock onto an eroded bedrock surface.

The volcanic rocks, named the Alverson Formation, are composed of dark-colored olivine basalts and lighter andesites associated with massive flows, breccia, air-fall cinder deposits, and minor volcanic sandstones. Good examples can be seen south of the Red Hill promontory (elevation 1,685 feet) along Lava Flow Wash. There is also evidence of Indian use in the flat areas and among the boulder-formed caves.

The Alverson Formation has been locally dated at about 18 million years old. Similar rock outcrops of the same age are found in the Fish Creek Mountains, Fossil Canyon, and Lava Gorge in the Coyote Mountains, Table Mountain, Jacumba Mountains, and Rockhouse Canyon. These may represent continuous events with the basalts of the Volcanic Hills. Combined, the volcanic activity records geologic events caused by the interaction of tectonic rifting in the Gulf of California, notably the initial rafting away of the tip of Baja California from the Mexican mainland.

45.6 Miles, Mortero Wash (right), Southeast of Mile Marker 55

This turnoff leads to the Volcanic Hills, Indian Hill, and Dos Cabezas. Four-wheel drive is strongly recommended.

46.2 Miles, Imperial County Line, Southeast of Mile Marker 56

Leave Anza-Borrego Desert State Park and enter BLM (U.S. Bureau of Land Management) lands. Imperial Highway S-2 continues southward another eight miles to its intersection with Interstate 8 at Ocotillo. Southeast of Ocotillo on Highway 98 is the fascinating Yuha Desert.

Slot canyons abound in the badlands such as this tributary to Canyon Sin Nombre. CP

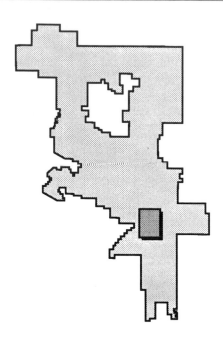

Palm Spring and Mesquite Oasis in the Vallecito Badlands. LL

FIELD TRIP NO. 5A

VALLECITO BADLANDS (Primitive Road)

Length:　　　　　　27.9 Miles (round trip from Highway S-2)

Road Conditions:　　Primitive road subject to wash-outs. Check with visitor center before proceeding. Four-wheel drive mandatory

Season:　　　　　　October through May

Route Summary:

Field Trip No. 5A turns off from Hwy S-2 (Field Trip No. 5) at the Vallecito Creek Turnoff (Mile Marker 43). The route proceeds along an established four-wheel drive roadway along Vallecito Creek to Arroyo Tapiado which it then follows, crossing over to and returning back down Arroyo Seco del Diablo, thence back to Highway S-2. The 1.5 miles to Palm Spring may be passable to passenger cars.

General Description:

The fossil record of the Vallecito-Fish Creek Basin is most complete, representing the longest continuous Pliocene and Pleistocene (0.9 - 5 MYA) shallow-water marine and continentally-derived terrestrial sequence known in North America. The Vallecito-Fish Creek Basin's rich vertebrate and invertebrate faunas continue to make Anza-Borrego the standard study section for Blancan and Irvingtonian Land Mammal Ages **biostratigraphy** (0.9 - 3.6 MYA). Several thou-sand fossils representing over 120 species have been recorded from the Palm Spring Formation alone. Over 700 localities from 250 stratigraphic levels are now known.

Cross-references to related fossil fauna include: Trip No. 2 (Borrego Badlands, "Borrego Local Fauna," Irvingtonian-Rancholabrean); Trip No. 4A (Sandstone Canyon, "Layer Cake Local Fauna," Hemphillian-Blancan); and Trip No. 5 (June Wash and Vallecito Badlands, "Vallecito Local Fauna," Blancan-Irvingtonian).

Keep in mind that all sediments exposed to view in the Vallecito Badlands have been tilted down to the west, therefore by driving in an easterly direction, you will be traversing, down-**dip**, back through the strata file of geologic time.

Route Log:

0.0 Miles, Mile Marker 43 on Hwy S-2

0.4 Miles, View of the Badlands Wash turnoff (left, northeast)
Proceed right (southeast). The low, surrounding hillsides are supported by the terrestrial Palm Spring Formation. It is aptly named for excellent rock expo-

STRATIGRAPHY OF THE VALLECITO BADLANDS

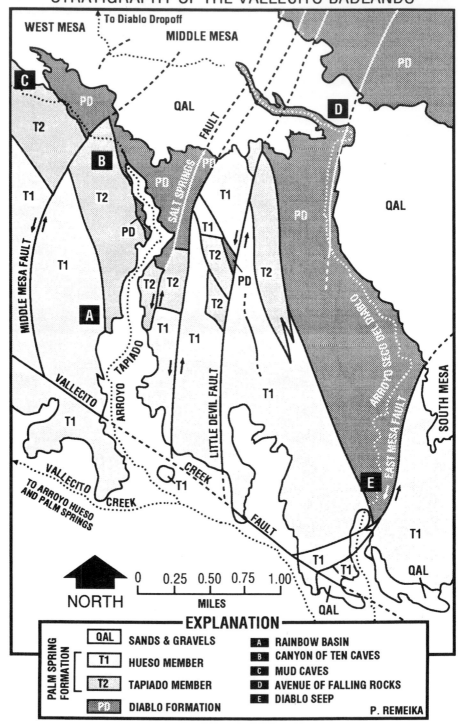

WEST MESA

To Diablo Dropoff

MIDDLE MESA

C MUD CAVES

PD

T2

T1

B

T2

PD

MIDDLE MESA FAULT

T1

A

T1

QAL

FAULT

SALT SPRINGS

PD

PD

PD

T1

T1

T2

T2

PD

T2

T2

T2

T1

T1

D

PD

QAL

ARROYO SECO DEL DIABLO

SOUTH MESA

EAST MESA FAULT

VALLECITO

ARROYO TAPIADO

T1

LITTLE DEVIL FAULT

T1

VALLECITO

TO ARROYO HUESO
AND PALM SPRINGS

CREEK

CREEK

T1

CREEK

FAULT

E

T1

T1

T1

QAL

QAL

NORTH

| 0 | 0.25 | 0.50 | 0.75 | 1.00 |

MILES

EXPLANATION

PALM SPRING FORMATION

QAL	SANDS & GRAVELS
T1	HUESO MEMBER
T2	TAPIADO MEMBER
PD	DIABLO FORMATION

A	RAINBOW BASIN
B	CANYON OF TEN CAVES
C	MUD CAVES
D	AVENUE OF FALLING ROCKS
E	DIABLO SEEP

P. REMEIKA

sures occurring in and around Palm Spring, Mesquite Oasis and View of the Badlands. The formation here consists predominantly of interbedded sandstone, claystone, and gravel conglomerate. Between Vallecito Creek and Arroyo Seco del Diablo, over 6,000 columnar feet of sediments belonging to the Palm Spring and Diablo Formations are exposed. The thick columnar section has been subdivided into two rock members from youngest to oldest: Hueso and Tapiado. In general terms of origin, the Hueso is riverine and the Tapiado is lakebed. Below this sequence are massive, fine grained, quartz-arenite, channel sandstones alternating with reddish-brown overbank deposits of the Diablo Formation (see Trip No. 4, Loop Wash and west, for more notes on the Diablo in this area. See below, Arroyo Seco del Diablo, notes on the Grand Canyon and Colorado River genesis of the Diablo).

Much of the western half of the Vallecito Badlands is the Hueso Member, a basinward derivative of the Pliocene-Pleistocene Canebrake Conglomerate. While land derived sediments were being shed, almost continuously, from highland sources into the Vallecito-Fish Creek Basin, basin-margin **alluvium in this area** was dominated by **braided-stream, lacustrine** and floodplain deposition of the Hueso Member.

Paleontological data suggest that the Palm Spring environment (during the time of Hueso deposition, 0.1 - 2 MYA) was that of a temperate savannah of rolling plains adjacent to meandering streams and shallow playa lakes. Riverine deposits were widespread with episodic flooding resulting in the accumulation of many cyclic overbank deposits. (See Trip No. 4A, Sandstone Canyon, for related notes on the Olla Member of the Canebrake Conglomerate.)

Badland Ridge, along View of the Badlands Wash, occupies a prominent **stratigraphic** position at the Pliocene-Pleistocene boundary. It has been **paleomagnetically** dated at 1.9 million years old.

1.0 Miles, Palm Spring Turnoff (left, northeast)

Continue straight ahead. Palm Spring, 0.6 miles up this spur road at Mesquite Oasis, served as a temporary way station, conveniently situated between the Carrizo and Vallecito Stage Stations, along the Butterfield Overland Mail Route.

Closer inspection reveals that the sediments (Hueso Member) that make up the Palm Spring badlands have been locally **folded** in a narrow belt, between Mesquite Oasis and Arroyo Hueso, along the northern side of the Vallecito Creek Fault.

2.3 Miles, Arroyo Hueso (left, northeast)

Proceed straight. The local scenery exposed along the mouth of Hueso Wash is made up of the Hueso Member (Spanish for "bone"). It is mostly a sequence of brownish-colored siltstones and silty sandstones of local origin.

2.6 Miles, Hollywood and Vine (left, northeast)

This outcrop and hidden cul-de-sac has become a favorite car-camping spot along Vallecito Creek. Note, in the road cut north of the entrance, that the strata consists of vertical-standing sandstones of the Hueso Member, deformed along the Vallecito Creek Fault.

4.6 Miles, Arroyo Tapiado (left, northeast)

Make a left turn (north) into Arroyo Tapiado, also known as Concretion

Wash, following the established roadway leading back into the Vallecito Bad-
lands. Arroyo Tapiado is an ephemeral stream incised into the tilted Palm Spring
Formation. It drains southward to Vallecito Creek from the southern flank of the
Pinyon Mountains.

This elongated arroyo is generally steep-walled and entrenched below the
surface of West Mesa throughout its lower half, and steep and V-shaped in its
upper half. The headwaters of Arroyo Tapiado are in the massive boulder and
cobble Canebrake **Conglomerate**.

Ahead, on the left and right, look for the conspicuous Vallecito Creek
Fault cutting through the Hueso Member in a northwest-southeast direction.
Sediments of the Hueso Member are tilted steeply to the southwest.

Concretions -
Accidents of Sedimentation

Sandstone concretions, the most varied shaped rocks of the sedimentary
world, arouse the curiosity of many park visitors. They vary from realistic
rounded, flattened, or cylindrical forms to imaginative shapes with imposing
names such as botryoidal (bunch of grapes), fusiform (like a spindle), and
ameboid (of the microscopic creature). They may form a mosaic on the bare
ground, more firmly cemented than the surrounding parent rock, all of which is
Diablo sandstone of ancestral Colorado River delta origin.

They apparently result from the tendency for particles of like composition
to concentrate around a common center, or nucleus, with a cementing agent of
silica, iron oxide, or calcite. This is a secondary process of chemical and
weathering changes after initial deposition of the sediment called "diagenesis."
Being more firmly cemented than the enclosing sandstone, concretions weather
out in myriad shapes that have been fancifully described as cannonballs,
pumpkins, dinosaur limbs, or bric-a-brac.

Local ensembles of concretions are widespread only in thick, hardened
channel sandstones of the Diablo Formation. Good examples can be seen in the
upper reaches of Arroyo Tapiado (Spanish word for "Concretion Wash"), in the
depths of Arroyo Seco del Diablo, Cannonball Wash, and Pumpkin Patch. They
appear as follows: in nodular patches; concentrated along bedding planes;
protruding from weathered cliffsides; randomly distributed over mudhills; or
perched on soft pedestals.

5.7 Miles, Rainbow Basin

Ahead and on the left, the open amphitheater of Rainbow Basin displays
highly eroded badland deposits that have been locally tilted to the west, revealing
an orderly yet complex progression of terrestrial sedimentation extending back
into the Pliocene Epoch (2 - 3 MYA). Here, the sediments were laid down as an
interbedded sequence of lakebed claystones and riverine sandstones along the
shallow-water shoreline of ancient Lake Tapiado. This lake is appropriately
named for massive lakebed siltstones and claystones exposed ahead that once
occupied the topographic low within the Vallecito-Fish Creek Basin during the
Later Pliocene Epoch (2 - 3 MYA). A modern analogy to the Lake Tapiado
environment might be Lake Henshaw, surrounded by the broad Valley of San
Jose which includes Warner Springs.

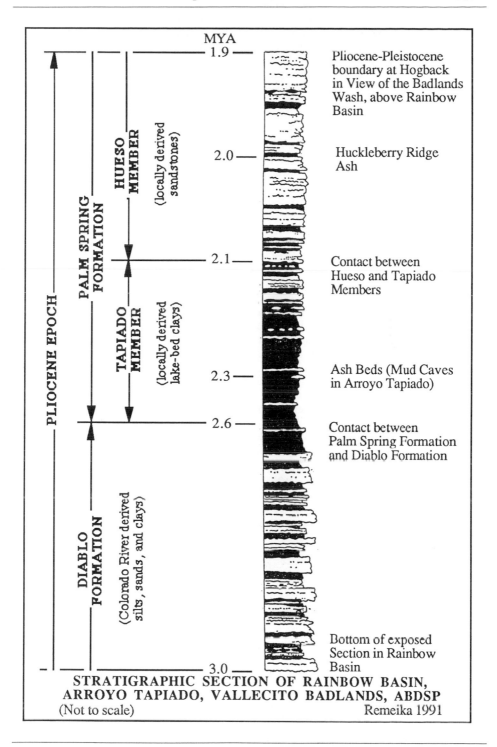

MYA

1.9 — Pliocene-Pleistocene boundary at Hogback in View of the Badlands Wash, above Rainbow Basin

2.0 — Huckleberry Ridge Ash

2.1 — Contact between Hueso and Tapiado Members

2.3 — Ash Beds (Mud Caves in Arroyo Tapiado)

2.6 — Contact between Palm Spring Formation and Diablo Formation

3.0 — Bottom of exposed Section in Rainbow Basin

PLIOCENE EPOCH

PALM SPRING FORMATION

HUESO MEMBER (locally derived sandstones)

TAPIADO MEMBER (locally derived lake-bed clays)

DIABLO FORMATION (Colorado River derived silts, sands, and clays)

STRATIGRAPHIC SECTION OF RAINBOW BASIN, ARROYO TAPIADO, VALLECITO BADLANDS, ABDSP

(Not to scale)   Remeika 1991

The vari-colored stack of sediments probably represents delta development. The presence of overbank deposits and channel sandstones suggest periodic flooding and abundant sediment input entering Lake Tapiado from the surrounding highlands. These sediments, which **prograded** (progressively graded) over the lake, are made up of alternating siltstones and sandstones of the Hueso Member. Vertebrate fossils occur in great abundance throughout the Rainbow Basin area.

6.7 Miles, Canyon of Ten Caves

On the left-hand side of the arroyo is the dry tributary identified by paleontologists as "Canyon of Ten Caves." Here, at cliffside, the Tapiado Member of the Palm Spring Formation consists of blue-gray, olive-green gypsum bearing mudstones and claystones with tan **calcareous** siltstones that record habitats of semiaquatic, marshy lake deposits of Lake Tapiado. Freshwater mollusks, amphibians, reptiles and mammals commonly became enmired in the shallow, muddy waters, now exposed to view as a hard entombing matrix. Northward, and up-section, the Tapiado Member eventually grades laterally into interbedded calcareous siltstones, sandstones and claystones of the Hueso Member.

On the right-hand (northeast) side of the arroyo, **conformably** underlying the Tapiado Member, is the contrasting Diablo Formation. It is made up of an alternating sequence of light-colored, crossbedded quartz arenite channel sandstones overlain by evenly-bedded, reddish-brown overbank mudstones. The massive Diablo sandstones yield many jumbled **fusiform** (spindle shaped), spheroidal and tabular concretions that are scattered over the surface. The sandstones resist erosion more than mudstones, forming prominent **strike-ridges.**

Between Canyon of Ten Caves and Cave Canyon of Arroyo Tapiado, look for evidence of the Middle Mesa Fault exposed in the canyon walls, particularly on the left side of the wash. Most of the Vallecito Badlands have been offset by a series of northeast-southwest trending **left-lateral** faults.

7.7 Miles, Cave Canyon (right, northeast)

"Cave Canyon," also known as Big Cave, is among the longest and largest natural mud cave formations reported in North America. The surrounding cave-forming terrain is called **pseudokarst** by analogy to true karst country where sinkholes and caves develop in limestone formation such as Carlsbad Caverns. Characteristic pseudokarst features here include recessed subterranean stream channel outlets and caves that have been internally eroded into halls, galleries, aisles, chambers and crawlways. Locally, Cave Canyon exhibits a channel length of over 1,500 feet. Other fascinating mud caves of unusual interest include the small slot of Plunge Pool Cave (adjacent on the right to Cave Canyon), Chasm Cave, Hidden Cave and Skylight Cave. These names are used by members of the National Speleological Society. Remember that all cave features in Arroyo Tapiado are subject to instantaneous collapse with no warning. Park visitors should always consider them dangerous and avoid entry.

Here, too, crossing the arroyo channel, are two essentially identical volcanic ash (tuff) layers. Stratigraphically separated by 78 feet, each is a unique datum marker. Newly discovered fossil footprints and bones belonging to the extinct camelid *Camelops* have been preserved between the ash. The oldest (lowermost) ash bed is 2.3 million years old.

Continuing ahead, up-canyon, is a long series of tight meanders that coincide with pseudokarstic topography that distinguishes Arroyo Tapiado. Upland surfaces are commonly defined by sunken valleys, blind valleys and low depressions (collapsed sink holes) formed by surface processes that are restricted generally to the swelling claystones and mudstones of the Tapiado Member. Basin Wash, in the Borrego Badlands, has similar though less extensive formations.

8.7 Miles, Ancient Lake Tapiado

On both sides of the arroyo, fluctuations of Lake Tapiado resulted in lakebed siltstones and claystones being **prograded** over by riverine sandstones and siltstones. Evidence suggests a progressive transition zone here, from shallow-water lakebed (Tapiado Member) into a more riverine environment (Hueso Member). Late Pliocene fossils include turtle, fish, camelids, peccaries, equids (horse-like), and other megavertebrates from these deposits.

10.5 Miles, Arroyo Tapiado Fork

The left-fork (main branch) continues straight ahead. Make a right turn, following the established roadway east along the right-fork of Arroyo Tapiado.

10.9 Miles, Cut Across Trail (right, northeast)

Cut across to Arroyo Seco del Diablo by climbing the short hillside route onto West Mesa. The smooth upland surface of West Mesa represents the remnants of an extensive **pediment** that once covered much of the area. It consists of about 10 feet of gravelly deposits, including conglomeratic sandstones in an unsorted sand and gravel matrix.

The lakebed and streamborne sediments of the Palm Spring Formation in Arroyo Tapiado have been compared to the present environment of Lake Henshaw and its surrounding green meadows, laced by streams. PR

13.1 Miles, Arroyo Seco del Diablo/Cut-Across Junction
Junction,"Dry Wash of the Devil." Continue straight, southeastbound.

13.2 Miles, Diablo Dropoff Turnoff (left, northeast)
Turn left onto established side-route 1.5 miles as it crosses Middle Mesa.

14.7 Miles, Diablo Dropoff (elevation 1,078 feet)
Here is a sweeping panorama of colorful earth strata and natural history, encompassing most of the Carrizo Badlands and Vallecito Mountain section of the state wilderness area. Exposed to view, like so many pages of an open book, the Vallecito-Fish Creek Basin began during Late Miocene-Early Pliocene times (5 - 6 MYA). Since then it has continually received marine, deltaic, and non-marine sediments from five million to 900,000 years ago, the latter eroded from the surrounding local mountains that surround it. Gravity measurements and other geophysical data indicate a total of nearly 14,000 feet of fill in the basin, almost three times that exposed in the Grand Canyon of Arizona.

In the distance to the east, the Fish Creek Mountains shape the skyline. They are discontinuously capped with frost-looking Fish Creek Gypsum. To the south are the Coyote Mountains, brooded over by 2,408 feet Carrizo Mountain. And to the north are the immense bulwarks of the Pinyon and Vallecito Mountains. In between are vari-colored badland canyons, weatherworn mudhills and flat-topped sunken mesas born not of the desert but of the sea. These are the marine sedi-ments of the Imperial Formation, gradationally overlain by successive "redbed" layers of delta and tributary-channels belonging to the Diablo Formation. Diablo sediments also cap the Diablo Dropoff, **striking** along the rim of Middle Mesa from Sandstone Canyon to Gert Wash. In this vicinity, they have been **paleo-magnetically** dated at about 3.1 million years old.

At this point, adventurous travelers may wish to extend their discovery journey back through time, exiting the Vallecito-Fish Creek Basin via Split Mountain Gorge. Proceed with caution. The narrow roadway drops steeply down from Middle Mesa several hundred feet into Dropoff Wash, intersecting with Fish Creek Wash after one mile. Four-wheel drive is mandatory. The Split Mountain Field Trip No. 4A can then be followed, backtracking from Dropoff Wash to Split Mountain Road. All the while, one is moving earlier and earlier back through geologic ages when proceeding northeastward to Split Mountain.

Others return back southwest to the intersection of the original road with Arroyo Seco del Diablo.

16.2 Miles, Diablo Dropoff Turnoff (again)
Back at the original turnoff (13.2 miles above), make a left turn, continuing southbound down Arroyo Seco del Diablo.

16.8 Miles, Avenue of Falling Rocks
For the next 2.4 miles, the entrenched roadway works its way down into the narrow confines of Diablo Canyon, entering the "Avenue of Falling Rocks." Note that through this section, the Diablo Formation and a small portion of the greenish-colored lacustrine Tapiado Member have been cut by several **transverse** faults, most notably the Middle Mesa, Salt Springs, Little Devil and Diablo Canyon Faults. These parallel, **left-lateral** fractures have broken up the Vallecito Badlands into elongated fault-blocks, suggesting a response to clockwise rotation of the Vallecito-Fish Creek Basin during the Middle to Late Pleistocene Epoch.

19.2 Miles, Colorado River Delta Deposits - Diablo Formation
This is a junction with a dry, unnamed tributary canyon on the right. During the Late Miocene-Early Pliocene, between 4 - 6 MYA, the ancestral Colorado River began to establish its present course, downcutting through the Grand Canyon and Colorado Plateau regions of Arizona and Utah. As a result, a vast amount of fine-grained **detritus** was transported and deposited by the river into much of the Anza-Borrego area.

One particular sequence of events, locally characterized by the Diablo Formation, represents the Colorado River delta-plain **alluvium** exposed here in the sheer walls of Diablo Canyon. With continued **progradation**, transitional tidal-flats of the older marine Imperial Formation (Camels Head Member) and younger river delta Diablo matured into delta-plains with meandering, riverine channels throughout much of the Vallecito-Fish Creek Basin. See latter entries in Field Trip 4A (Fish Creek Badlands) for additional notes on the Camel's Head Member, and Diablo Formation in this area.

Locally, the rock sequence includes alternating layers of very distinctive, pale-orange tributary-channel sandstones (with scoured bases) and reddish-brown **overbank** claystones and siltstones. These thick-bedded sandstones may be **cross-stratified**, and commonly yield fragments of petrified wood and an abundance of concretions which weather out in bizarre shapes. All told, the Diablo Member was laid down during the Early and Middle Pliocene Epoch, 3-4 MYA. The duration of deposition, based on paleomagnetic data, covered a time span of 1.2 million years.

Throughout, sediments that were buried over several miles deep during the Pliocene Epoch are exposed to view, at cliffside, 800 feet above sea level.

21.0 Miles, Diablo Seep
Ahead in the canyon walls, note a change in rock structures. The East Mesa Fault crosses the wash, passing east of Arroyo Seco del Diablo in a northeast-trending direction. It has brought the older reddish-brown river delta Diablo Formation into fault contact with the younger, deformed, tan-gray fluvial sandstone of the Hueso Member (exposed along the mouth of the arroyo). The very presence of the water seepage here is another expression of fault activity.

22.0 Miles, Vallecito/Arroyo Seco del Diablo Junction
Turn right (northwest) to return to pavement.

23.5 Miles, Vallecito/Arroyo Tapiado Junction (again)

28.1 Miles, County Hwy S-2 at Mile Marker 43

*A member of the Society of Vertebrate Paleotology investigates trackways on
"Camel Ridge" in the Vallecito Badlands. LL*

PART III - APPENDICES

GLOSSARY OF SELECTED GEOLOGICAL TERMS

THESE TERMS ARE SELECTED FOR THEIR APPLICABILITY TO ARID AREA GEOLOGY.

AEOLIAN: (*Aeolus*, Greek god of the winds.) Wind deposited. (Sometimes Eolian.)

AGGLOMERATE: A rock composed of volcanic fragments similar to sedimentary conglomerate in appearance.

ALLUVIUM: Coarse to fine deposits made by water runoff; does not include underwater sediments of seas and lakes.

ALLUVIAL FAN: A fan-shaped deposit of **alluvium**, generally at the mouth of a canyon.

AMPHIBOLITE: A dark, metamorphic **rock** including the aluminum silicate mineral amphibole (typically **hornblende**). May represent regional metamorphism.

ANDESITE: A gray to dark gray volcanic rock, intermediate in composition and color between light rhyolite and dark **basalt**. **Plutonic** equivalent is **diorite**.

ANTICLINE: A fold, generally convex upward, where older rocks are found towards the core or axis.

ANTECEDENT: Having existed before the present topography.

APLITE: A whitish plutonic **dike** rock composed of quartz and feldspar with a sugary, fine grained texture.

ARENITE: A well-sorted, well-cemented "clean" sandstone with little clay with a high percentage of (or exclusively) quartz.

ARKOSE: A clayey, generally coarse, sandstone with a relatively high percentage of feldspar.

ASTHENOSPHERE: The weak and spongy layer of the earth's mantle below the **lithosphere** upon which tectonic **plates** move. Starts about 100 km (60 miles) below the earth's surface.

BAJADA: An alluvial plain; A broad apron extending out from the base of mountain ranges formed by the intersection of **alluvial** fans, and having a generally undulating topography.

BARRANCA: A deep gully or canyon with steep sides.

BASALT: A dark **volcanic** mafic rock, generally oceanic, with high percentages of heavy minerals such as olivine and pyroxene. Plutonic equivalent is **gabbro**.

BATHOLITH: (Greek, "deep rock.") A major granitic mass of mountain range or greater size with no known depth that cooled and solidified beneath the earth's surface and may be partially exposed due to erosion. See **pluton**.

BEHEADING: The capture and diversion of a drainage system's headwaters to another headward-cutting drainage system; stream piracy, headward erosion.

BIOSTRATIGRAPHY: Differentiation of sedimentary rock units based on the fossils contained in the strata.

BIOSTROME: A distinctly bedded sediment composed of the remains of sedentary organisms such as oysters and clams.

BIOTITE MICA: Dark, flaky, aluminum silicate rock forming mineral with magnesium and iron; black **mica**.

BRAIDED STREAM: A stream that divides into an interlacing network of shallow streams separated by islands or channel bars; esp, an overloaded stream in a wide channel or floodplain.

BRECCIA: A course, **clastic** rock composed of angular fragments held together by a mineral cement; may be igneous, sedimentary, metamorphic, or mineral fragment.

CALCAREOUS: Containing calcium carbonate. Often a prefix indicating organic origin.

CATACLASTIC: Rock structures formed by intense mechanical stress during fault movement and dynamic metamorphism; e.g. fault breccia or gouge.

CLAST: A fragment formed by the disintegration of an earlier and larger rock.

CONFORMABLE: Strata in which the layers are formed one above the other in parallel and are uninterrupted by other deposits.

CONGLOMERATE: A sedimentary rock composed of coarse **clastic** or fragmented material cemented together.

COUNTRY ROCKS: The preexisting bedrock of a region into which molten **igneous** rocks **intrude**.

CRYSTALLINE: Minerals with molecules in a fixed arrangement. Visible crystals are a defining characteristic of **plutonic** rock. Opposite, amorphous.

DACITE: A medium light colored, fine-grained **volcanic** rock with a composition like that of **andesite,** but with more quartz. Plutonic equivalent is quartz-diorite (tonalite).

DELTA or DELTAIC: The flat land at the mouth of a river resulting from the accumulation of river-supplied sediment.

DETACHMENT FAULT: A complex low-angle, large-scale **normal fault** with displacement measured in miles.

DETRITUS: Broken up rock material and rock debris.

DIKE: An intrusion of magma that cuts across the grain of existing rock, generally through cracks or joints.

DIORITE: A grainy **plutonic** rock, intermediate in composition and color to light granitics and dark **gabbro.** Volcanic equivalent is **andesite.**

DIP: The angle between a layer of rock and the horizontal, measured perpendicular to the line of **strike.**

DIP-SLIP FAULT: See **normal fault.**

DISTAL: Far from the point of origin or attachment (opposite - see **proximal**).

EN ECHELON: Geologic features, especially faults, in a staggered, overlapping, or offset arrangement of rows.

EPHEMERAL: Seasonal; short-lived.

EPICENTER: The point on the earth's surface directly above the point of origin (focus) of an earthquake.

ESCARPMENT: A continuous steep cliff, or line of cliffs, formed as the result of erosion or faulting.

EXHUMED TOPOGRAPHY: A topological feature, once buried under younger material, that has been exposed by erosion or faulting.

EXTRUSIVE or EXTRUDE: see **volcanic** and **igneous.**

FACET: A planed-off surface, especially an inverted V at the end of a spur or ridge, indicating lateral motion along a fault.

FACIES: A distinct set of characteristics in a rock group, different from adjacent groups, series, or suites.

FANGLOMERATE: ("Alluvial fan conglomerate") Solid rock composed of sediments originally deposited in an alluvial fan and since cemented together.

FAULT: A fracture in a rock or the earth's crust where movement has occured.

FAUNA (or FLORA): The animal (or plant) life in a region, period of time, or geologic strata.

FELDSPAR: An aluminum silicate that is the most abundant mineral on earth's surface and is therefore the most common **rock-forming mineral**. Potassium feldspars (e.g. microcline and orthoclase) tend to occur in lighter, more **felsic** rocks while plagioclase feldspars (containing sodium and calcium) tend to occur in darker, more **mafic** rocks.

FELSIC: (Feldspar plus silica quartz). Light colored, igneous rocks, generally of continental origin. Opposite, see **mafic**.

FLUVIAL: Of or pertaining to rivers; created by river flow.

FOLD: A bend in rock due to forces operating after the consolidation of the rock.

FOLIATED ROCKS: Metamorphic rocks characterized by color layering; not as regular as the layering of sedimentary rocks; more specific than **lineation**.

FOOTWALL: The mass or face of rock below an inclined fault. Opposite, see **hanging wall**.

FORAMINIFERA: Single-celled marine animals that secrete a **calcareous** shell. Some limestones are composed almost completely of foraminifera.

FORMATION: A **lithologically** distinct rock body or deposit that is large enough to be recognized, named, and mapped.

FOSSILIFEROUS: Containing fossils.

FUSIFORM: Spindle shaped; tapering at either end from a swollen middle.

GABBRO: A grainy, dark, **mafic, plutonic** rock, generally with olivine or pyroxene. **Volcanic** equivalent is **basalt**.

GEO: (*Gaea*, Greek goddess of the earth.) Combining form of "earth."

GNEISS: A course-grained, high grade metamorphic rock in which bands of dark and light-colored rock alternate. Discrete layers of **foliated** minerals.

GRABEN: A block of the earth's crust dropped down between two faults steeply inclined inward. Opposite, see **horst**. Generally equivalent to trough, basin, or sink.

GRANO - or GRANITE: A combining prefix or generalized term for granite-like, **felsic**, light colored, plutonic **crystalline** rock. Volcanic equivalent is **rhyolite**. Granitics in eastern Peninsular Ranges tend to be quartzdiorite (tonalite) or granodiorite.

GRUS: Decomposed granitic rock; "DG" in construction industry.

HANGING WALL: The mass or face of rock above an inclined fault. Opposite, see **footwall**.

HORNBLENDE: Dark colored variety of the rock forming mineral **amphibole**.

HORST: A block of the earth's crust uplifted between faults. Opposite, see **graben**.

IGNEOUS ROCK: A rock formed by the solidification of **magma**; appearances vary from smooth basalt to grainy granite. Divided into **intrusive** (plutonic) and **extrusive** (volcanic) rock. Compare, **felsic** and **mafic.**

IMBRICATION: (*Imbrica*, Latin, "brick") Overlapping structures such as rocks in a streambed.

INCLUSION: A fragment of older rock within an igneous rock; a **xenolith** (Greek, "stranger rock").

INSELBERG: (German, "island hill") A remnant hill, around which erosion has lowered the surface as atop a **pediment**.

INTERCALATED: Inserted between or among existing layers or elements.

INTERMONTANE: An area in the mountains, or between mountain ridges.

INTRUSION: The injection of magma into or between preexisting rock formations. A **plutonic** process.

JOINT: (Latin, *jugum*, "yoke") A fracture in a rock along which no significant slip has occurred; provides entry for roots and organic acid-bearing waters that cause weathering in the rocks. See **fault.**

JUXTAPOSITION: The position of being side to side or close together.

KARST: Topography over limestone, gypsum, or dolomite where rocks, dissolved by groundwater, leave features such as sinkholes, caves, and underground drainages.

LACUSTRINE: (Greek, *laccus*, "pond) Of or related to or growing in lakes.

LATERAL FAULT: See **strike-slip.**

LEFT-LATERAL, (OR RIGHT-LATERAL), FAULT: A fault in which the opposing block seems to be displaced to the left (or right).

LEFT STEP (OR RIGHT STEP): The offset direction of a **step fault.**

LINEATION: A general term for linear features in a rock, broader than **foliation.**

LITHIFY: (Greek, *lithos*, "stone") To turn to stone; to consolidate to solid rock.

LITHOLOGY: The study of rocks; the physical character of a rock.

LITHOSPHERE: The outer 100 km of the earth's surface which appears to be relatively strong and brittle and is comprised of the crust and rigid, outer layer of the mantle. Lies between the atmosphere (or hydrosphere), and the **asthenosphere** and is fragmented into tectonic **plates**.

MAFIC: (magnesium plus ferric/iron) Dark colored, igneous rocks, generally of oceanic or deep origin. Opposite, see **felsic**.

MAGMA (MELT): Molten rock within the earth; usually rich in silicon and oxygen. Lava is magma solidified on the surface of the earth.

MEGABRECCIA: Very large angular blocks of same or similar rock united by a common cement.

MEMBER: A distinct part of a **formation**.

METAMORPHIC ROCK: An unmelted rock which has undergone significant change of its properties as a result of heat, pressure, and chemical activity, generally at depth. (e.g. slate was once clay, quartzite was once sandstone).

METASEDIMENTARY ROCK: A metamorphosed sedimentary rock.

MICA: A common rock-forming aluminum **silicate** mineral with well developed cleavage in one direction and parallel sheets with color ranging from colorless (see **muscovite**) through rose or lilac (lepidolite) to black (see **biotite**).

MICRO: Prefix, meaning small.

MICROSEISMICITY: Feeble motions in the earth that are unrelated to an earthquake.

MIGMATITE: A mixed rock with igneous and/or metamorphic materials, or **clasts**.

MINERAL: A natural, inorganic solid compound, composed of one or more elements, with definite physical, chemical, and crystalline properties.

MOHO or MOHOROVICIC DISCONTINUITY: Boundary between the earth's crust and rigid upper portion of the mantle, within the **lithosphere**. Depth is shallow below oceans, deep below continents.

MUSCOVITE MICA: Transparent or light flaky silicate mineral with abundant potassium and aluminum; white **mica**, isinglass.

MYA: Millions of Years Ago. MYBP (before present) also used.

MYLONITE: A hard, dark, fine-grained **cataclastic** rock with flow patterns.

MYLONIZATION: Deformation of a rock by severe stress and fragmentation due to mechanical forces applied in a definite direction, but without significant chemical change. Compare **metamorphic** and **cataclastic**.

NORMAL FAULT: A fault in which the overhanging block (the **footwall**) has moved down the inclined plane; dip-slip fault. Opposite, **thrust fault**.

OROGENY: (*Oro* plus *geny*, Greek, "mountain producing or genesis") Process by which mountains are formed; especially by folding of the earth's crust.

OVERBANK: The flat surface adjacent to a stream, over which streams spread in time of flood. A local variation of a floodplain.

OVERTURNED FOLD: A fold which has one limb that has been rotated past the perpendicular; overfold.

OVERPRINTED: Overlayed.

PALEO-: Prefix meaning ancient.

PALEOMAGNETISM: The study of fossil magnetism in rocks in order to determine the direction and intensity of the earth's magnetic field in geologic past.

PALEONTOLOGY: The study of life in geologic time based on plant and animal fossils.

PEDIMENT: A gently sloping bedrock surface produced by erosion at the foot of a mountain range.

PEGMATITE: (Greek, "congealed or fixed rock") A course-grained igneous rock with a composition similar to granite; usually found as irregular dikes or veins at the margins of **batholiths** and intruded after the matrix or surrounding rock has cooled.

PHYLLITE: An intermediate grade metamorphic rock, beyond slate and before mica schist.

PLATE TECTONIC THEORY: The theory that the earth's **lithosphere** is divided up into huge plates that move and interact with one another. See **spreading zone, transform fault**.

PLUTON: (*Pluto*, ancient god of the underworld) An igneous intrusion of a "balloon" of molten rock into solid, overlying **country rock**. Generally one of many units of a **batholith**. May be a few to many miles wide.

PLUTONIC ROCK: Intrusive, coarse grained igneous rock which formed underground when **magma** cooled and solidified; usually of a grainy **granitic** texture. Generally equivalent to visible **crystalline** rock. Opposite, see **volcanic**.

PREBATHOLITHIC: Having existed before the **batholith**.

PROGRADE: "Progressive Grading." To be built outward by deposition and accumulation (e.g. an alluvial fan).

PROXIMAL: Close to the point of origin (opposite - see **distal**).

QUARTZ: Silicon dioxide. Compare **silicate, rock-forming minerals, felsic, granite.**

QUARTZDIORITE: Also tonalite. A medium to light colored plutonic, **felsic** rock. Volcanic equivalent is **dacite**.

REVERSE FAULT: See **thrust fault.**

RHYOLITE: A light colored or reddish **felsic volcanic** rock, often with flow bands or small pits filled with quartz or feldspar. **Plutonic** equivalent is granite or granodiorite.

RHYTHMITE: An individual unit of a rhythmical succession of strata.

RIFT: A long belt of faulting of regional extent.

RIGHT-LATERAL FAULT (OR RIGHT-STEP): See **left-lateral.**

RILL: A rivulet or streamlet.

ROCK: A natural aggregate composed of one or more **minerals.**

ROCK-FORMING MINERALS: A group of about 15 common minerals generally silicates, including quartz, feldspars, micas, amphiboles, pyroxenes, and olivine. Carbonates and iron oxides are also important.

ROOF PENDANT: **Country rock** which overlies an igneous **intrusion**

SAG POND: A body of water or depression along a fault where recent activity has made drainage impossible; generally **left stepping** on a **right lateral** fault (or vice versa). Opposite is pressure ridge.

SCARPLET: A small-scale scarp (**escarpment**).

SCHIST: A **foliated** metamorphic rock with relatively thin individual folia (layers) and an intermediate grain size.

SEDIMENTARY ROCK: A layered rock which results from the consolidation of sediment (**clastic** or organic material or precipitated salts).

SIDE-STEPS: See **left step** and **left lateral.**

SILICATE: Compound with silica and oxygen in a definite **crystalline** structure; most common of the **rock-forming minerals** including quartz and feldspar.

SLIP: Distance of displacement along a fault.

SLOPE WASH: Rock material transported down a slope due to gravity and water that is not confined to a channel.

SPREADING ZONE, OR CENTER: The area where sea-floor spreading takes place and the oceanic crust is increased by the upwelling of **magma**. One of three types of tectonic plate boundaries; a constructive plate margin.

STEP FAULT: One of a set of parallel, closely spaced faults over which the entire stress is distributed, and offsetting to the left or right generally **en echelon**.

STRIKE: The compass direction of a surface feature, perpendicular to **dip**.

STRIKE-SLIP FAULT: A fault in which the relative displacement is primarily lateral (sideways) rather than up and down; a lateral fault.

SUPERPOSED (SUPERIMPOSED) STREAM: A stream that maintained its course as it eroded through layers of different character and composition; downcutting of a stream into uplifting terrain.

SWALE: A depressed area of land in a region of level land; often wet.

TECTONIC: Pertaining to the deformation of the earth's crust due to forces internal to the earth.

TERRESTRIAL: Of or relating to the planet Earth; also used to distinguish dry land from marine environments.

THRUST FAULT: A fault in which the **hanging wall** appears to have been raised above the **footwall**; same as a reverse fault. Opposite, **normal fault**.

TOMBOLO: A sandbar that connects an island to the mainland or another island.

TRANSCURRENT OR WRENCH FAULT: See **strike-slip fault**.

TRANSFORM FAULT: A major **strike-slip** fault, generally associated with a plate boundary or **spreading zone**. The San Andreas Fault Zone is an example.

TURBIDITE: A sediment deposited by a **turbidity** current; characterized by graded bedding. Turbid water is "not clear" water.

TURBIDITY CURRENT: A current created by a mass of water made more dense by suspended sediment that flows swiftly within another body of water, often along or near the bottom.

VOLCANIC ROCKS: (*Vulcan*, ancient god of fire). Extrusive, fine grained igneous rock which cooled and solidified after eruption or "extrusion" onto the surface of the earth. Opposite, see **plutonic**.

Font's Point Sandstone, representing a semi-arid environment of deposition, caps the alluvial fan-floodplain deposits of the Ocotillo Conglomerate which in turn overlies the ancient lakebed deposits of the Borrego Formation. The whole terrestrial series has been uplifted due to tectonic forces within the San Jacinto Fault Zone. PR

EARTHQUAKE ALMANAC

Salton Trough's Biggest Temblors Since 1850

DATE	LOCATION	RICHTER MAG.	FAULT ZONE (OR FAULT)
Nov. 29, 1852	Imperial Valley	M6.5	San Jacinto
Dec. 16, 1858	San Bernardino	M6.0	San Jacinto
Nov. 15, 1875	Imperial Valley	M7.0	San Jacinto
Feb. 09, 1891	San Jacinto	M6.3	San Jacinto
July 30, 1891	Colorado River Delta	M7.0	San Andreas
Feb. 23, 1892	Laguna Salada	M7.0	Elsinore*
May 28, 1892	San Jacinto	M6.3	San Jacinto
Oct. 23, 1894	Mts. east of San Diego	M5.6	Elsinore
July 22, 1899	Cajon Pass	M6.5	San Andreas
Dec. 25, 1899	Hemet, Riverside Co.	M6.8	San Jacinto
Jan. 23, 1903	Colorado River Delta	M7.0	San Andreas
Apr. 19, 1906	Imperial Valley	M6.0	San Jacinto
Sept. 20, 1907	San Bernardino	M6.0	San Jacinto
June 23, 1915	Imperial County	M6.3	San Jacinto
Nov. 20, 1915	Cerro Prieto	M7.1	Cerro Prieto
Apr. 21, 1918	San Jacinto	M7.2	San Jacinto
July 23, 1923	Riverside County	M6.2	San Jacinto
Dec. 31, 1934	Mexicali Valley	M7.1	San Jacinto
Mar. 25, 1937	Clark Lake/Buck Ridge	M6.0	San Jacinto
May 18, 1940	El Centro	M7.1	SJ (Imperial)
Apr. 09, 1941	Gulf of California	M6.0	San Andreas
Oct. 21, 1942	Carrizo Badlands	M6.5	San Jacinto
Dec. 04, 1948	Desert Hot Springs	M6.5	San Andreas
Nov. 04, 1949	Northern Baja Calif.	M5.7	Cerro Prieto
June 13, 1953	Imperial Valley	M5.5	San Jacinto
Mar. 19, 1954	Arroyo Salado	M6.4	San Jacinto
Nov. 12, 1954	Northern Baja Calif.	M6.3	Cerro Prieto
Feb. 09, 1956	El Alamo, Baja Calif.	M6.8	Cerro Prieto
Apr. 09, 1968	Borrego Mountain	M6.5	SJ (Coyote Creek)
Apr. 28, 1969	Borrego Valley	M5.8	San Jacinto
Oct. 15, 1979	Imperial Valley	M6.6	San Jacinto
Apr. 26, 1981	Westmoreland	M6.4	San Jacinto
July 08, 1986	Palm Springs	M5.9	SA (Banning)
Nov. 23, 1987	Elmore Ranch	M6.2	San Jacinto
Nov. 24, 1987	Superstition Hills	M6.6	SJ (Superstition Hills)
Jan. 25, 1988	Sierra Juarez Mtns.	M5.1	Laguna Salada
Apr. 22, 1992	Joshua Tree Nat. Mon.	M6.1	San Andreas
June 28, 1992	Landers & Yucca Valley	M7.5	San Andreas**
June 28, 1992	Big Bear	M6.6	San Andreas

* Strongest historic quake felt in San Diego County.
** Salton Trough's strongest historic quake

Selected California Earthquakes Since 1850
(not including those listed above)

DATE	LOCATION	RICHTER MAG.	FAULT ZONE (OR FAULT)
Jan. 09, 1857	Ft. Tejon, Kern Co.	M8.0	San Andreas
May 27, 1862	San Diego coast	M5.9	(Rose Canyon)
Mar. 26, 1872	Lone Pine	M8.3	Owens Valley
Apr. 18, 1906	San Francisco	M8.3	San Andreas
June 29, 1925	Santa Barbara	M6.3	(Sur-Nacimiento)
Mar. 10, 1933	Long Beach	M6.3	(Newport-Inglewood)
July 21, 1952	Tehachapi, Kern Co.	M7.7	(White Wolf)
Mar. 27, 1964	Alaska	M9.2	Turnagin Sound*
Feb. 09, 1971	San Fernando	M6,6	(San Fernando)
May 02, 1983	Coalinga	M6.7	San Andreas
Oct. 01, 1987	Whittier Narrows	M6.1	Elsinore
Oct. 17, 1989	Loma Prieta	M7.1	San Andreas
Apr. 25, 1992	Ferndale (near Eureka)	M6.9	San Andreas

* Earthquake was centered in Alaska, however, its induced tsunami devastated Crescent City, Calif.

THE RICHTER SCALE (Compiled by P. Remcika)

The Richter scale, named after Dr. Charles F. Richter of Cal Tech, is the best known scale for measuring the strength, or magnitude, of an earthquake at its source. This scale ascribes a measurement, or magnitude index, to the ground motion of an earthquake. This measurement is expressed as a number preceded by "M" (e.g. M5.2, M6.0, etc.). By Richter's definition, the scale is logarithmic; thus, an earthquake with a magnitude of 5.0 is 10 times as strong on the scale as an M4.0 and 100 times more violent than a M3.0. Theoretically, there is no upper level or lower limit to the Richter Scale. (It is possible to have measurable negative magnitudes.) The lowest magnitude normally felt is about M2.0, while the strongest earthquake ever recorded in North America was the Good Friday Alaskan Quake of 1964, at M9.2.

The Richter magnitude of an earthquake is obtained by measuring the height (amplitude) of ground waves with seismograph instruments. For example, the amplitude of ground motion during the 1965 Borrego Mountain Earthquake (estimate at M6.5) was about 10 times greater than that of the 1953 Imperial Valley Earthquake (M5.5).

Measurement of the ground motion provides an indirect measurement of the energy radiated by a seismic event. According to this scale, the energy increases approximately 30-fold with each index of magnitude. Thus an M7.0 earthquake releases about 30 times the energy of a M6.0 and about 900 times as much as a M5.0.

RICHTER SCALE	DESCRIPTION
Magnitude -3	Smallest recorded quakes
Magnitude 2	Smallest quake normally felt by residents
Magnitude 3	Quake may cause slight damage
Magnitude 4	Quake may cause moderate damage
Magnitude 5	Quake may cause considerable damage
Magnitude 6	A "large" earthquake; can cause severe damage
Magnitude 7	A "major" earthquake; capable of widespread damage
Magnitude 8	A "great" earthquake; capable of tremendous damage
Magnitude 9.2	Highest recorded temblor in North America (Alaska, 1964); almost total destruction

The EARTHQUAKE ALMANAC was compiled by P. Remeika and L. Lindsay. Sources were:

D. Agnew, SDAG   *Earthquake History of San Diego* (1979)
   GSA Field Trip

S. Goter, NEIC   *Seismicity of California* (1988)

P. Kern   *Earthquakes and Faults in San Diego County* (1989)

R. Wallace (editor)   *The San Andreas Fault System,* USGS Professional Paper 31515 (1990)

K. Bullock   *It's Your Fault* (1992)

SELECTED RECENT ABSTRACTS - GEOLOGY AND PALEONTOLOGY OF THE ANZA-BORREGO REGION

The following abstracts represent papers developed by Paul Remeika or presented by others at one of the Desert Symposia at Borrego Springs, sponsored by the Anza-Borrego Foundation and organized by Dr. James and Grace Rickard. They are offered as examples of available material for researchers and students in these fields in the Anza-Borrego region.

MARCH 11, 1989 SYMPOSIUM

GEOLOGY FROM JULIAN TO INDIO

Herb Arkin (U.S. Forest Service)

A transect from Julian to Indio crosses the Elsinore, San Jacinto and San Andreas Fault zones at about right angles. Right lateral slip on these faults since the late Miocene, 5 million years ago, is at least 25 km for the Elsinore, 15 km for the San Jacinto and 200 km for the San Andreas.

For 70 km of the 90 km transect it crosses the Cretaceous, 90-110 million year old, Peninsular Ranges Batholith. Roof pendant metasediments of Triassic age, about 210-240 million years old, overlay the batholith for 32 km at random along the transect. These metasediments include the Julian Schist of interbedded quartz-mica schist and quartzite, and quartz-biotite gneiss.

Batholithic rocks are exposed for 18 km along the transect and consist of granite, granodiorite, tonalite or diorite. They are gray medium to coarse-grained rocks and weather to exfoliated boulders.

The remainder of the transect is of Pleistocene and Holocene age, less than 2 million years old, and includes alluvium, the Salton Trough and the Martinez Mountain Rock Avalanche. The Salton Trough is a graben with several thousand meters of terrestrial strata. The 2000 meter high granite Martinez Mountain slid down to the northeast for 8 km about 20,000 years ago. This avalanche includes 240 x $(10)^6$ m3 of rock (Baldwin, 1980).

A PRELIMINARY REPORT ON HALF-A-MILLION-YEAR-OLD CUTMARKS ON MAMMOTH BONES FROM THE ANZA-BORREGO DESERT IRVINGTONIAN

George J. Miller, Paul Remeika, Julia D. Parks, Betty Stout, and Vern Waters (Imperial Valley College Museum)

Bones of an adult male mammoth (*Mammuthus* sp.), closely related to the Imperial mammoth, have been discovered in the Anza-Borrego Desert State Park, San Diego County, California. The nearly complete skeleton was found *in situ* in Irvingtonian Land Mammal Age sediments (Late Pleistocene). A rib bone with V-shaped cuts was found 2.51 meters below the top of the Pleistocene beds. Studies of the cuts show that they were made with a chopping motion. It is suggested that the cuts were made by early hominids using a primitive stone chopper or hand axe.   Radiometric, faunal and paleomagnetic dates show the site to be from 300,000 to 720,000 years old.

BAT CAVE BUTTES - AN ISLAND IN HOLOCENE LAKE CAHUILLA

Neil J. Maloney (Department of Geiological Sciences, California State University, Fullerton)

Bat Cave Buttes, located about a mile east of Highway 111 along the Riverside and Imperial County line, was an island during the last filling of Lake Cahuilla 1200 - 400 years ago. The buttes form the highest points, 31 meters above sea level, of an elongated hill that was uplifted along the east side of the San Andreas fault. You walk to the buttes over the lake bottom which consists of the eroded surface of Borrego and Shavers Well Formations.

Shoreline features including beaches, tufa lines and erosional shoreline angles occur at elevations of 12.1 to 16.0 meters. The extensive development of wave eroded surge channels on the northwest and together with the deposition of sand to the east of the buttes show that the principal wind direction was from the northwest.

The almost four meter variation in the elevation of the shoreline features could have resulted from recent deformation along the San Andreas fault located to the west. An erosional surface occurs on top of the buttes at an elevation of about 30 meters. This may be a small uplifted segment of an older lake bottom.

EARTHQUAKE HISTORY OF THE SAN JACINTO FAULT

G. Simila and C. Wang (Department of Geological Sciences, California State University, Northridge, CA 91330)

The historical record for the San Jacinto fault during 1890-1986 reveals that this fault has been the most seismically active zone in Southern California. Investigators believe that at least 6 to 10 magnitude 6 or greater events have occurred. In addition, the Anza to Coyote Mountain region has been identified as a seismic gap capable of a M6.5 future earthquake. This zone is between the 1918 San Jacinto and 1968 Borrego Mountain ruptures. The region is not aseismic, and the level of microseismicity indicates that several branches of the main fault are active. The general style of faulting is right lateral strike slip, The general seismicity patterns from near San Bernardino to the Imperial Valley will be presented.

APRIL 13, 1991 SYMPOSIUM

DROUGHT CYCLES IN THE SOUTHWESTERN UNITED STATES - AN HISTORIC PERSPECTIVE

David Harbison, (Coachella Valley Water District)

The major controlling factor of weather in the Western United States is the Mid-Pacific high pressure system. The position of this high pressure system controls the flow of moisture across the Pacific Ocean, where storms generate and where they meet the west coast.

The normal position of this high allows the majority of storms to hit from San Francisco to southern Canada. As the high pressure moves the storm track moves in reaction, allowing Pacific storms to hit different parts of the west coast.

A major factor in storm generation from the Pacific Ocean is water temperature. Weather scientists still do not fully understand the causes and cycles of the ocean temperature.

The record of storms and drought in the West is found in soil profiles and in tree rings. Each major storm brings down more alluvial material from the mountains and hills then distributes it in an interwoven pattern across the alluvial plain. High on the alluvial plain is deposited the most coarse material. Farther out the medium material is deposited and finally the last material deposited is silt and clay particles. The strength of a given storm and the wetness of the soil determine how far down on the alluvial plain the material is deposited.

Tree rings give the best record of rainfall during the growing season. Very thin rings indicate very poor growing conditions whereas thicker rings indicate more growth because of more available moisture.

Tree ring studies indicate that in the West the normal weather pattern is periods of drought offset by periods of ample water. The drought period may be short or in some cases drought appears to have persisted for 30 to 50 years when a period of several centuries is studied.

The tree rings do not tell why a weather pattern has persisted for a period of time.

The current drought in the West seems to be a normal occurrence when viewed from a historic perspective. This current drought shows the critical need for planning water supplies to match the needs of a growing population, otherwise we are going to have to learn to live with less water in our lives.

DESERT CLIMATES AND ANZA-BORREGO

W. G. Hample (Sunbelt Publications)

The author is a state registered mechanical engineer who, as a second career, publishes outdoor books. He travels at least once per month between his office in Bakersfield and the publishing office in San Diego, via the Mojave and Colorado Desert areas with which he has had a love affair since the days of his early youth. Over this period many questions have come to mind. If elevation, temperature and maximum precipitation are defining criteria, why are not areas such as the Bakersfield region, where measured values are similar to those of Borrego Springs, considered deserts? Why does the Anza-Borrego Desert region differ from other California desert regions? Finally, are there derivations which can be obtained from the reams of commonly measured precipitation, temperature, and elevation data which might define and categorize regions in California as specific desert types? The author presents the results of analyses of regional California data.

STATUS REPORT ON THREE MAJOR CAMELID TRACKSITES IN THE LOWER PLIOCENE DELTA SEQUENCE, VALLECITO-FISH CREEK BASIN, ANZA-BORREGO DESERT STATE PARK, CA.

B. W. Stout, P. Remeika (Anza-Borrego Desert State Park and Imperial Valley College Museum)

The latest discovery of Neogene ichnites (footprints or tracks) from the Hemphillian-Blancan transition provides vertebrate paleontologists with a rare opportunity to study tetrapod (four footed) trackmakers in a stratigraphically continuous section.   This project involves the description and interpretation of three lower Pliocene track-bearing sites in the Vallecito-Fish Creek Basin: Hanging Tracks Wash, Fish Creek Wash (new), and Camel Ridge.

Exposures in Hanging Tracks Wash include large cloven-hoofed tetrapod footprints, indentified as belonging to the Hemphillian-Blancan camel *Megalytopus*. Fish Creek Wash contains footprints which compare favorably with *Megalytopus*, and a second camelid trackway representing the Blancan camelopine *Camelops*. In the same horizon are recently discovered tracks tentatively described as *Hypolagus*. Of the many footprints studied at Camel Ridge two sized compare favorably with *Camelops* and the llama *Hemiauchenia*.

This important site has been assigned a paleo-magnetic date of 3.08 MYBP and also yields rare avian (bird) and felid (cat) footprints.

EXPLORATIONS IN GEOLOGIC TIME - EIGHT FIELD TRIPS IN ANZA-BORREGO
Lowell Lindsay (Grossmont College -- Extended Studies)

The three major regimes of Paleozoic metamorphism, Mesozoic batholithic intrusion, and Cenozoic volcanism and sedimentation are presented through the medium of eight field trips developed for Sunbelt Publications' desert natural history series. This series is being field tested for user interest and comprehension through Grossmont College Extension programs in Anza-Borrego Desert State Park and the surrounding desert region.   Major interpretive perspectives have been provided by Regional Administrative Officer Fred Jee (geology) and Park Naturalist Mark Jorgensen (interpretive technique).

A PRELIMINARY REPORT ON CALCAREOUS TUFA DEPOSITS FROM THE PALO VERDE WASH AREA: EVIDENCE FOR THE EXISTENCE OF A PRE-LAKE CAHUILLA STRANDLINE IN THE BORREGO BADLANDS
Paul Remeika (Anza-Borrego Desert State Park)

At least one earlier Pleistocene ice-age lake left behind evidence of a pre-Lake Cahuillan strandline (beachline). Recently discovered calcareous tufa deposits near Palo Verde Wash are the first evidence and identification that a much larger pluvial lake existed within the Salton Trough at ca. 800 feet above sea level. Two distinctly layered beach cobblebeds have been found, *in situ*, with thin imbricating laminae of microcrystalline calcium carbonate encrusting the alluvial clasts.

Faulting associated with movements along the Clark Fault have raised, rotated and deformed the tufaceous beds, dipping 36 degrees to the southwest. The exposures are buried by relic alluvial geomorphic surfaces washed from the fan-frayed Santa Rosa Mountains. They range in age from approximately 7-13 ky (Onken and Rathburn, written comm., 1988). The presence of calcareous tufa not only documents the existence and desiccation of a vanished lake but suggests a combination of tectonic uplift, Late Quaternary glacial-interglacial climatically-induced warming and increased aridity were fundamental variables in the desertification of Anza-Borrego prior to the terminal Pleistocene.

FORMATIONAL STATUS FOR THE DIABLO REDBEDS; DIFFERENTIATING BETWEEN COLORADO RIVER AFFINITIES AND THE PALM SPRING FORMATION

Paul Remeika (Anza-Borrego Desert State Park)

Recognition of locally-derived basin-margin sediments (Palm Spring Formation) versus Colorado River-derived sandstones (Diablo Member of the Palm Spring Formation) is useful in establishing correct nomenclature and stratigraphic control. For example, in the Vallecito-Fish Creek Basin these two distinct depositional suites form unrelated genetic-stratigraphic affinities that can be readily identified in the field. The Diablo redbeds are pale orange, fine grained, well sorted, quartz-rich arenite sandstones, with subordinate claystones, that form conspicuous strike ridges. In marked contrast, the overlying Palm Spring sediments are tan-gray, coarse to fine grained, poorly sorted, feldspar-rich, arkosic sandstones with gravelly conglomerates. Both units are sedimentologically, stratigraphically and paleontologically dissimilar.

Diablo-like lithologies are very distinctive in appearance. They are the most extensively exposed Neogene sedimentary unit in Anza-Borrego and not genetically synonymous with the Palm Spring Formation that is restricted in outcrop to the Vallecito Badlands. Based on petrographic evidence alone, I herein recommend the Diablo be reclassified into the ranks of the compositionally similar Colorado River-derived deltaic package and recommend its elevation to formational status.

ADDITIONAL CONTRIBUTIONS TO THE NEOGENE PALEOBOTANY OF THE VALLECITO-FISH CREEK BASIN AND VICINITY

Paul Remeika (Anza-Borrego Desert State Park)

Lower Pliocene palm fronds from the Vallecito-Fish Creek Basin mark the first occurrence of fossil leaf material in Anza-Borrego. The specimens were discovered, *in situ*, from cross-stratified paleochannel sandstones between the Diablo facies and Olla Member of the Canebrake Conglomerate (IVCM 1856). Until now, no evidence of petrified palm has been found in Anza-Borrego. Collected specimens resemble the extant fan palm *Erythea brandegeei* of Baja California in appearance.

In 1986, George Miller and the author produced the first significant fossil samples of the Dudley Willow *Salix gooddingii* known to science. These were recovered from lacustral claystones of pluvial Lake Cahuilla (Later Pleistocene to Holocene). Until now, the oldest specimen preserved was collected in 1845 by John C. Fremont during his expedition to California. Today *Salix gooddingii* is a common species of willow, widespread throughout the southwestern United States and Mexico; Paleoenvironmentally, *Salix gooddingii* preferred the riparian distribuary channels of the Colorado River and confirms a climate of arid temperatures.

STRATIGRAPHIC REVISION AND DEPOSITIONAL ENVIRONMENTS OF THE MIDDLE TO LATE PLEISTOCENE OCOTILLO CONGLOMERATE, BORREGO BADLANDS

Paul Remeika (Anza-Borrego Desert State Park); Jarg R. Pettinga (University of Canterbury, New Zealand)

We recognize three lithofacies that establish stratigraphic control and age determinations for the Middle to Late Pleistocene Ocotillo Conglomerate. In ascending order, they are the Mammoth Cove Sandstone (new name), Inspiration Wash (new name), and Font's Point Sandstone (new name).

The fossiliferous Mammoth Cove Sandstone represents a locally-derived distal alluvial fan facies. It thins basinward into sheetflood deposits along the Ocotillo Rim. Torrential bedding, lenticular bandings of sediment and climbing ripple lamination indicate rapid deposition. The basal contact with the Borrego Formation is 1.25 MYA (Schueing, written comm., 1991). Extinct vertebrates, heretofore undescribed in the paleontological literature, index the Irvingtonian Land Mammal Age.

Inspiration Wash consists of fluvially-deposited channel sands, gravels and lacustral silts and clays. Recently discovered ash beds represent the Bishop Tuff at 0.73 MYA, marking the Matuyama-Bruhnes geomagnetic boundary. The extinct megafauna is Late Irvingtonian-Rancholabrean in age. The upper contact is defined by an erosion surface having a paleomagnetic signature of 0.37 MYA (Schueing, written comm., 1991).

The Font's Point Sandstone represents the reddish caprock of the Font's Point promontory. It is crudely-bedded and locally conglomeratic. Distinctive mottled zones of caliche indicate a semi-arid environment of deposition during the Late Pleistocene.

REVIEW OF PALEOBOTANY AND PALYNOLOGY, 56 (1988)

LOWER PLIOCENE PETRIFIED WOOD FROM THE PALM SPRING FORMATION, ANZA-BORREGO DESERT STATE PARK, CALIFORNIA

Paul Remeika, Irwin W. Fischbein, and Steven A. Fischbein

ABSTRACT

This investigation identifies the abundant petrified wood found in the basal Diablo Member of the Palm Spring Formation, Anza-Borrego Desert State Park. Three families of temperate hardwood trees are recognized from the fossil wood cell structure. The *Lauraceae* represented by *Umbellularia,* the *Salicaceae* with specimens of *Populus* and *Salix,* and the *Juglandaceae* represented by *Juglans.* A review of the paleontologic and paleomagnetic literature established the base of the Diablo Member at approximately 3.8 m.y. B.P. with continued deposition for 1.2 m.y.

The unique paleobotanical assemblage found in the Diablo Member together with the floral ecology of present-day equivalents reflects a temperate climate with ocean influence and predominantly winter rainfall in this region during the Lower Pliocene Epoch.

INTRODUCTION

The purposes of this study are to identify the fossil wood found within the basal Diablo Member of the Palm Spring Formation and to decipher the paleo-habitat which reigned during the accumulation of these ancestral Colorado River sediments. This will add to the overall picture of the Pliocene paleomammology and chronology for this region established by Downs and White (1968).

The Palm Spring Formation is notable for a number of reasons: (1) The stratigraphic sequence yields one of the richest records of Blancan-Irvingtonian fossil vertebrate faunas in North America (Downs and White, 1968); (2) its extensive dimension, vertical thickness and lateral extent (Woodard, 1963); (3) it spans a locally documented magnetic polarity biochronologic framework (Opdyke et al., 1977); (4) the untouched, remote, arid, uninhabited terrain preserves and protects a high content and quality of surface petrified wood and other fossil materials.

The area of study encompasses the broad west-central part of the Vallecito Basin, in the southern Anza-Borrego Desert, 43 km south of Borrego Springs.

FROM THE MOJAVE DESERT QUATERNARY RESEARCH SYMPOSIUM, 1992

PRELIMINARY REPORT ON THE STRATIGRAPHY AND VERTEBRATE FAUNA OF THE MIDDLE PLEISTOCENE OCOTILLO FORMATION, BORREGO BADLANDS

Paul Remeika, (Paleontology Coordinator, Anza-Borrego Desert State Park)

The vertebrate-bearing Ocotillo Formation (redesignated) represents a locally-derived Middle Pleistocene continental fluvial-floodplain sequence of gravelly sandstones, silts and clays exposed throughout the western half of the Borrego Badlands and Coyote Badlands. The stratotype is located in the Arroyo Otto-Mammoth Cove section, above and below the Ocotillo Rim north of the Inspiration Point Fault. To establish stratigraphic control and age determinations, Remeika and Pettinga (1991) recognized two previously undefined lithofacies for the Ocotillo Formation. This report includes a lacustrine facies. In ascending order they include a 74 meter thick distal alluvial fan sequence (Mammoth Cove Sandstone Member), a 87 meter thick series of freshwater lacustrine beds (unnamed), and a 216 meter thick mixed composition fluvial-floodplain interbeds (Inspiration Wash Member). The contact with the underlying Borrego Formation, at 1.25 MYA (Schneing, pers. comm. 1989), is gradational. In the Borrego Badlands, the Ocotillo Formation is overlain by thick alluvial plain deposits of the Late Pleistocene Font's Point Sandstone.

Work initiated in the 1970s by Ted Downs, Harland Garbani (LACM), and the late George Miller (IVCM) led to cyclic prospecting and recovery of a rich vertebrate megafauna, represented by 33 mammalian genera. This Borrego Local Fauna (new name) is a heretofore unreported fossil assemblage of at least 5,000 catalogued specimens, collected from more than 400 paleontologic localities in the Ocotillo Formation. Most of the composite fauna (Table I) is based upon fragmentary remains and only a few articulated specimens have been found. Diagnostic species include *Camelops huerfanensis, Equus (Dolichohippus) enormuus, Mammuthus imperator, Smilodon gracilis, Equus (Dolichohippus) simplicidens, Borophagus sp., and Arctodus sp.* A Late Irvingtonian Land Mammal Age (LMA) is indicated. The occurrence of *Microtus californicus, Mammuthus columbi, Equus (Equus) sp. indet., Lepus cf. L. californicus,* and *Ovibos moschatus* appear only in the youngest levels of the Inspiration Wash Member (possible early Rancholabrean LMA) above a recently discovered tephra which may correlate to the Bishop Tuff (Adams, pers. comm. 1992). Equids and camelids are the most common taxa. In addition, various-sized tetrapod footprints comparable to the coeval ichnogenus *Pecoripeda (Ovipeda)* occur in the unnamed lacustrine beds. These require further study and may be attributable to *Camelops* and larger *Gigantocamelus.*

TABLE I
BORREGO LOCAL FAUNA (COMPOSITE)

Clemmys sp.	western pond turtle
Accipiter cooperii	Cooper's hawk
Phoenicopterus sp.	playa-like flamingo
Nothrotheriops shastensis	small ground sloth
Glossotherium sp.	giant ground sloth
Lepus sp. cf. L. californicus	jackrabbit
Microtus californicus	California vole
Geomys sp.	pocket gopher
Borophagus sp.	bone-crushing hyaenoid dog
Canis dirus	dire wolf
Arctodus sp.	short-faced bear
Felis (Lyns) rufus	bobcat
Panthera atrox	North American lion
Smilodon gracilis	gracile sabertooth cat
S. californicus	Californian sabertooth cat
Mammuthus columbi	columbian mammoth
M. imperator	imperial mammoth
Equus (Equus) sp. indet.	western cabaline horse
E. (Dolichohippus) enormuus	giant Anza-Borregan zebra
E. (D.) simplicidens	American zebra
E. (D.) sp.	small zebra
E. bautistensis	western horse
E. hemionus	half ass
Camelops sp.	American camelopine
C. huerfanensis	early dromedary camelopine
C. hesternus	western camel
Gigantocamelus sp.	giant camel
Hemiachenia sp.	llama
Odocoileus sp.	mule deer
Tetrameryx sp	4-tined pronghorn antelope
Capromeryx sp.	small pronghorn antelope
Ovibos moschatus	ox
Euceratherium sp.	shrub-oxen

Author Paul Remeika sketches the Pliocene delta shoreline history of the Diablo Formation in the Vallecito Badlands for members of the Society of Vertebrate Paleontology. LL

Fossil skull of the American Zebra (Equus or Dolichohippus simplicidens) in Ocotillo Conglomerate in the Borrego Badlands. PR

SELECTED BIBLIOGRAPHY
EARTH SCIENCES IN THE ANZA-BORREGO REGION

1.   Abbott, P.L. and Abbott, J.V., eds. 1977. *Geologic Hazards in San Diego County*. San Diego Society of Natural History.
2.   Abbott, P.L. "Geology and Deserts" in *Environment Southwest, Summer 1988*. San Diego Society of Natural History.
3.   Abbott, P.L. "The Rose Canyon Fault" in *Environment Southwest Winter/Spring 1989*. San Diego Society of Natural History.
4.   Abbott, P.L., and Todd, V.R., eds. 1979. *Mesozoic Crystalline Rocks: Peninsular Ranges Batholith and Pegmatites, Point Sal Ophiolite*. Dept. Geol. Sciences, San Diego State University. 286p.
5.   Bartholomew, M.J. "San Jacinto Fault Zone in the Northern Imperial Valley" in *Geological Society of America Bulletin, V. 80*. October 1970.
6.   Berger, J., and Wyatt, F. "Measurements of Strain Accumulation Between the San Andreas and San Jacinto Faults" in *Proceedings of the Conference on Tectonic Problems, V. 13, 1973*. pp. 80-85. Stanford University Publications, Geological Sciences.
7.   Brown, A.R., and Ruff, R.W., eds. 1981. *Geology of the San Jacinto Mountains. Annual Field Trip Guidebook No. 9*. South Coast Geological Society, Santa Ana, California. 219p.
8.   Crowell, J., and Sylvester, A.G., eds. 1979. *Tectonics of the Juncture Between the San Andreas Fault System and the Salton Trough, Southeastern California. A Guidebook*. Dept. Geol. Sciences, University of California, Santa Barbara. 193p.
9.   Demere, T.A. "Paleontology and Our Local Desert" in *Environment Southwest, Summer 1988*. San Diego Society of Natural History.
10.   Estavillo, W. "Treasures of the Peninsular Range" (2 parts) in *Environment Southwest, Fall 1988, Fall 1989*. San Diego Society of Natural History.
11.   Evans, J.R., ed. 1988. *Landslides in Crystalline Basement Terrain*. San Diego Association of Geologists.
12.   Gastil, R.G., Phillips, R.P., and Allison, E.C., 1973. *Reconnaissance Geology of Baja California*. Geological Society of America.
13.   Greeley, R., Womer, M.B., Papson, R.P., and Spudis, P.D., eds. 1979. *Aeolian Features of Southern California* including "Geological Aspects of the Salton Trough," "Field Trip to Dunes at Superstition Mountain," "Geological Field Guide to the Salton Trough." *Dept. of Geology, Arizona State University, Tempe. Office of Planetary Geology, NASA, Washington D.C.: USGPO*.
14.   Guptil, P.D., Gath, E.M., and Ruff, R.W., eds. 1986. *Geology of the Imperial Valley. Annual Field Trip Guidebook, No. 14*. South Coast Geological Society, Santa Ana, California. 225p.
15.   Hart, M.W., and Dowlen, R.J., eds. 1974. *Recent Geological and Hydrologic Studies, Eastern San Diego County and Adjacent Areas. A Guidebook*. San Diego Association of Geologists. 101p.
16.   Jahns, R.H., ed. 1954. *Geology of Southern California Bulletin 170*. California Division of Mines and Geology.

17. Jee, F. "Geology of Anza-Borrego: A Window to the Past" in
     Environment Southwest, Autumn 1985. San Diego Society of Natural
     History.
18. Johnson, P.R. "The Desert Beckons" in *Environment Southwest,*
     Summer 1988. San Diego Society of Natural History.
19. Krinsley, D.H., and Dorn, R.I. "New Eyes on Eastern California Rock
     Varnish" in *California Geology May 1991.* California Division of Mines
     and Geology.
20. Lindsay, D.L. 1973. *Our Historic Desert.* San Diego, California: Copley
     Press.
21. Livingston Jr., A. 1968. *Geological Journeys in Southern California.*
     Dubuque, Iowa: Wm. C. Brown Co.
22, Merriam, R. 1958. *Geology and Mineral Resources of Santa Ysabel*
     Quadrangle Bulletin 177. California Division of Mines and Geology.
23. Miller, G.J. "A Look Into the Past of the Anza-Borrego Desert" in
     Environment Southwest, Summer 1985. San Diego Society of Natural
     History.
24. Morton, P.K. 1977. Geology and Mineral Resources of Imperial County,
     California *County Report 7.* California Division of Mines and Geology.
25. Norris, R.M., Webb, R.W. 1976. *Geology of California.* New York:
     John Wiley.
26. Oakeshott, G.B., 1971. *California's Changing Landscape: a Guide to the*
     Geology of the State. New York: McGraw Hill, Inc.
27. Powell, C.L. 1986. *Stratigraphy and Bivalve Molluscan Paleontology of*
     the Neogene Imperial Formation in Riverside County, California. M.S.
     Thesis, San Jose State University. 275p.
28. Pridmore, C.L., and Frost, E.G. "Detachment Faults - California's
     Extended Past" in *California Geology Jan. 1992.* California Division of
     Mines and Geology.
29. Remeika, P. 1990. *Landscapes of Time. Outcroppings, Paleontology and*
     Geologic History of Anza-Borrego Desert State Park. Unpublished
     Manuscript, Anza-Borrego Desert Natural History Association. 336p.
30. Remeika, P., Fischbein, I.W., and Fischbein, S.A. 1988. "Lower
     Pliocene Petrified Wood from the Palm Spring Formation" in *Review of*
     Paleobotany and Palynology, V. 56, pp. 183-198.
31. Rigsby, C.A. 1984. *The Imperial Basin--Tectonics, Sedimentation and*
     Thermal Aspects. Pacific Section, S.E.P.M., Los Angeles, California.
32. Schmidt, N. "Plate Tectonics and the Gulf of California Region" in
     Arizona Geology Summer 1990. Arizona Geological Survey, Tucson.
33. Sharp, R.V. 1967. "San Jacinto Fault Zone in the Peninsular Ranges of
     Southern California" in *Geol. Society of America Bulletin, V. 78,*
     pp. 705-730.
34. Walawender, M.J., and Hanan, B.B., eds. 1991. *Geological Excursions*
     in Southern California and Mexico. Guidebook. Geological Society of
     America, San Diego, California. 503p.
35. Wallace, R.E., ed. 1990. *The San Andreas Fault System.* USGS
     Professional Paper 1515, Washington D.C.: USGPO.
36. Weber, F.H. 1969. *Geology and Mineral Resources of San Diego*
     County, California. California Division of Mines and Geology.

37.   White, J.A., Lindsay, E.H., Remeika, P., Stout, B.W., Downs, T., and
        Cassiliano, M. 1991. *Society of Vertebrate Paleontology Field Trip Guide
        to the Anza-Borrego Desert.* Society of Vertebrate Paleontology, 51st
        Annual Meeting, San Diego, California. 23p.
38.   Winker, C.D. 1987. *Neogene Stratigraphy of the Fish Creek-Vallecito
        Section, Southern California: Implications for Early History of the
        Northern Gulf of California and Colorado Delta.* PhD. Dissertation, Univ.
        Ariz., Tucson. 494p.
39.   Woodard, G.D. 1963. *The Cenozoic Succession of the West Colorado
        Desert, San Diego and Imperial Counties, Southern California.* PhD
        Dissertation, Univ. Of California at Berkeley. 173p.

MAPS

1.   Jennings, C.W. 1967. *Salton Sea Sheet of the Geologic Map of
        California.* Calif. Division of Mines and Geology. Scale 1:250,000.
2.   Morton, P.K. 1966. *Geologic Map of Imperial County, California.* Calif.
        Division of Mines and Geology. Scale 1:125,000.
3.   Rogers, T.H. 1965.   *Santa Ana Sheet of the Geologic Map of California.*
        Calif. Division of Mines and Geology. Scale 1:250,000.
4.   Strand, R.G. 1962. *San Diego - El Centro Sheet of the Geologic Map of
        California.* Calif. Division of Mines and Geology. Scale 1:250,000.

*Bubbling mudpots, volcanic outcrops, and geothermal wells on the southeast
shore of the Salton Sea are evidence of molten magma nearing the surface, there
to cool and create new crustal material. Anza-Borrego lies on the western edge of
this creation. LL*

RECOMMENDED READING LIST
GEOLOGY AND GENERAL GUIDES TO THE ANZA-BORREGO REGION

The following books and maps are currently in print (1992). Many are available at the Anza-Borrego Visitor Center and all are available at major bookstores in Southern California. Contact Sunbelt Publications, telephone (619) 258-4911, for more information. These titles are recommended as a general introduction to the desert region and earth science in the southwest with annotations that relate the title to Anza-Borrego.

Key natural history guides and maps of Baja California are included because of the geologic and biologic continuity of the Peninsular Ranges, Sonoran Desert, and Salton Trough/Gulf of California natural provinces across the international border. "To understand Borrego, you must understand Baja."

ADVENTURING IN THE CALIFORNIA DESERT Foster 0-87156-721-0
(Sierra Club)
Best single reference to the natural history and destinations in the local deserts including numerous walks and drives in Anza-Borrego, Yuha Desert, and Salton Sea. Excellent chapters on desert climate and geology "Reading the Rocks."

AFOOT AND AFIELD IN SAN DIEGO COUNTY Schad 0-89997-057-5
(Wilderness Press)
Over one-third of this best-selling guide is allocated to desert and desert mountain hikes and walks with extensive commentary on trailside natural features and geological points of interest.

AGENTS OF CHAOS Harris 0-87842-243-9 (Mountain Press)
This exploration of earthquakes, volcanos and other natural disasters reminds us that our planet, subject to chaotic forces, pulsates like a living organism. Its geographic emphasis is California and the West Coast.

ANZA-BORREGO DESERT REGION, 3rd ed. Lindsay 0-89997-129-6
(Wilderness Press)
Latest updates to the comprehensive guide to Southern California's most popular desert playground. Includes detailed map (also available separately). Features overviews of natural history by topic and area with details at checkpoints.

ANZA-BORREGO DESERT STATE PARK Johnson, Jorgensen, Daniel
0-910805-01-6 (ABDNIIA)
A book of stunning color photographs with text that captures, with acute sensitivity, the geology, scenery, and ever-shifting moods of Anza-Borrego's varied desert landscape in all seasons of the year and times of the day.

AUDUBON FIELD GUIDE TO NORTH AMERICAN FOSSILS Thompson
0-394-52412-8 (Random House)
The 474 color plates are keyed to basic fossil shape and color with detailed descriptions to aid in field identification. Fossil bearing rock formations are also described and pictured to facilitate location.

AUDUBON FIELD GUIDE TO NORTH AMERICAN ROCKS & MINERALS
Chesterman 0-394-50269-8 (Random House)
The 794 color plates are organized for quick identification of all important rocks, gems, and mineral species in their many variations of color and crystal form. Additional keys based on hardness, cleavage, streak, and environment.

AUDUBON POCKET GUIDE TO FAMILIAR FOSSILS OF NORTH
AMERICA 0-394-75791-2 (Random House)
Eighty of the most abundant fossils, representing 12 basic groups of invertebrates and plants, are illustrated in color and described in this handy volume. Introductory essays and a glossary round out the basics of the subject.

AUDUBON POCKET GUIDE TO FAMILIAR ROCKS AND MINERALS OF NORTH AMERICA 0-394-75794-7 (Random House)
Pictured are 68 common minerals and 12 rocks with important field marks, colors, crystal form, and environment. Introductory text and many clear charts differentiate various classes of rocks and minerals and facilitate identification features.

BACKCOUNTRY ROADS AND TRAILS: SAN DIEGO COUNTY Schad
0-911518-72-X (Touchstone)
One-third of this economical book describes the natural environments and points of interest in San Diego's desert areas. The well-known author is a community college physical science instructor and popular outdoor guide.

BAJA CALIFORNIA PLANT FIELD GUIDE Roberts 0-9603144-0-7 (Natural History Press)
This popular guide contains an excellent introduction to Baja's plant environment with discussions on geography, geology, and climate of the peninsula of which the Anza-Borrego region is geologically a part.

BAJA HIGHWAY: A GEOLOGY AND BIOLOGY FIELD GUIDE FOR THE BAJA TRAVELER Minch and Leslie 0-96321090-0-6 (John Minch & Associates)
This may well be considered THE natural history guide along Baja's highways with a clear summary of its geologic development and numerous diagrams of geological features applicable to arid areas throughout the Southwest.

BAJA SATELLITE MAP No ISBN (Map Centre)
A 38" x 14" high gloss color enhanced satellite image of the entire Baja peninsula taken from an altitude of 580 miles, including the Salton Trough, Anza-Borrego, and the coast and mountains of San Diego County.

CALIFORNIA LANDSCAPE: ORIGIN AND EVOLUTION Hill
0-520-04849-0 (Univ. of Calif. Press)
A survey of the recent history of California landforms as they have been shaped in the last 10,000 years, describing the constructive process of mountain-building and destructive process of erosion with a chapter on "The Dynamic Desert."

CALIFORNIA DESERT RECREATION MAP 1-56575-006-3 (Compass Maps)
The only general utility map that shows the Salton Trough region as a whole

including San Diego, Imperial, and Riverside Counties. Accurate roads, trails, and natural features are displayed.

CALIFORNIA, NEVADA...PAST, PRESENT, FUTURE   No ISBN (Raven Maps and Images)
A novel map of this shifting region, including a projection 5 million years into the future, when the Gulf of California once again extends north to Palm Springs and west into the Anza-Borrego region. Printed in five colors. 29" x 43".

EARTHQUAKES AND FAULTS IN SAN DIEGO COUNTY Kern
0-9622845-0-5 (Philip Kern)
This popular guide discusses earthquake hazards, prediction, and preparedness techniques. Descriptions of historic quakes and active faults in the county lend credibility and timeliness to the account. Abundantly illustrated.

EARTHQUAKE COUNTRY: TRAVELING CALIFORNIA'S FAULT LINES
Ayer 1-55838-120-1 (Renaissance House)
A new and lively, full color description with maps of the geologic setting of earthquakes, the San Andreas system and other major faults, an historical account of the state's major quakes, and where to travel the faults.

EARTHQUAKE SURVIVAL GUIDE Calhoun 0-9625335-0-5 (Magnet Press)
Comprehensive procedures and checklists on pre-quake planning and emergency supplies, survival response during the event, and coping with post-event conditions. Discusses earthquake insurance. Bibliography.

FIRST AID AND SURVIVAL GUIDE - Phone Book (White Pages)
Pacific Bell
There are 12 detailed pages of vital information, including earthquake safety, often overlooked but readily available in every home, phone booth, and office in the state with additional pages on government emergency assistance agencies.

GEOLOGY FIELD GUIDE, SOUTHERN CALIFORNIA Sharp
0-8403-1272-5 (Kendall/Hunt)
Best general book on geological structures and processes in the region. Road guides emphasize desert geology: Mojave, Owens Valley, Death Valley, and Riverside to Palm Springs. Many maps.

GEOLOGY FIELD GUIDE, COASTAL SOUTHERN CALIFORNIA Sharp
0-8403-1863-4 (Kendall/Hunt)
Geology road guides from San Luis Obispo to San Diego and I-15 from Riverside to Tijuana. Chapters on building-up processes (tectonics) and tearing-down processes (agents of erosion), shoreline processes and features.

GEOLOGY OF ANZA-BORREGO: EDGE OF CREATION Remeika and Lindsay 0-932653-17-0 (Kendall/Hunt)
A new guide, introducing the Southern California desert enthusiast to a region where new earth crust is created within the Salton Trough. Eight field trips journey through deep time in the desert with numerous maps, photos, and charts.

GEOLOGY OF PEÑASQUITOS CANYON Northrup 0-808158-49-X
(J. Northrup)
The story of this area north of Miramar recaps much of the geologic history of
theSan Diego coastal plain with sedimentary layers and metavolcanic outcrops
exposed. Clear introductory text with photos and a colored geological map.

GEMS AND MINERALS OF CALIFORNIA Estavillo 1-155838-118-X
(Renaissance House)
A great amount of information is contained within this small volume by the
Curator of Mineralogy. Features mineral identification by hardness and color
tests, rock identification by color and texture tables, and mineralization by area.

GEOLOGY OF ARIZONA Nations and Stump 08403-2475-8
(Kendall/Hunt)
"The basics of minerals, stratigraphy, paleontology and tectonics, teaching
universal principles by use of concrete descriptions." An excellent introduction to
geology in the arid Southwest, typical of Anza-Borrego deserts and mountains.

IT'S YOUR FAULT: THE SAN JACINTO VALLEY FAULTS
Bullock, (B & D Training)
One of a series of community-specific books on local faults focusing on the area
northwest of Anza-Borrego which shares the region's major fault zone. Major
quakes on the San Jacinto, related faults, and the personal preparation plan.

MINES OF JULIAN Ellsberg 0-910856-44-3 (La Siesta Press)
A popular little book which outlines the geology and history of San Diego's own
gold rush country on the desert slopes of the Laguna Mountains with specific
descriptions of the more successful mines.

PAGES OF STONE: GEOLOGY OF WESTERN NATIONAL PARKS AND
MONUMENTS
A superb series, richly illustrated with color and black and white photos, maps,
charts. Each title includes an introduction to different geologic concepts with
examples in America's finest natural areas. Highlights include:
> #1: ROCK MOUNTAINS AND WESTERN GREAT PLAINS -
> Badlands National Park, Dinosaur National Monument. 0-89886- 095-4
> (Mountaineers)
> #2: SIERRA NEVADA AND PACIFIC COAST - Cabrillo National
> Monument, Channel Islands National Park. 0-89886-114-4
> (Mountaineers)
> #3: DESERT SOUTHWEST - Death Valley National Monument, Joshua
> Tree National Monument, White Sands National Monument. 0-89886-
> 124-1 (Mountaineers)
> #4; GRAND CANYON AND PLATEAU COUNTRY - Arches National
> Monument, Capitol Reef National Monument. 0-89886-155-1
> (Mountaineers)

PEACE OF MIND IN EARTHQUAKE COUNTRY Yanev 0-87701-771-9
(Chronicle Books)
The tectonic environment, fault mechanics, and measurement of quakes. Major

faults and quake history in the West including the San Andreas, San Jacinto, and Elsinore Fault Zones. Information sources and bibliography.

ROCKS AND MINERALS OF CALIFORNIA 3rd ed. Brown 0-911010-58-0 (Naturegraph)
Convenient field manual with physical and chemical tests and a key to common minerals. Charts facilitate rock identification and geologic history of the state. Topographic map key locates mineral sites in terms of survey sections.

SAN DIEGO BACKCOUNTRY RECREATION MAP Harrison
1-877689-00-9 (Tom Harrison Maps)
A superb full color map for outdoor enthusiasts and naturalists who need East County's mountains and deserts on one handy and frequently updated map.: Features topographic information, water features, roads and trails, campsites.

SAN DIEGO: AN INTRODUCTION TO REGION 3rd ed. Pryde
0-8403-3233-5 (Kendall/Hunt)
Latest update to THE reference to the natural environments and cultural patterns of the county. Earth science topics include: Geology, Climate, Soils, Vegetation, and Wildlife; The Most Essential Resource - Water Supply.

WEATHER OF SOUTHERN CALIFORNIA Bailey 0-520-00062-5
The classic introduction to the subject including climatic regions, desert conditions, wind circulation, drought, and precipitation. One of the acclaimed Natural History Guides by University of California Press.

WEEKENDERS GUIDE: ANZA-BORREGO 2nd ed. Johnson 0-910805-05-9 (ABDNHA)
Walks along desert roads and trails with all-color photos by a veteran Anza-Borrego naturalist and professional photographer. Detailed maps supplement descriptions with post mile markers carefully locating highway points of interest.

Anza-Borrego Desert State Park
RULES and REGULATIONS

The following are excerpts from some of the State laws which apply in Anza-Borrego:

VEHICLES

The established roadways in the park are Highways. All Vehicle Code sections are enforced, including:

- All vehicles must be highway legal.
- All vehicles (including bicycles) must remain on established roads.
- All drivers must have a driver's license in their possession.
- It is illegal to have an open container of alcoholic beverage in a vehicle.

CAMPFIRES

Groundfires are illegal. You may have a fire in a metal receptacle that completely contains the fire. Flames or smoke may not blacken or damage any feature. Fire debris must be taken with you. Gathering vegetation (dead or alive) is prohibited.

FIREARMS

Firearms must be unloaded, inoperative, and in a case while in the park.

NATURAL AND CULTURAL FEATURES

All features are fully protected. Nothing may be removed from its place or disturbed (including rocks, plant material, or Indian artifacts).

DOGS

Dogs are allowed only on roadways and in campgrounds. They are not allowed on trails or in natural areas. They must be kept on a leash no longer than six feet and under the immediate control of a person. At night dogs must be kept in a tent or vehicle.

INDEX

Page numbers highlighted in **bold type** refer to related Glossary definitions or annotation.

Massive Diablo river delta sandstones in Arroyo Seco del Diablo reveal some of the story of the Colorado River during Pliocene times as it transported sediments from the Grand Canyon area to the sea. PR

Volunteer naturalist Jean Morley indicates fossil camel track castings in Diablo sandstone in the badlands. LL

Detail of track castings shown above, revealed by separation of layers along bedding plane in overhanging sediments. LL

Oyster shells from the marine Imperial Formation in Fish Creek Wash. PR

Lake Cahuilla, which last evaporated about 1500 A.D., left its highwater mark or "bathtub ring" at 42 feet above sea level at numerous locations around the Salton Trough including this site near Trestle Road in the Fish Creek Mountains. Compare this to the present surface of the Salton Sea at minus 235 feet below sea level. CP

Map of Salton Trough Province; M--Mecca, N--Niland, PS--Palm Springs, SC--Salton City, TR--Travertine Rock. (From **Geology Field Guide to** *Southern California by Robert P. Sharp, copyright 1975, reprinted by permission Kendall/Hunt Publishing Co.)*

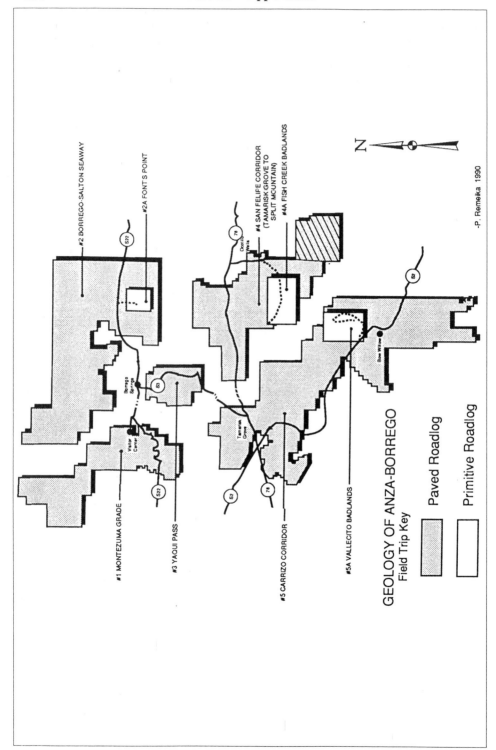

GEOLOGY OF ANZA-BORREGO
Field Trip Key

Paved Roadlog

Primitive Roadlog

#1 MONTEZUMA GRADE
#2 BORREGO-SALTON SEAWAY
#2A FONT'S POINT
#3 YAQUI PASS
#4 SAN FELIFE CORRIDOR (TAMARISK GROVE TO SPLIT MOUNTAIN)
#4A FISH CREEK BADLANDS
#5 CARRIZO CORRIDOR
#5A VALLECITO BADLANDS

Borrego Springs
Visitor Center
Tamarisk Grove
Ocotillo Wells
Bow Willow

-P. Remeika 1990